ESSAYS IN HEGELIAN DIALECTIC

ESSAYS IN HEGELIAN DIALECTIC

Quentin Lauer, s.j.

New York
Fordham University Press
1977

Printed in the United States of America

CONTENTS

Abbreviations

In-text and footnote references to the works of Hegel are indicated as follows:

BDG   *Vorlesungen über die Beweise vom Dasein Gottes,* ed. Georg Lasson (Hamburg: Himmelheber, 1966).

BS   *Berliner Schriften, 1818–1831,* ed. Johannes Hoffmeister (Hamburg: Meiner, 1956).

"Diff."   "Differenz des Fichteschen und Schellingschen Systems der Philosophie," *Jenaer kritische Schriften,* edd. Hartmut Buchner and Otto Pöggeler (Hamburg: Meiner, 1968).

EGP   *Einleitung in die Geschichte der Philosophie,* ed. Johannes Hoffmeister (Hamburg: Meiner, 1940).

EPW   *Enzyclopädie der philosophischen Wissenschaften,* edd. Friedhelm Nicolin and Otto Pöggeler (Hamburg: Meiner, 1959).

GP   *Vorlesungen über die Geschichte der Philosophie,* ed. Hermann Glockner, 3 vols., Sämtliche Werke xvii–xix (Stuttgart: Frommann, 1928).

GW   *Glauben und Wissen,* ed. Georg Lasson (Hamburg: Himmelheber, 1962).

JL   *Jenenser Logik, Metaphysik, und Naturphilosophie,* ed. Georg Lasson (Hamburg: Meiner, 1967).

PG   *Vorlesungen über die Philosophie der Geschichte,* ed. Hermann Glockner, Sämtliche Werke xi (Stuttgart: Frommann, 1928).

Phän.   *Phänomenologie des Geistes,* ed. Johannes Hoffmeister (Hamburg: Meiner, 1952).

PR   *Vorlesungen über die Philosophie der Religion,* ed. Hermann Glockner, 2 vols., Sämtliche Werke xv–xvi (Stuttgart: Frommann, 1928).

SP   *System der Philosophie,* ed. Hermann Glockner, 3 vols., Sämtliche Werke viii–x (Stuttgart: Frommann, 1929).

TJ   *Theologische Jugendschriften,* ed. Hermann Nohl (Frankfurt: Minerva, 1966).

WL   *Wissenschaft der Logik,* ed. Georg Lasson, 2 vols. (Hamburg: Meiner, 1963).

Introduction

AT THE VERY BEGINNING of an enterprise such as the present one a rather simple (but serious) question must be asked: Is the author justified in digging up a series of studies which have issued from his pen over the past twelve years and collecting them within the covers of one book? The question is not whether it is worthwhile to publish one more book—even one more collection of essays—on Hegel. A look at the rapidly growing list of books which the thought of Hegel has called forth in recent years would seem to answer the latter question adequately. What has to be justified is giving to this collection of articles a unity they do not of themselves possess by simply putting them together in this way. Each was, after all, written independently of the others, and each was intended to stand on its own feet. Many of them do, of course, complement each other, as the numerous cross references from one to another will indicate, but of itself that does not answer the question. When one writes of Hegel, whose own thought is so systematically unified that every aspect of it implies every other aspect of it, one inevitably multiplies such cross references. But perhaps the answer to the question is contained right there: Hegel himself provides the unity which justifies gathering together what can seem to be disparate attempts to come to terms with one or another aspect of his thought.

No one more than Hegel, it can safely be said, has made more gigantic efforts to bring all being and all thought into a unity. To put it negatively: no one saw more clearly than Hegel the futility of fragmentation, of disconnectedness, whether it be the political fragmentation of a Europe which Napoleon had vainly sought to unify by force, the cultural fragmentation of an intellectual community caught in the grip of Romantic individualism, the social fragmentation of a civil society whose members were becoming alienated from each other through the fierce competitive activity of production, the moral and religious fragmentation of a mob scene of sheer selfishness, or the intellectual fragmentation of a world dominated by the power of scientific abstraction. The entire Hegelian endeavor was dedicated to the task of reintegrating the dismembered world in which Hegel found himself. Yet he did not see his mission as that of the activist crusader who would change the world by revolutionary activity. Nor could he be satisfied with simply ensconcing himself in the ivory tower of abstract thought and criticizing the world as it passed beneath him. As he saw it, his task was, rather, that of educating his people—and through them, he would hope, the whole of humanity—to the existential vocation of realizing a humanity which would be thoroughgoingly human, which is to say, thoroughly rational in the best sense of that term. That he should see this task as specifically a philosophical one was due to his conviction, first, that what is most characteristically human is rational thought and, secondly, that human thought is most supremely rational when it occupies itself with thought, with what thought reveals regarding man. This last is important enough to bear emphasis. Hegel was interested in thought, not because its investigation constituted the most interesting of all intellectual games, but because it threw light on that most significant of beings, man. If he could bring man to a consciousness of all that it is to be human, his philosophical task would be accomplished—and the world would be a better place for man to live in. It may, of course, be considered naïvely utopian to believe that if men think rationally they will live rationally, but that may not be too wide of the mark; it is certainly not irrational to say that the failure to live rationally is a sign that men fail to think rationally—not to *live* rationally is to *be* irrational. In any event, it was Hegel's conviction that philosophy's task is to grasp in thought (*begreifen*) the structure of rationality (*Begriff*) and that by being in service to philosophy the philosopher is in service to humanity.

THE SYSTEM

Phenomenology. In a very significant sense, then, Hegel's whole philosophy—which he considers not to be *his* philosophy but simply philosophy systematizing itself—is in all its complexity essentially a philosophy of man, of the essential spirituality of the characteristically human. The problems to which this philosophy addresses itself are the perennial problems of human thought; nor are the problems and their solutions separable from each other. The first question philosophy has to answer regards itself: Just what is philosophical thinking? Is it conjectural, emotional, intuitive; or is it scientific, in the sense that it is knowing in the strictest and fullest sense of that term? If philosophy is to be scientific, are we to determine antecedently what "scientific" means and then see to it that philosophy confine itself within the limitations of what can possibly be scientific; or are we to allow human consciousness to show us what it itself is by developing one after the other all the implications of being conscious at all until we see that it cannot stop short of an absolute subject knowing an absolute object? The answers to these questions Hegel attempts to give us in his *Phenomenology of Spirit*, which in one sense is the introduction to the System, unfolding as it does the very possibility of there being a system. In another sense it is the constant underpinning of the System, since the unfolding of the total interconnectedness of all thought and all being is already contained in the process whereby merely objective consciousness develops into that thoroughly rational self-consciousness wherein an absolute subject which can only be spirit grasps comprehensively an absolute object which can only be Spirit.

Logic. The next question to be asked concerns what thought thinks. It would, of course, be simply out of the question that any philosophy —or philosophy itself—could provide us with a catalogue of all that human thinking thinks or can think, knows or can know. It is not out of the question, however, that in thinking itself thought could elaborate the framework within which all that can be thought fits. It is this which Aristotle sought to do from the point of view of thinking in his *Organon* and from the point of view of what is thought in his *Metaphysics*. The framework he thus provides is genial but static. It is this framework which Kant sought to provide—at least in regard to "speculative" thought—in his *Critique of Pure Reason*, but the framework allows for only a mundane, finite content. It is this framework which Hegel seeks to fill out in his *Science of Logic*, where the being which thought thinks—if there is to be thought at all—elaborates itself into all the determinations under which being can be thought. The framework is dynamic; its structure is conceptual, which is but another way of saying that any other structure of either thought or reality is inconceivable—a rather large order, but Hegel makes a good case for it. We might put it this way: as Hegel sees it, reality is inconceivable except as the product of infinite thought, and it is inconceivable that finite thought should conceive (comprehend) reality except by stretching out beyond its own finitude to *re*-produce an object which is infinite—or is not at all.

Since it would obviously be futile to construe the infinity either of thought or of the world of reality which thought thinks in such a way as to deny the finitude of each human thinker and of each object of his thinking, infinity must be so conceived as not to eliminate finitude, just as finitude must be so conceived as not to eliminate infinity. The key to this reconciliation of the finite and the infinite, Hegel is convinced, is contained in his *Logic*, wherein the inescapable finitude of the particular is intelligible only in light of the infinity of the universal, and the abstractness of the universal is concretizable (determinable) only in and through the determinateness of the particular. The Hegelian system of total interconnectedness of all thought and all reality is inconceivable save in the framework of a dynamic logic. But that logic itself is condemned to the emptiness of sheer abstraction if it cannot be shown that its unity of concept and idea is verified in the totality of reality which thought thinks—from the tiniest atom to the infinite totality which is divine being.

Here it is that Hegel has been accused of having constructed a Procrustean bed into which the whole of reality must willy-nilly be made to fit. But has he in fact done something so very unusual? From the beginning thinking man has constantly come up with conceptual frameworks into which he feels justified in expecting the reality he experiences to fit. Reason has always worked this way, Hegel contends, but because each successive conceptual framework has been only partial, accounting in its own way for only a segment of reality, reason has been one constant struggle to overcome the abstractness which plagues it. Only a conceptual framework which will account for the totality of reality, he is convinced, will have overcome the abstractness of the partial, and the blueprint for this total conceptual framework he has sought to elaborate in his *Logic*. That he should expect the unity of the logical idea, therefore, to be verified in the reality we experience is not necessarily unusual—even though those who fear that the reality of the partial will be swallowed up in a whole such as this may continue to consider it illusory. In any event, Hegel is convinced that, having established the unified framework of thought, he can look at a world of reality and justifiably expect that the dynamic unity of the logical idea will there be verified.

Philosophy of Nature. The process of verification begins with nature, which is simply the sum total of whatever is not spirit, whether this nature be organic or inorganic. The interest of an Hegelian philosophy of nature, however, is focused not on nature itself—that can be left to the sciences of nature. The philosophy of nature focuses, rather, on the manner in which thought is embodied in nature, which is not to say that it consists in an epistemology of scientific thinking—however fruitful that too might turn out to be. Very early in his career, in his doctoral dissertation, "De orbitis planetarum," Hegel pointed out that even the scientist can come to terms with nature only by conceptualizing it, by translating nature into thoughts and then consulting those thoughts to find there what nature reveals of itself. Prior to thought, the very intelligibility of nature is only potential, not actual. If in the actuality of thought, however, nature reveals itself to be rational, then its rationality is antecedent to the thinking of any scientific thinker who formulates in thought the laws which regulate nature's behavior. But for Hegel it cannot make sense to speak of a rationality of nature which is antecedent to thought itself—certainly not logically antecedent. Nor does it make sense to speak of a rationality of nature which reveals itself only in the partial ideas of this or that aspect of nature.

Only in the total interrelatedness of one rational idea does it make sense to speak of nature as a totality at all. Thus, nature itself bespeaks more than nature, and the systematic verification of the logical idea in reality must move on.

Philosophy of Subjective Spirit. From an examination of how thought comes to grips with nature as an interconnected whole, Hegel now turns to an examination of the human, standing over against nature, capable of transforming nature, and constantly in the process of becoming all that it is to be human. To be human is to be a spiritual agent, but human spiritual activity is unintelligible except as rooted in human nature (anthropology). What counts in the long run, and that to which Hegel devotes the major portion of his philosophical endeavor, is what the human subject does. But, that man is capable of doing what he does, what no mere being of nature does, is due to a nature which is uniquely his. He shares, it is true, certain features with all living beings, but even these features are present in man in a unique way, precisely because alone in nature man is a spiritual being. From the point of view of man as a subject acting, then, two characteristics are outstanding: man is conscious (phenomenology), with all that that implies of an awareness that conscious activity is not a being acted upon, and man is free (psychology), with all that that implies of determining himself to do what he does and to become what he is.

Philosophy of Objective Spirit. To say that man acts consciously and freely, however, is not yet to say that man acts humanly in the fullest and best sense of that term; he is adequately human only when he acts rationally. Here, once more, we are back with the Hegelian idea, the idea of what it is to be human. Man can and does, it is true, act inhumanly, irrationally; but to say this is to say that man can know what it is to act humanly, rationally, that he can know what is the morally right and what the morally wrong way of acting (morality). Since man, even as an individual, cannot be an isolated subject but must live in concert with others, the right and the wrong way of acting cannot be separated from the rights which men as men have (politics). This means that man is essentially a social being, but it also means that ultimately the society in which man lives must be that in which human rights are secure: namely, political society. Man is essentially a political being.

The result of the investigation up to this point is that Hegel sees verified, not only in all that is distinctively natural, but also in all that is distinctively human, the spiritual, the complete interrelatedness of the logical idea. But, presented in this way, the result runs the risk of obscuring a very important distinction between the natural and the spiritual. As Hegel sees it, nature is the sphere of the essentially repetitive; its laws function undeviatingly, its classifications are constant. Spirit, on the other hand, is the sphere of emerging novelty, of unpredictable self-determination. Yet the exposition thus far would seem to imply that the rationality of the human is essentially fixed; that the moral, social, and political requirements for authentic human living can be antecedently determined and rigidly applied. This could be true were it not for another facet of the human which now begins to assume enormous importance in Hegel's philosophizing—even though it was abundantly foreshadowed from the beginning in the *Phenomenology*. Man is essentially an historical being (history), not merely in the sense that the events of human existence are sequential, not even in the sense that man makes history; but human self-determination is a process of human self-development, intimately bound up with man's activity of transforming nature. The question remains, however, whether this introduction of the historical really gets Hegel off the hook or whether it simply causes the unity of the logical idea to explode in his face. Can Hegel really have his cake and eat it too? It is all very well to see reason manifest itself in nature with its necessary laws; how can reason manifest itself in history if man both makes history and is free in so doing? The question, says Hegel, can be asked only from the point of view of abstract understanding, which sees only the irreconcilability of contradictory opposites and thus refuses to entertain the possibility of reconciling freedom and necessity in human history. From the point of view of reason, on the other hand, whose function is precisely to reconcile the inevitable contradictions of dynamic reality, it is no more rational to expect nature to operate rationally (to make an act of faith, as Whitehead puts it, in the decency of the universe) than it is to expect history to unfold rationally.

The problem, of course, is to determine just what it can mean to say that history unfolds rationally. If it means that in the course of history nothing irrational ever happens, it is quite obviously nonsensical. By the same token, if it means there are no contingent events, it is simply untrue. But if it means that there is a rational principle which grounds the intelligibility of history, the statement at least bears looking into. This rational principle Hegel finds in what he calls teleology. Looking at history—world history—he finds in it an orientation which, despite the contingency of individual events, or of individual purposes, ineluctably works itself out. That this purpose, which he sees as the gradual process of human self-realization in freedom, is progressively fulfilled Hegel takes as proof that the process is rational.

The argument is something like this. Since it is characteristic of reason that it act with a purpose, where there is reason there is purpose. Conversely, where purpose is discernible there is reason; purpose becomes the criterion of reason. If, then, in history there is discernible an overall purpose, there is an overall reason whose purpose need not coincide with the purposes individuals who reason set for themselves. The unity of overall purpose bespeaks the unity of overall reason, a unity of which philosophers in the West since the pre-Socratics have been convinced, but which Hegel is assured can be concretized only under the rubric of purpose. Admittedly, the argument thus sketchily presented is not very convincing, but the point here is not to convince; it is to emphasize the importance of historical process in Hegel's attempt to give a rationally "scientific" account of the totality of reality. What Hegel does not say in so many words is that it does not make a great deal of sense to speak of purpose which is not *someone's* purpose and that, thus, the overall reason to which he concludes is in some sense personal (he does equate it with "providence"). There are those, of course, who will want to see in Hegel's notion of one overall reason —even in his notion of Absolute Spirit—only some vast impersonal force of which finite human spirits are the vehicles; but the coping stone of Hegel's system, the philosophy of Absolute Spirit, does not make a great deal of sense from that view. This is not the place to solve this problem (more will be said about it in the course of the present volume), but this much can at least be said. The interpreter who takes Hegel seriously wants Hegel to make sense—even if the interpreter will ultimately reject that sense. If, then, to equate Reason or Absolute Spirit with a God whom the interpreter has decided to reject does not make sense, the interpreter is quite sure that Hegel is not making this equation. If, on the other hand, an interpreter is convinced that not to make the equation does not make sense, the interpreter is free to take Hegel at his word and thus to see him struggling with and not brushing aside a real issue. One way or the other, it is quite clear that from Hegel's point of view man has not come to terms with thought or with himself until he has come to terms with the ultimate object of that thought, the Absolute.

Philosophy of Absolute Spirit. It may very well be that the choice of a term such as "absolute" or "the Absolute" is unfortunate. The term says at once too little and too much: too little, because it can mean pretty much what the user of the term wants it to mean; too much, because it includes all possible meaning, and that is rather vague. Hegel's point in using the term is just that: it is at once all inclusive and completely determinate in its meaning—provided its determinateness become progressively more manifest. To put it negatively: the absolute neither is nor is known, nor does it act relatively to something other than itself; there simply is no other to which it could be related. This is not to say that relation is inconsequential. Nothing could be further from the thought of Hegel; for him relation is all-embracing, it is constitutive of all being, of all intelligibility, all determinateness. Relatedness is constitutive even of the absolute, but this is not a relatedness of the absolute to something other than itself; it is the internal interrelatedness of the totality which is the absolute itself. It is not too difficult to see what this can mean when Hegel speaks of the "world" as absolute. The world is the totality of reality, outside of which there is no reality to which it might be related, within which there is no reality which is not related to all other reality. To know the world, then, is to know the totality of its interrelatedness. This is not to say that, in knowing, the knower has an infinity of fragments of information which he relates to each other in thought. It does say that to know at all is to know comprehensively, i.e., in a framework which can be no less than the totality of the knowable. It is for this reason that Hegel can call for an unending process of inquiry—which he is convinced will be very hard work—inquiry into thought, into nature, into the progress of the human spirit, in the conviction that the inquiry will constantly manifest the overall unity of the idea elaborated in his *Logic*.

When we turn, with Hegel, to a consideration of the Absolute as God, it is not difficult to see why so many have accused Hegel of out-and-out pantheism. If the world is the absolute, and God is the absolute, and there is only one absolute, then God and the world must be identified. To which Hegel replies, yes, God and the world are identified, but the identification is a dialectical one, not the identification of abstract thought with its "either–or": either identical or different, not both. The world is other than God, it is "created" by God; but it is God's self-othering, which is to say that to know God is to know the world, to know the world is to know God, and to know either without the other is to know neither. If one is accustomed to think of creation—whether one accepts it or rejects it—in the mode of causal efficacy, of "making," it is not easy to think of it in the mode of self-thinking divine thought, but it is also difficult to make any sense whatever out of creation. To set an infinite God over against a finite world is to finitize both, since each limits the other by being what the other is not.

The answer, it would seem, lies in the absolute which Hegel calls "soul," the sum total of rational activity, which as absolute is spirit. This is the spirit which reason becomes when it realizes in itself the truth that it "is all reality," that in knowing reality it knows itself, and that in knowing itself it recapitulates the divine self-knowing which is creative of all reality. To know self is to know God is to know the world—is to know absolutely, but not to know without the possibility of growing in knowledge.

As we said before, the focal point of Hegel's concern as a philosopher is man, the human spirit. But since the human spirit is the vehicle of Absolute Spirit, concern for man has to take into account what man does when face to face with the absolute, and this Hegel does in three final stages of his philosophizing, each manifesting within itself an historical process of coming to terms with the absolute as its content, each coming to terms with the absolute in a form which supersedes the one preceding it, each retaining an autonomy in the systematic integration of all three. Each of the three seeks to express the absolute in a way peculiar to itself. The first of these (no chronological order is implied) is *art*, which seeks to express the infinite beauty of the absolute by clothing it in a form which can be sensibly perceived. The second is *religion*, wherein the God whom the human spirit worships is presented in the form of figurative representation, a form not yet adequate to the full presence of absolute Spirit in man. The third is *philosophy*, wherein the divine Spirit is present in human thinking; divine self-knowing and human self-knowing are integrated in a comprehensive grasp of beauty, goodness, truth—Spirit.

Nothing so sketchy as this schematic presentation of Hegel's philosophy of absolute spirit can convey the riches of his monumental lectures on the philosophy of art, the philosophy of religion, and the history of philosophy. What emerges from them is an engrossing picture of man's colossal achievement of bringing forth the divine Spirit which dwells in the human. It has been argued, of course, and it will continue to be argued, that Hegel is not talking about the divine Spirit at all but only about the human, the infinite dimensions of which are beyond comprehension. In one sense at least this is true: what Hegel is talking about is the achievement of human thought. The question is whether it would be an achievement at all if it stopped short of the divine.

SUMMARY

When all this has been said, and the elaborate achievement of the Hegelian system has been sketched even as inadequately as it has been here, we seem to have come around full circle with a non-answer to the question with which we began as to the justification of gathering these essays within the covers of one book. Are there not so many gaps in the presentation that the picture we come up with is that of a truncated Hegel—a Hegel who is no Hegel at all? Nothing is said in these pages of Hegel's philosophy of nature, nothing of his philosophy of art (except in connection with his philosophy of religion). Little is said of his moral, social, and political philosophy, and but little more of his philosophy of history. Just what is the overall unity which warrants this collection? There are two essays devoted to Hegel's phenomenology, one concerned with his early endeavors, one on his treatment of the history of philosophy, five dealing with his philosophy of religion, and two which do not speak directly of Hegel or of his philosophy at all.

One possible answer to the question is that there is about as much unity and completeness in this collection as there is in most anthologies of essays on Hegel. Another is simply that completeness is not what is being sought; no one book can dispense the reader from coming to grips with Hegel himself, and that can be done only through an extensive (and intensive) reading of Hegel's own works. What is being presented is a series of attempts to show how Hegel wrestled with philosophical issues, not by isolating one from another and then giving to the whole the rather fragile unity of a unified method of inquiry, but by entering into the ongoing life of a philosophy whose unity is organic, whose history is a process of continuous growth, whose past is always an integral part of its present. There is no such thing as presenting the complete Hegel; no one has yet succeeded in doing that. What one can do is to show Hegel at work in his constant effort to overcome rationalist intellectualism in a healthy regard for experience, to combat romantic intuitionism by focusing on a rational standard of objectivity, to avoid a crassly empirical interpretation of experience by including in it the whole spiritual life of man. No one was more keenly aware than Hegel of the dual danger of a fragmented, disconnected reality or of an attempt to overcome that by an appeal to an abstract, undiversified absolute which unifies reality at the cost of blurring its outlines. Hegel sees the first danger eliminated in the dynamic conceptual unity of thought and reality, the second eliminated in the broadened conception of an experience which itself is a systematic whole.

It is not without reason, then, that the present volume begins with an essay on Hegel's treatment of what Dewey calls "the stretching of experience" (chapter 1). The *Phenomenology of Spirit* traces the development of experience from an initial abstract contact with the surface of material reality in sensation to the comprehensive rationality of self-conscious spirit through an unbroken chain of implications emerging from the very awareness of being-conscious (*Bewusst-sein*). To speak of "phenomenology" in a contemporary context, however, inevitably calls to mind the phenomenological movement inaugurated by Edmund Husserl and carried on by a large group of contemporaries who draw their inspiration from him. Hence a second essay (chapter 2) endeavoring to make clear what a Hegelian phenomenology is and is not by comparing it with Husserl's phenomenology. That there are enormous differences should be clear to anyone even minimally acquainted with the two endeavors. That there are similarities, particularly in the efforts of both Hegel and Husserl to come to grips with the autonomy of that essentially spiritual activity which is consciousness, may be much less obvious. That the two "phenomenologies" complement each other in such a way that each makes the other more intelligible has only rarely been noted at all.

The excuse for including in this collection a review of Henry Harris' book on Hegel's early development (chapter 3) is twofold. There is reason to call attention once more to an excellent book which by this time should have become standard reading for anyone seriously interested in understanding Hegel. In addition the review permits the present author to comment on Hegel's intellectual biography in such a way as to throw light on much of what is to follow in these essays. There follows a study of the manner in which Hegel elucidates the history of philosophy (chapter 4). If we are to understand Hegel's conception of philosophy as a "system" which reconciles the logical and the empirical, it is essential that we familiarize ourselves with his *Lectures on the History of Philosophy*. In the *Science of Logic* with which the system begins, Hegel elaborates through a process of dynamic logical entailment—what he calls "speculative thinking"—the structure of thought which alone, he is convinced, will enable the human spirit to be possessed of the rational standard of objectivity in the framework of which reality can be authentically comprehended. In the *Lectures on the History of Philosophy* he seeks to verify "empirically" philosophy's own elaboration of that very same structure of its own thinking. Thus it is that Hegel sees in history the temporal unfolding of the atemporal structure of thought revealed in his *Logic*. This is not, as it might seem, a downplaying of the significance of the individual or of his thought, but it does serve notice that the individual can have significance only as integrated in the overall (universal) process of unfolding. This is to be verified, however, not only in the historical elaboration of the structures of thought, but in the unfolding of the structures of human purposes which constitute the overall purpose of world history and in the progressive effort of man through artistic expression to embody ultimate truth (the absolute) in sensible form. Neither Hegel's philosophy of history nor his philosophy of art is expressly treated in these essays, but they cannot be completely absent from what is treated at some length, the philosophy of religion.

That the philosophy of religion should be treated at greater length is due not to a preference on the part of the author for this one aspect of Hegel's philosophizing. It is due, rather, to a conviction that the religious is not simply one aspect of that philosophy; it suffuses the whole. An initial attempt to bring this out is contained in a study of the role which religious consciousness plays in the march of consciousness toward knowledge of the absolute (chapter 5). In the *Phenomenology of Spirit* we see human consciousness progressively coming to an awareness of what it is to be authentically rational in its activity. But human consciousness can do this only by becoming aware that its activity is thoroughgoingly spiritual, and this awareness in turn is simply inconceivable apart from an awareness of God as Spirit, not as some abstractly unsatisfactory "supreme Being." Just as Hegel can see his *Logic* as a "presentation of God as he is in his eternal essence," so he can see in his "System" a philosophical elaboration of man's awareness of the divine. This is highlighted in the relatively brief review of Emil L. Fackenheim's *The Religious Dimension in Hegel's Thought* (chapter 6), the upshot of which is the contention that Hegel's philosophy will never be comprehended for what it is if it is not comprehended as essentially religious.

It is this last contention which is worked out in considerable detail in three essays dealing with God, not only as the ultimate object of philosophical thought, but as the only object which can rescue that thought from the abstractness and fragmentation which constantly menace all attempts either to safeguard the scientific rigor of philosophical thought by making it stop short of a divine content or to attain to the divine by going beyond the scientific rigor of conceptual thinking. Hegel is convinced not only that human thought can attain to God but also that a thought which does not attain to God has been untrue to itself as thought. He takes "proofs" for the existence of God seriously (chapter 7), not because an inference from the existence of the finite to the existence of the infinite imposes itself, but because only if the being of the infinite imposes itself does it make sense to speak of the finite at all. The human spirit is finite, it is true, but its very finitude makes sense only as oriented to infinity. It is here that Hegel most seriously takes issue with Kant (chapter 8). Because for Kant human reason is essentially finite, it cannot have as its object infinite being—only faith can do that. Hegel will agree that where finite and infinite are mere categories of the understanding they mutually exclude each other. For reason which is dialectical in its movement, however, finite and infinite mutually imply each other: a finite reason which did not infinitize itself in a movement toward infinity would not even be reason; an infinite being which would simply be over against all that is finite would finitize itself in being limited by what is other. It is for this reason that Hegel can contend that the ultimate object (the content) of philosophical thought and of religious consciousness are one and the same (chapter 9). A philosophical thought which does not attain to the only God there is, the God who is concrete Spirit, is not true to itself as philosophy; and a religious consciousness which does not seek to penetrate the veil of figurative representation under which God appears to it, in order to find God present in thought, is a religion which has abdicated its vocation to be authentically human. Nor does this mean that religion is swallowed up in philosophy; it means that religion cannot be satisfied with a God who is present to it in an inadequate form, just as philosophy cannot be satisfied with the presence in thought of an inadequate God.

Although the last two essays in this volume are not directly concerned with Hegel's thought, there is little need to search for an excuse to include them. If a philosophical way of thinking is to be more than a curiosity, it must offer at least a viable possibility of coming to grips with contemporary problems. Such a possibility, I am convinced, Hegel's philosophy offers. More than that, I am further convinced that one cannot over a long period of time (twenty-six years) occupy oneself seriously with Hegel's thinking without having that thinking rub off. This does not mean that one inevitably becomes a Hegelian—any more than one becomes a Platonist, an Aristotelian, or a Spinozist by taking Plato, Aristotle, or Spinoza seriously. Still less does it mean that one seeks to be a "neo-Hegelian"—which would be about as un-Hegelian as one could be. What it does mean is that a serious study of Hegel provides one with resources for the approach to problems which Hegel himself did not explicitly face. This is particularly true when the problems in question are problems of change, of development, of novelty—without ceasing to be perennial problems. There is no question that the problems of changing social patterns of thought, of authority as a dynamic principle in the very concept of society, of changing attitudes toward the reality of God, are problems made to order, so to speak, for an Hegelian approach. This is not to say that an Hegelian solution imposes itself; it is to say that one can justifiably expect the Hegelian mode of thought to be fruitful in an approach to problems such as these.

There can be no question that changes in social structures, in social patterns of thinking, in the image of man which a given society or a given historical period projects, do not wait upon the elaboration of a philosophical underpinning before they take place (chapter 10). The changes precede philosophical reflection. The questions which have to be asked, then, regard the degree to which such changes color philosophical reflection itself, the degree to which the dynamic concept of man—or what Hegel would call the structure of the logical idea—can provide the criteria for evaluating change, or the degree to which change itself affects concreteness of the concept. If we follow Hegel in seeing the concept as inseparable from the historical context of its manifestation, we may not have answers to all these questions, but then again we may well discern directions in which to look for answers. If nothing else, we may have better insights into the nature of the problems posed.

The problem of authority (chapter 11) is surely not unique in our own generation; nor is it necessarily a different problem today from what it was in the days of Plato, of Thomas Aquinas, or of Kant. Solutions to the problem have varied down through the centuries, however, and the variations have kept pace with variations in the concept of man, of society, of the state, of the church. Thus the very concept of authority has evolved, and forms of authority which were once taken for granted are no longer acceptable. The authority of an Oriental potentate which, in the Bible, for example, no one thought to question is now inconceivable. There have been throwbacks, of course, as in totalitarian conceptions of political society, but the evolution of the concept has been on the whole steady, as steady as man's evolving consciousness of human freedom, which, as Hegel sees it, is the orientation of history.

There can be no doubt that, for Hegel, philosophy was not an academic discipline to be included among other disciplines in a university curriculum. For him philosophy was a human commitment to which every ounce of his energy was dedicated, a commitment to seeking a comprehension of what it is to be human and to holding up before society the image thus comprehended so that society might discover whether it finds itself mirrored there. Nor is there any doubt that Hegel could not conceive of the philosopher's task as that of speaking or writing *about* philosophy. That task can only be to think philosophically. This means, moreover, that there is no legitimate way one can speak or write about *Hegel's* philosophy; one can only think along with him. To think along with, however, is not necessarily to agree with; it is to think through the reality in which we are immersed—man, the world, God—with the same thoroughness as did Hegel. Whether or not we accept his solutions to the problems we think through, we can still find in him a reliable guide to the thinking-through, a model for the dedicated quest for truth.

Over the millennia there has been little improvement on the Delphic oracle's designation of the human task as that of knowing self. There is no knowing self, however, except through the mediation of what is not self. Here it is that Hegel, the "absolute idealist," is in truth the incorrigible realist; he is convinced that when man really, i.e., rationally, knows himself he knows reality as it really is—there is nowhere to look but in reason for the truth of reality. The point, however, is not to know *that* the truth of reality is to be sought in reason but to engage in the Herculean task of finding it there. Hegel is not making the absurd claim that his philosophy—or even philosophy as such—has found it all. He does claim, however, that whatever is found—or will be found—will be integrated into the dynamic contours of the concept and that the finding will not be separate from the conceptual process of seeking. What a serious study of Hegel's thought, then, can do for us is not to give answers to the perennial questions which philosophy asks but to unfold before us the integral pattern of seeking.

It is my hope that in the following pages that Hegelian pattern of seeking may be at least partially unfolded. In the unfolding not everything will be abundantly clear, but, paradoxically enough, that is as it should be; there is a risk that in making things clearer than Hegel himself did one will falsify the thought one seeks to elucidate. On the other hand, because the serious student can rarely be satisfied with the clarity manifested in the available translations of Hegel's works, I have throughout given my own translation of his words. This may have the disadvantage of the arbitrariness of any translation; it will have the advantage of consistency—be it the consistency of arbitrariness. One final caution: precisely because each of the following essays was originally intended to stand on its own, there is a sense in which the overall effect will be to take Hegel apart; it will be the task of the reader to put him together again.

1

The Phenomenon of Reason

IN THE PEDAGOGY of the physical sciences it has become relatively easy in modern times to define, prior to scientific investigation, the particular science with which one is concerned or to which one wants to introduce students or readers. Nor does this kind of defining express merely what the individual teacher or writer *means* by a term when he uses it in a particular universe of discourse; within the scientific community there is substantial agreement as to what each science is and as to where its boundaries lie, so that the individual is not free to present it in a way which does not correspond with the common agreement. Despite certain family disputes the same is true with regard to mathematics; before beginning, one can say what one does when one does mathematics.

In regard to philosophy, however, this is not the case. Here, we might say, we cannot be told ahead of time what philosophy is because the very doing of philosophy is a prerequisite for understanding what one is doing, and defining philosophy is itself a philosophical task, in a way in which defining science or mathematics is not a scientific or mathematical task. Nor is it self-evident that the many peculiar human activities which have at one time or another paraded under the name of philosophy simply do not belong there, any more than one can with certainty dispute the right of some of our contemporaries to give philosophy a meaning of their own and then to deny that what others call philosophizing deserves to come under this heading.[1] But if we look at the question historically, we can, I think, say that philosophy began when men first sought to explain rationally what had previously been explained by an appeal to authority, to myth, to tradition, or simply to common opinion. By this criterion, then, philosophy is not so much a discipline, a method, or a body of knowledge, as

An earlier version of this chapter appears in *The Isenberg Memorial Lecture Series, 1965–1966* (East Lansing: The Michigan State University Press, 1969), pp. 163–92.

[1] Not too many years ago a nationwide philosophical convention featured a session entitled in the program "The Meaning of Negative Existential Statements." In this session a group of grown men spent two hours discussing the proposition "There is no Santa Claus." I have serious misgivings as to whether I could engage in such a discussion and think that I am philosophizing, but I cannot dispute the right of others to do that sort of thing and call it philosophizing—so long as they do not magisterially tell me that what I am doing is not philosophy.

an attitude which human beings bring with them in approaching the reality in the midst of which they live. This attitude we might call a determination to *know* reality (as opposed to opining or believing), understanding "knowing" to mean having adequate rational grounds for affirming or denying what we do in regard to reality. Such an attitude is philosophical even when, as in the case of skepticism, it results in the conviction that reality cannot be known.[2]

Without prejudicing the issue we can, I think, say that reality has always been looked upon as that which is present to man when he experiences—no matter how vague and fluctuating his notion of experience may have been and no matter how convinced many have been that reality is present as reality only when experience is supplemented by thought, or that experience which has not been taken up into thought is not really experience. In this context, then, the philosophical attitude (or impulse) might tentatively be defined as the determination to understand or, better still, to grasp through reason what experience presents.[3] This would mean that the very attitude which lies behind the impulse to scientific thinking is itself a philosophical one. But such a definition simply brings us face to face with another problem, which may well turn out to be the most fundamental of all philosophical problems: What is reason, or when is man being rational in his thinking? It should be fairly obvious that this question is inseparable from the question as to what is experience—neither question is answered unless both are. Neither question, however, is easily answered—it is even doubtful that they can be asked separately.

At the very beginning of his *Discourse on Method* Descartes mentions that "common sense" is the one gift of God of which no one complains that he has not been given enough.[4] This we might call the common sense notion of common sense (one needs a great deal of it in order to be able to admit that one does not have enough of it). By the same token there is a common sense notion of rational thinking, and it can be somewhat crudely described as the way I think—as op-

---

[2] There are, of course, various kinds and degrees of skepticism. Very rarely in history has this taken the form of denying that there is knowledge, since this is equivalent to saying "I know that there is no knowing." Most often it takes the form of denying that what people (or philosophers) call knowing is really knowing (in which form it constitutes a very important and necessary step, as Hegel says, in the process of coming to know). Or it can take the Humean form of insisting that if one defines knowing very narrowly (on the basis of logical necessity), one will seek in vain for philosophical knowledge.

[3] We can, for the moment, prescind from the question as to whether or not one can justifiably separate experience and thought. It would seem, however, that an experience which excludes thought falls short of being experience, and a thought which excludes experience is but a truncated thought.

[4] *Discours de la méthode* (edd. Adam–Tannery) VI 1–2.

posed to the way those think who disagree with me. How often in ordinary conversation do men use the expression "It stands to reason"? The expression is admittedly not very precise, but it seems to mean at least this: "Anyone who is not prejudiced must see that my way of seeing things is correct." When we stand off from such a statement (or attitude) we can laugh at it, but behind this common sense notion is hidden a profound truth of human experience: we do—and perhaps we must—look at our own seeing as a criterion for the way things are; or, to put it another way, *if* we really do *see* that this is the way things are, then this is the way they are, and they cannot correctly be seen otherwise. Human beings are often irrational, but more often than not they are so in the name of reason; they are convinced that if others would only think correctly (the way they do) they would see that this *is* the way things are—or should be (witness political thinking). Thus, professed irrationalists write books to show that the only rational thing to do is to have no confidence in reason (which non-confidence, incidentally, is really no less rational than the confidence of the professed rationalist). The more truly rational attitude, of course, would be that which says "My thinking is clearly not rational enough, nor will it ever become rational if it stays where it is."

Looked at historically, the notion of the rational is seen in a somewhat different light. Rational thinking, we might say, begins when a distinction is made (often unconsciously) between grounds which are arbitrary and therefore unworthy of commanding human affirmation and grounds which are discernibly relevant and therefore worthy of commanding such an affirmation. This kind of rational thinking is already present when men plow the ground and plant seed instead of simply imploring heaven for food. Such rational behavior obviously can and does exist side by side with non-rational forms of behavior— it is not even necessary that there be anything irrational about the coexistence of such forms of behavior.

Philosophy, then, begins when a conscious effort is made to explain (rather than merely to handle) reality on rational rather than on mythical, religious, or merely traditional grounds.[5] The pre-Socratics— with whom we say philosophy (Western philosophy) began—explained the world in a rational way, and this in a double sense: (1) the principles of explanation are sought in that which is to be explained (the κόσμος); and (2) the explanation is seen as somehow imposing itself on correct thinking (however vague this notion may at first be). This

---

[5] *What* one calls reality and *how much* of it one seeks to explain continues to be somewhat vague. Thus the first Western philosophers are called "materialists," not because this term expresses a universal theory of reality, but because the material world was all they sought to explain.

kind of rational thinking reaches its apogee with Parmenides and Zeno, for whom the demands of thought must be affirmed, even when they apparently contradict experience or common sense.

With Socrates and Plato rational explanation is based on grounds which correct thinking cannot refuse (it is not amiss to remark that the capacity to do this kind of thinking is seen as a "divine spark" in man).[6] It is true that in the writings of Plato this kind of rationality most frequently manifests itself negatively, as again and again Socrates shows that common opinions—or opinionated opinions—have no adequate foundations. This meant not that those opinions were not "true" (in a somewhat naïve sense), but that those who held them had no adequate grounds for so doing.[7] Out of this negative procedure came the conviction that the adequate ground ($\alpha i \tau i \alpha$) was an insight into the essence ($\epsilon i \delta o s$) of things as distinguished from their appearances ($\phi \alpha \iota v \acute{o} \mu \epsilon v \alpha$). Though Plato does not develop it formally, the result of this endeavor is a "logic," i.e., a set of rules calculated to ensure that thinking is adequately grounded (or to manifest that what goes under the name of thinking is not so grounded). Once again, as formal logic this sort of thing is primarily negative in its working: it does not show that thinking corresponds with reality—or that reality corresponds with thinking (Parmenides)—but it does show that a failure to think thus rigorously will make it impossible to determine whether there is such a correspondence.[8] One can distinguish here between a formal logic whose concern is the correct relationship between grounds and conclusions and a material logic whose concern is the adequacy of grounds.

Logic as such appears with Aristotle (not merely in his *Organon*). It consists of a set of well-worked-out rules for determining when thinking is indeed rational. When it is, its result is *knowledge*; when it is not, its result is mere *opinion*. It might be remarked that of itself this kind of logic is quite ideal and not incompatible with the non-existence of knowledge at all—except the knowledge that the thinking itself has been correct. Even those who find fault with the Aristotelian *logic* agree with Aristotle's basic presupposition: that there are discoverable rules which are valid for *all* reasoning (at least for all that

---

6 Cf. *Meno* 99D–100B.

7 In the naïve sense an opinion is true when a proposition which is affirmed *happens* to correspond with a state of affairs. In this sense a *guess* can be true, even though the guesser has no grounds for his affirmation and does not really *know* whether or not it corresponds with a state of affairs. Philosophy concerns itself with such "truth" only indirectly, if at all.

8 Only late in his life (with the *Timaeus*) did Plato concern himself with the reality of the world. His primary concern throughout a long philosophical career was with the reality (or truth) of moral and political judgments. Even the universe ($\kappa \acute{o} \sigma \mu o s$) is significant as a totality of ultimately moral order.

one is willing to *call* reasoning). Ideally at least (but only ideally) reason thus becomes the most universal of all universals—it can always be distinguished from what is not reason. This permitted Aristotle to hand down to posterity the most fateful of all definitions, that of man as a "rational animal." [9]

Revolutionary as he may have been in other respects—and we can scarcely call any other intervening mode of thought revolutionary in the rational sense [10]—Descartes does not change the basic Aristotelian conception of the rational. He merely changes the emphasis; with Descartes the rational becomes *more* subjective (it had always been fundamentally subjective). When the individual thinker sees things as clearly as he does in mathematical reasoning (the camel's nose), then he knows that his thinking has universal objective validity and that anyone who sees objectivity otherwise is not thinking rationally. The ultimate basis for Descartes' reasoning is still the going cause–effect metaphysics, and the primary opponent is authority. The ground of human assent can never be someone else's *mere* say-so; it must be the subject's own rational insight into the truth of his own assertions, secured by a tested "method" of reasoning. (To Descartes' credit, he saw that reason could not ultimately justify itself—it contains no built-in guarantee that it is not condemned to be deceived—and so he appeals to the decency of a God who would not permit man to deceive himself when acting at the summit of his potentiality.) Since it was fairly obvious, even to Descartes, that not everyone can know everything (though there was less to be known in those days), presumably there were for him ways of determining whether someone else's say-so was backed up by an adequate method of reasoning. (In contemporary thinking not every member of the scientific community personally checks whatever any other member of the community says, but there is confidence that in the long run everything will be—or has been—checked.) In any event, through the influence of Descartes the ultimate criterion of truth became the individual's own rational insight, and the model for rational investigation became the physical sciences with their mathematico-physical method—without too much

---

[9] To some this definition has meant that man is a being who reasons syllogistically, à la Aristotle (though Aristotle's own conception is not nearly so narrow). To others it has meant, much more broadly, that all the activities which characterize man as man (his religion, art, science, politics, economics) must have the stamp of reason on them—in the assumption, of course, that one can determine what the stamp of reason is.

[10] The advent of Christianity, it is true, produced a revolution which has influenced *all* subsequent thought (even non-Christian) in the West. Still, this was a change not so much in the manner of rational elaboration as in the manner of experiencing reality. In a very real sense Hegel was the first to realize consciously that the Christian way of experiencing changed the very concept of philosophical reasoning (cf. *Phän.* 523–31, 544–45; PR II 193–94; PG 41, 378–79, 384–90, 546).

concern as to whether the subject matter under investigation lent itself to the application of such a method, or whether, in fact, the subject matter itself could dictate the method of investigation. The important thing was to know reality by discovering the "laws" which governed its functioning. (Only later did the assurance that one was *knowing* become more important than *what* one knew, but Descartes laid the foundations for this.)

Because Descartes emphasized both the *subjective* aspect of rational insight and the *objective* aspect of detailed experiment (as a method of arriving at rational insight), two seemingly antipodal movements arose in response to his endeavors, "Rationalism" on the continent and "Empiricism" across the channel. Opposed as these tendencies were, they were one in their conviction that the task of philosophy is to determine what rational thinking is and how it is to be assured, since only through rational thinking can man achieve certainty as to the truth of his affirmations.[11] Ultimately the main difference between the two camps seems to center in a somewhat pragmatic dispute over the extent to which rational certainty is achievable: the empiricists wishing to limit it to the empirically verifiable, and the rationalists wishing to set no limits at all—the *a priori* vs. the *a posteriori* approach. It was Hume who tossed a mortar shell into both camps: he narrowed the rational down to such an extent that he denied to rationalists and empiricists alike the right to think that they *know* much, if anything at all. Only if it steers clear of reality can knowledge be called "knowledge," and if it does steer clear of reality, who wants it? What is needed, then, is an effective substitute for rational knowledge, and this Hume finds in "belief." Having thoroughly undermined the old cause–effect metaphysics, which in one way or another was basic to the positions of all his predecessors, Hume left the philosophic community faced with two possibilities: either begin all over again and construct philosophy on a new base, or renounce rational certainty and be content with as high a degree of probability as unremitting and conscientious scientific effort can achieve. The first option did not wait long to materialize, and it took the form of German idealism, inaugurated by the rational critique of Immanuel Kant. The second alternative was slower in maturing, but its effects have been lasting. It produced an attitude which still dominates the scientific community and has caused a good part of the philosophical community to abridge its efforts.[12]

---

[11] Cf. Franz Schnabel, *Deutsche Geschichte im 19. Jahrhundert* (Freiburg: Herder Taschenbuch, 1965), I 40–41.

[12] We might add that it has resulted in a situation in which practically the whole of the scientific community and a good part of the philosophical community have lost any understanding of what the other part of the philosophical community is doing.

The reaction to Hume which we call "German Idealism" took up his challenge on two fronts: it sought to restore rational *knowledge* of reality without resorting to a cause–effect metaphysics (leaving to various forms of "materialism" the task of salvaging this sort of "realism"); and it asserted that in so doing it was achieving "scientific" knowledge. The key to these efforts can, I think, be found in the one certainty which Hume admitted (apart from rational tautologies), i.e., appearances (or phenomena), provided they were recognized as appearances, and only that.

Kant began the campaign by placing all the emphasis of his investigations on the act of knowing (he admits that his *Critique* is a preparation for philosophy, not philosophy itself).[13] If it is possible to establish the requisites for completely rational thinking, and if, when one is completely rational in one's thinking, one is knowing, then both knowing and reason have been saved. It may be, of course, that they have been saved at the cost of very severe limitations, but Kant's concern was to save knowledge, not to guarantee its relationship to reality. On one point he went along with Hume much further than his immediate successors would be willing to do; he refused to see any establishable connection between appearances and reality. In regard to "speculative" reason (which he arbitrarily identifies with theoretical reason, i.e., knowing what *is* as opposed to what *should be*), Kant feels that it can be saved only if its content is limited to the phenomenal (appearances). But, in doing this, he is convinced that he has established the absolutely necessary laws of experience, thus enabling man to *know* how reality must *appear*, which is all that science requires, though it leaves metaphysics out in right field. The consequences have been lasting: philosophers are still trying to show how philosophy can be "scientific"—usually by jettisoning metaphysics. As an absolutely certain concomitant of all experience, Kant sees an awareness of the self as the central function of experiencing (not the *ergo sum* of Descartes). As an absolutely necessary concomitant of experiencing, this awareness of self becomes a *condition* of experiencing.[14] Logically speaking, however, a condition is a pre-condition (it is prior to the conditioned), with the result that to speak of knowledge is to speak of self-knowledge, the ultimate source of all knowledge worthy of the name.

Kant's most significant followers (Fichte, Schelling, Hegel) are united both in their negative and in their positive reactions to him.

---

13 One can, of course, wonder (along with Hegel) how one guarantees the validity of philosophic reasoning without reasoning philosophically (cf. *Phän.* 63–64), but the problem seems not to have bothered Kant at all.

14 This is the renowned "transcendental unity of apperception" (cf. Kant, *Kritik der reinen Vernunft,* B132–36; WL II 222), which in one way or another became the straw to which Kant's successors clung in their efforts to reconstruct a "system" of knowledge.

Negatively they agree in refusing the radical Kantian separation of appearance from reality (and of sense from intellect), which would leave the ultimate reality of things unknown; and positively they agree that the solution to the problem of knowing is somehow to be sought in knowledge of the self. This solution presents itself in its most radical form in the thought of Fichte, who seeks to derive (dialectically) all objective knowledge of reality from knowledge of the self (he is quite sure, incidentally, that there is extra-mental reality and that his *Theory of Knowledge* permits him to know it). Schelling takes as his point of departure what had always been recognized as essential if there was to be knowledge at all, the identity of reality as it is and reality as it is thought. Since this kind of identity is possible only if nature (reality) and spirit (thought) are two sides of the same coin, Schelling simply postulates this identity: in knowing one, one knows the other. Knowledge of nature, however, is not *derived* from knowledge of the self; rather, the science of nature (with which he was quite familiar) is shown to be genuinely knowledge, because it is at the same time knowledge of the self.[15]

Hegel took upon himself the enormous task of continuing, criticizing, and improving upon all three of his illustrious predecessors. This he did by simultaneously affirming what they had said and negating it (thus employing the "dialectical" method of simultaneous affirmation and negation, which is at once so well known and scarcely known at all). Hegel agrees with Kant that the content of rational knowledge is provided in appearances (phenomena) which are presented in experience. He disagrees with Kant by refusing to separate these appearances from reality, knowledge from experience. He agrees with Fichte in affirming that the process of knowing (science) is dialectical in its movement and that all knowledge is ultimately self-knowledge. He disagrees with Fichte by denying that one can arrive at objective knowledge (of reality) by *beginning* with knowledge of self; one must recognize, he contends, that every step forward in the consciousness of reality is a step forward in consciousness of self—the "logical" priority of condition over the conditioned is only a red herring. Thus, though the process of knowing is indeed dialectical, the movement results in, does not start from, a knowledge of self which is identical with the knowledge of reality. Hegel agrees with Schelling in affirming the ultimate identity of reality and thought reality (nature and spirit). He disagrees with Schelling by insisting that this identity cannot be a point of departure—which would be empty of content and out of

---

15 Hegel (*Phän.* 17–18; cf. *Phän.* 180–81) calls this a subterfuge: simply taking what is already considered to be known and throwing over it the cloak of "scientific system," without ever showing that the system is genuinely scientific.

which no amount of effort could carve a content. Rather, this identity is only gradually revealed in a painstaking passage from the first awareness of objectivity in sense perception to the ultimate knowledge of all this initial step implies (phenomenology), which knowledge can then be filled out by working in the opposite direction, i.e., from general to particularized knowledge (logic). We shall grasp Hegel's gigantic effort to solve the dilemma of thought *vs.* reality only if we see how he grasped the Humean (and Kantian) bull squarely by the horns. He will begin where Hume says one must begin, with the certainty of appearances (phenomena), but he will go where Hume said one cannot go, to a knowledge of reality, because he refuses to separate appearances from reality. Sense perception is not distinct from knowledge; it is the beginning of a process, the whole of which ultimately reveals itself to be knowledge. The cause–effect metaphysics, which he rejects (as do Hume and Kant), had seen appearances as produced by and revelatory of reality—and as produced by, therefore separate from, the reality which they reveal. Rather than try to put this Humpty-Dumpty together again, Hegel will see the appearing of reality as integral to the being of reality, and the process of working this out he will call "phenomenology"—not in the sense that phenomena provide all the evidence which is needed for grasping the "essence" of reality, but in the sense that the total process of experience is identical with the total process of knowledge and that the *appearing* of reality is the same movement as the *consciousness* had of it.

In recent years the term "phenomenology" has become familiar even to those who merely dabble in philosophy. What the term really signifies, however, is familiar to relatively few, whether it is used in the contemporary Husserlian or in the earlier Hegelian sense. Although it would not be without value to compare the two uses of the term (and the disciplines which they designate)—to see how they differ and how, in some ways, they supplement each other—we shall have to content ourselves here with a description of the Hegelian phenomenology, hoping that its efforts to solve the riddle of the relationship between experience and reason may contribute to an understanding of phenomenology in its other manifestations.

Although it is true that the name "philosophy" has been reserved for that which is pre-eminently a rational discipline, and though history has accorded the title "philosopher" only to those who have contributed to the rational elaboration of human experience, it is equally true that the greatness of the *great* philosophers does not rest on the inner consistency or on the convincing power of such rational elaborations. Rather, their greatness consists (as does that of the great poet or great artist) in the quality of their experience, its capacity to reveal in a new way the possibilities of human experience. The analyses and explanations which the philosopher provides are precisely the provisional in his contribution, but they do serve to point up the significance of the experience to which he is a witness and whereby he leaves his mark on the experiences of those who come after him. Although we continue to marvel at the monumental rational structures they have bequeathed to us, the influence of a Plato or an Aristotle, a Kant or a Hegel, even of a Husserl or a Wittgenstein, is to be discovered not in these structures but in the profundity of an experience which the penetration of their philosophical genius has made possible and which the lucidity of their elaboration has enabled them to communicate. Their experience, in its turn, is significant not because it is experience—as though this were some sort of universal for which a unified "logic" could be prescribed—but because it is the experience of a genius, whose capacity for experience is in a very special way his own. We can say, I think, that each great philosopher has had a very special way of experiencing experience and through this special way has enriched the sum total of human experience. Thus, experience is not significant simply because it is experience; what is significant is who does the experiencing.

Applying this to the Hegelian manner of experiencing, we can, I think, say that it is characterized by an extraordinary confidence in reason. This is obviously opposed to the "Romantic" glorification of emotion and intuition, which Hegel constantly characterized as an unwarranted short-cut to knowledge. Not so obviously but equally vigorously it is opposed to the sentimental rationalism of the "Enlightenment," which first deified human reason and then knelt down in adoration before it (cf. *Phän.* 388). Nor, finally, was it the confidence of a Kant or a Fichte, who purchased their confidence by handing over to faith the ultimate concerns of human living and limited reason to mundane considerations (cf. GW 2, 6, 14). Hegel's was rather the confidence of a Plato or an Aristotle, who saw reason as that which in the highest degree distinguishes man as man and which should, therefore, characterize man when he is engaged with that which is of the highest interest to him. Like those who went before him, Hegel saw reason as infallible, in the sense that what reason saw to be true simply had to be true; and, like those who went before him, he saw reason as absolutely one, in the sense that what any human reason saw to be necessarily true had to be true for any other reason which was truly reason. This conviction, of course, was properly speaking a pre-philosophical conviction—neither, strictly speaking, self-evident nor philosophically verifiable. It was not, then, the starting point of Hegel's philosophizing, but it did influence his whole manner of thought, never letting him rest until his painstaking pursuit of experience should lead him to a reason which, he felt, had shown itself to be one and infallible in the very process which experience goes through in becoming reason. Whether or not we think that this pursuit has been successful depends on the judgment we make after we have followed Hegel through the tortuous intricacies of his *Phenomenology of Spirit*. If nothing else, Hegel's approach has the advantage of not trying to establish the unity of reason by employing a reason which is simply assumed to be adequate to the task.

As we said before, characteristic of any phenomenology—except the negative sort which preceded Hegel's, remnants of which are still detectable in Kant's thought (cf. *Phän.* vii–xvii)[16]—is the conviction that philosophy not only must begin in experience but must never become detached from experience, if it is not to lose itself in unwarranted "rational" vagaries.[17] There are, however, two characteristics which mark the Hegelian concept of experience and which distinguish it from those conceptions of experience which are current in most of the "phenomenologies" inspired by Husserl. For Hegel whatever is inevitably implied in any experience (it never stands still) is integral to that experience in its totality, no matter how far it may advance beyond the merely empirical. In accord with this, reason is not distinct from experience; it is not even the result of experience; reasoning is simply the highest form of experiencing. Secondly, experience is historical, not merely in the sense that it develops (each experience conditioning each subsequent experience), but also in the more profound sense that human history is integral to human experience and that the great events of human history are landmarks in the progress of human experience, as the spirit advances toward full consciousness of what it is to be spirit. We can illustrate the difference at this point with but one telling example. Not only as a nineteenth-century man was Hegel impressed by the enormous historical significance of the French Revolution (as were all his thinking contemporaries), but as a philosopher he saw in it the most significant contemporary phenomenon in the steady march of the human spirit through history (the first practical attempt in history to build a political community founded on a rationally conceived idea of man as such and of his essential freedom). For Hegel any attempt to philosophize in abstraction from the French Revolution was a refusal to be "timely" in one's thinking and, therefore, a refusal really to philosophize.[18] On the other hand, Husserl experienced World War I more immediately than did Hegel the French

---

[16] Kant (*Kritik der reinen Vernunft*, B86) calls ancient dialectic a *Logik des Scheins*, and (B87) transcendental dialectic a *Kritik des dialektischen Scheins*; cf. B349–50.

[17] Hegel was unalterably opposed to what he called "rationalism": "In regard to both content and form rationalism is contrary to philosophy" (GP I 112).

[18] Cf. Joachim Ritter, *Hegel und die französische Revolution* (Frankfurt: Suhrkamp, 1965).

Revolution. We may assume that as a man Husserl saw in it the end of an era in human thinking and human living. So far as I have been able to determine, however, there is no evidence that as a philosopher he ever thought of it at all; in his sense of the term it had simply no significance for "phenomenology." It may have been integral to human experience (though one doubts that he saw this); it had nothing to do with philosophical experience—the assumption being that one can justifiably distinguish between "human" experience and "philosophical" experience.[19]

All this is said, not by way of criticizing Husserl, who had his own reasons for not according the "contingent" any philosophical significance, but in order that we may better understand the phenomenology of Hegel, rooted as it is in the whole of human experience, not merely in his own or that of his associates or, for that matter, in that of philosophers as a whole. Nor is it concerned with some sort of abstraction simply labeled "experience." The *Phenomenology of Spirit* is historical, not in the ordinary sense of presenting a chronological record of a series of events (it is not chronological at all), but in the sense that it sees the whole of human history as important for the development of human consciousness, and in the sense that it contends we shall not understand man until we have examined the various forms which this developing consciousness has taken in the course of history—even though Hegel does not examine them in the order in which they occurred (they keep recurring). Nor is the *Phenomenology* a history of philosophy. It seeks to take into account all the forms of human consciousness which have been manifested in the course of history, through which and in which spirit gradually comes to a realization that all history is its history. Though it is difficult to follow him in this, it is Hegel's contention that if we begin with the simplest of all experiences, that of a single individual faced with an unrelated object of sense consciousness, we shall find that this simple act of consciousness demands for its elucidation—or self-elucidation—the whole process of human consciousness, not only on the individual but also on the social and historical levels.

It is generally admitted that Hegel's *Phenomenology of Spirit* is one of the great masterpieces of philosophical literature (although not too many can say why). It is also admitted, even by those who know it best, that it is one of the most difficult of all the works in this literature.

19 It would not have been impossible for Husserl to have initiated a "phenomenology of love" or a "phenomenology of religion" insofar as these are phenomena which can be analyzed, investigated, and explained, and whose "essence" can be discovered. But it would have been quite impossible for him to look upon love or religion as experiences of the human spirit and, as such, integral to the very process of philosophizing. Among "Husserlian phenomenologists" the nearest approach to this sort of thing is to be found in the works of Max Scheler (e.g., *On the Eternal in Man*).

For many, of course, the main difficulty is to be found in the language which Hegel employs, and since they rarely get beyond this they excuse themselves from the kind of effort which would bring them face to face with the true difficulty of following it through. It is difficult because of the enormous philosophical, literary, cultural, and historical erudition needed in order merely to enter into its universe of discourse. It is difficult to habituate oneself to the involuted style of writing and to the peculiar use of concepts which one may have thought familiar. It is difficult because its contents reflect Hegel's own vast erudition, which he somehow sought to squeeze between the covers of one book. But the chief difficulty of all is that of staying with the method from beginning to end and trying to understand why the author thinks that every step necessarily implies every other (cf. *Phän.* vi). If we do make the effort, however, though we may not at the end be convinced that Hegel has fully proved his point, we shall not be likely to think that the torture was in vain.

From Descartes to Fichte, those who sought to guarantee the validity of human reasoning were in search of some indubitable truth or principle from which the movement of knowing could begin and which would be the constant support of all knowledge derived from it. For Hegel, on the contrary, it is a matter of indifference whether we begin with truth or error, since a beginning (precisely because it is a beginning) is never either 100 per cent true or 100 per cent false. The important thing is that we begin and that we then follow with the utmost fidelity the movement of successive implication which this initial act of consciousness involves, provided, of course, that the beginning is truly a beginning and not a continuation. Even error will imply its own truth, because as an act of consciousness it carries within itself, so to speak, its own built-in corrective (one is reminded of the rational optimism of Peirce, James, Dewey). It is precisely this inner principle of truth in all consciousness, however, thoroughly distinct as it is from the subjective certainty one has regarding the object of consciousness, which makes the movement of the *Phenomenology* so difficult to follow. It is, on the other hand, this conviction of the truth in all consciousness which permits Hegel to take the somewhat discredited title of "phenomenology" and apply it to his own approach to philosophical knowing. In the German tradition which preceded Hegel, *appearances* had always been suspect because of their capacity to deceive, and phenomenology had been a method of detecting the fallacy of appearances and thus avoiding deception. Hegel, however, looks upon appearances as the bearers of truth, as long as the unremitting effort of thinking permits them to purify themselves of the element of error which is inseparable from partial truth.

If, then, science is the methodical procedure through which human thinking moves in arriving at a grasp of truth, we can understand why Hegel calls science the movement we have so summarily described. Its goal is knowing—Hegel calls it "absolute knowing"—but science is not merely the knowing; it is the whole process of coming-to-know. Short of the *whole* process there is no science. It is for this reason that Hegel calls his *Phenomenology* a "science"—the original title had been *Wissenschaft der Erfahrung des Bewusstseins* ("Science of the Experience of Consciousness"). It should be remarked, incidentally, that he does not intend it as a science which has as its object a "faculty" called "consciousness." Rather, it is a science in the double sense (*a*) that it rationally examines the process which consciousness goes through in becoming all that consciousness is and (*b*) that the process of experiencing through which consciousness goes consists of a series of steps each of which entails the next and all of which culminate in knowing in the strictest sense. It is a science precisely because the movement of experience is itself scientific (only when, of course, arbitrary subjective associations have been eliminated and none but the inevitable implications of consciousness are allowed to assert themselves). Reality *appears* in consciousness, and the series of these appearings is *experience*. This does not mean that what appears is some sort of reality behind the appearing (as it is for Kant), but rather that appearing is what reality does when it truly is. Thus, just as the shining of light is not something other than light, the appearing of reality is not something other than reality. If the appearing is cut short at any stage in the process, it is not the true being of reality. This last is what most clearly distinguishes the Hegelian from the Husserlian phenomenology; only in the total process of appearing is reality discoverable as what it is, and what it is is not some "essence" contained *in* the appearing; it is the sum total of appearing as process.[20]

We have now reached the point, I think, where we can see all this illustrated in the text of Hegel's *Phenomenology of Spirit*. It is the record of the experience of consciousness, and as such it is historical in character—although, as we said, it does not present an historical account in the sense in which we have come to understand that term. It is also "systematic," in the sense that it is a gigantic effort to put order into the totality of forms in which human experiencing has manifested itself.[21] But the "system" is not a pre-established framework

[20] Obviously this should not be taken to mean that the "essence" is *not* grasped in the process. Insofar as the essence is present to consciousness, it too is *experienced*. It is significant, however, that for Hegel knowledge of essence is only a stage along the way toward the fullness of knowledge (cf. WL II 213–14).

[21] Cf. Walter Kaufmann, *Hegel* (New York: Doubleday, 1965), pp. 146–49. One gets the impression in reading the *Phenomenology* that Hegel's head was just bursting with the erudition he had gathered over the years and on the significance of which he had meditated profoundly.

into which the sum of experiences is made to fit; [22] rather it is an order, which we may frequently have difficulty in recognizing as order, of the forms which the human spirit takes in passing from minimal consciousness to the fullness of knowledge. This is not, be it remarked again, a passage from experience to knowledge; the whole movement is experience—even to know is to experience knowing (just as to love is to experience loving). If we are to know science, then, science must appear (in Hegel's terms it must be *Erscheinung*), but the appearing of science is not other than the being of science, any more than the appearing of pain (its being experienced) is other than pain. [23]

The process begins with simple, naïve, immediate consciousness of a sensible object (the Humean paradigm of all consciousness), which is no sooner present than it reveals to itself that it is not the knowledge it thought it was. [24] In order to pass beyond this eminently unsatisfactory stage, consciousness must negate its own inadequacy, which is but another way of saying that it must negate the immediacy (and "certainty") which makes it satisfied to stand still where it is. [25] Thus, at the very beginning, the mainspring of the process is introduced as negation, negating that immediacy which we might call experience's dead-end street and which Hegel qualifies as "abstract." In this sense the process will be a negative one throughout; it will be process at all only to the extent that consciousness repeatedly denies itself the illusory satisfaction of clinging to the certainty which immediacy promises but never gives. Hegel is convinced that if we follow this negative process conscientiously, it will repeatedly reveal its further positive content and will not let us stop until it has become knowledge in the truest and fullest sense of the term (one suspects, of course, that he was convinced of this *before* he went through the process, but he is con-

---

22 Just the reverse would seem to be the case. Hegel was convinced that all the forms of experience he had collected were significant; the task was to put them into some sort of order which would bring out this significance.

23 The example is taken from Locke, who seems to have been on the brink of a discovery similar to Hegel's. Unfortunately, he did not carry this insight beyond its application to the perception of sensible qualities.

24 In what follows we shall attempt to present the thought movement of Hegel in a language which will (we can hope) make up in familiarity for what it loses in technical accuracy. Those who are familiar with Hegel's text should have no difficulty recognizing the details in the broad outlines of this summary. One must bear in mind, of course, that an interpreter can scarcely avoid reducing Hegel's thought to the limits of his own understanding. The fact that an interpreter's principles do not permit him to understand Hegel's principles does not necessarily speak against Hegel. Any fool can to his own satisfaction make a fool out of Hegel.

25 Hume had recognized the negative character of the process whereby consciousness goes from the immediacy of sense impressions to the mediacy of thought. But since for him sense impression was the paradigm of consciousness, the movement in question was purely negative, betokening a *loss* in concreteness and, therefore, in validity. Hegel, as we shall see, moves in exactly the opposite direction: the more immediate, the more abstract; the process of mediation (negation of immediacy) is a process of concretization.

tent nevertheless to let the process speak for itself). The point is that the degree of certainty in consciousness is in inverse proportion to its content, and that the significance of knowledge is in direct proportion to its content, not to the certainty we have regarding it.[26] Of course, if *all* this meant only a progressive loss of certainty, the knowledge at which Hegel aims would turn out to be empty. It means, rather, a progressive regaining of certainty in the realization that the immediate certainty of sense consciousness is sterile without the mediation of thought. The fatal mistake, Hegel feels, is the opinion that to *think* what was at first only sensibly perceived is to introduce an element foreign to the reality which is perceived (cf. *Phän.* 63–64). Thinking is foreign neither to sensation nor to reality; it is integral to the process in which alone both are what they *really* are. Hegel is further convinced that in conscientiously observing this process of experiencing we will see that thought is integral to it, i.e., that thought reality is more real than reality which is not thought.[27]

Hegel is as aware as is anyone else that thinking is an operation of the subject who thinks. Where he differs from others is in insisting that it is at the same time an activity of the object which is thought,[28] if it is truly thought and not merely imagined or represented. This can be illustrated by a simple example which Hegel himself gives. When we say that one thing is distinguished from another, we are saying that the one distinguishes itself from the other, in the sense that the one really has a character or determination which is different from what the other has and which makes the one really different from the other. Determination, however, is that whereby things are manifest to consciousness as this or that. Thus, the determinations of things are at one and the same time in things and in the consciousness one has of things (in this case in *thought*). At the same time difference *from* another is relation *to* another, and relation is inseparable from thought. When the thought which relates one thing to another as different is true thought, then, the two things are really different from each other.

---

26 Hegel is not opposed to abstraction; he recognizes it as a necessary step in human thinking (cf. *Phän.* 29). Abstraction makes the real unreal (mental), but it does so in order to reinstate reality at a higher level. It is characteristic of his thought (even in the *Logic*) that he sees reason as primarily concerned with concrete reality, not with necessary (abstract) judgments. The bond between abstractness (usually triviality) and certainty has not ceased, even in our day, to be a close one.

27 This, in somewhat more modern dress, reiterates the insight of Plato, who saw more genuine reality in "ideas" than he did in sense impressions.

28 Heidegger, with his flair for manipulating language, has partially recaptured this in speaking of "the thinking of Being" (*das Denken des Seins*), where the "of" governs "Being" as both an objective *and* a subjective genitive—when man thinks Being, it is Being which thinks.

Thought, then, means initially the effort to "understand" what is thought, and Hegel sees the effort to understand as an effort to explain why things are experienced the way they are (he feels that this is as far as Kant went). This effort manifests itself in the positing of some hidden "essence" or "force" within things, which explains their being outwardly the way they appear (the example is taken from Newtonian physics). If this "essence" or "force" is outside consciousness, however, it will be thoroughly sterile since it cannot explain what is *in* consciousness (short of an indemonstrable cause–effect relationship). Once more, then, consciousness makes the effort to overcome sterility, and this carries it beyond understanding, at the same time revealing the inadequacy of considering only the object of consciousness; consciousness must turn to an examination of itself, and this is self-consciousness.[29]

At this point the *Phenomenology of Spirit* becomes really difficult, and the difficulty increases as we continue in our efforts to follow the movement of self-experiencing consciousness which it describes. Just as on the level of mere objective consciousness there was a first immediate stage which revealed itself as inadequate to its own object, so here on the level of self-consciousness there is a first immediate stage, which we can call the stage of individual self-consciousness, which in turn reveals itself as inadequate and relatively sterile.[30] That the individual be genuinely conscious of himself he must be conscious of being recognized as a self, which recognition he can find only in other selves, whom he in turn recognizes as selves.[31] Not only is coming to consciousness of self a process, it is a long process and, like the process we have already seen, it is a process of mediation (negation). Experience has already found that consciousness of objects is empty without

29 The danger of superficiality in making this jump so rapidly is obvious. We should not forget that this whole negative process is a "struggle," a "torture" (cf. *Phän.* 12–13).

30 Obviously any but the very first step in the process is not fully immediate, only relatively so, i.e., relative to the fullness of the consciousness achieved on any level and to the (absolute) fullness of consciousness which is revealed only at the end. Yet self-consciousness can be considered immediate in that very first relation to its object whereby it turns away from the object to itself. This first step, Hegel tells us, is mediated through "appetition" (*Begierde*), a relation which is not "objective" in the same way as cognition is, since the former turns out to be self-referential in a way in which the latter is not.

31 The whole section of the *Phenomenology* entitled "Self-Consciousness" has something of the character of a digression—but a necessary digression. Objective consciousness is revealed as truly objective only when it is also consciousness of self (cf. "transcendental unity of apperception"), but this requires that self-consciousness be given its full significance, which means far more than that the individual have himself as the object of his consciousness. It is far from easy to grasp that a self (essentially *subject*) should be the *object* of consciousness; it is impossible if the only self there is to grasp is one's own. This sort of self-consciousness requires a complex movement of mutual recognition, in which subjects are to each other both objects and subjects.

the mediation of thought originating in the subject; now it will find
that consciousness of self is little more than the grasp of another kind
of object, when it is not supplemented by the mediation involved in
the mutual recognition accorded in a community of selves.[32]

From here on, then, the individual, even as an individual, cannot
progress by merely experiencing its own experience; it must take in
the experience of others and not stop until its own experience blends
with the collective experience of humanity (in its history). Thus it is
that the Hegelian phenomenology becomes historical in a way in
which no contemporary phenomenology is (including that of Heidegger, Sartre, Merleau-Ponty, or even Scheler). Man begins to recognize
himself progressively for what he really is, a rational being whose
grasp of reality is identified with the autonomy of his own conceptual
life. Consciousness of rationality, then, goes hand in hand with consciousness of freedom, neither of which is present on the level of
merely "natural" (naïve) consciousness, but is acquired in the process
of becoming a "human" consciousness, or in the process of developing
into spirit, as opposed to mere nature. Later, when he looks back from
a different vantage point, Hegel will be able to entitle his work a
Phenomenology of Spirit; up to the present point he can know only
that it is still a "Science of the Experience of Consciousness."

Consciousness has now begun to experience itself as free (autonomous, self-determined). But as an immediate experience of freedom
(or an experience of immediate freedom), consciousness experiences
not true freedom but only independence, which immediately reveals
itself as independence *of* others; this on careful examination turns out
to be dependence *on* others—the "of" means a necessary relation *to*
others and manifests the meaninglessness of freedom in isolation *from*
others. Man is free only in community *with* other men, which by implication means that man is rational only in common with other men,
not as isolated (even in thought) from them.[33] Hegel was never willing
to see genuine freedom in mere freedom of thought (whether in the
form of stoicism, skepticism, the Enlightenment, or Romanticism—
"stone walls do not a prison make"). More often than not (as Marx
saw so well) freedom of thought is a poor substitute for the effort to
realize freedom in action (its result in our own day is that the best

---

[32] Negation, for Hegel, is never merely mutual opposition. To say that the subject as
other than the object is the negative of the object is not to say that the negative of the
subject is merely the object as other; there would be no *movement* in this. Rather, the
significant negative of the subject must be another other, i.e., another subject.

[33] Franz Schnabel has pointed out how German scholars in the nineteenth century were
encouraged to great freedom of thought (in science) to keep them from realizing their
lack of political freedom (cf. *Deutsche Geschichte im 19. Jahrhundert*, v 160).

heads are not doing the most important thinking—they are producing the instruments which can destroy the world).[34]

Historically speaking, the search for an adequate guarantee of individual reason (from Descartes to Fichte) had been unable to survive the rejection of the cause–effect metaphysics. If the activity of a cause cannot guarantee the universal validity of reason's conclusions, then the guarantee (if such there be) must come from elsewhere, and the only answer to this seems to be some sort of idealism, where thinking finds within itself the guarantee of its own validity. Hegel's point is that reason will never acquire this guarantee of universal validity if all it is is individual reason (an abstract universalization of which, à la Kant or Fichte, is no more than an assertion of universality, not a guarantee). It is all very well to say that what I rationally know to be true is necessarily true for everyone who reasons correctly, but Hegel will see things in the reverse order: if common reason (the reason of man as such) prescribes that things be seen in a certain way, then it prescribes that my individual reason see things the same way. The problem, however, is not to see that this is the case; it is, rather, to know when it is common reason which speaks (just as Rousseau's problem, which he never solved, was to know when the "general will" speaks). Hegel's search, then, is for something (by way of example) whose validity is the product of the community and not of any individual member of the community.[35] Once more he borrows a page from Rousseau and finds this common product in *law* (involving, of course, a somewhat idealized picture of democracy according to which its laws, if genuinely laws, are in truth legislated by the whole of the people). Actually Hegel realizes that if this is seen merely on the level of positive law, the picture is far too ideal ever to be true. When he contemplates the moral law, however, he finds an initial realization of that which is a product of reason and still not a product of the individual, except to the extent that the individual really sees that in so thinking both he and others are thinking the same.

But even this realization, which in principle is justified, has its concrete vicissitudes. What one would merely like to be true can present

[34] It is conceivable that an abstract consideration of man might reveal that all men are essentially free. It is doubtful, however, that such a consideration could reveal that those who are *de facto* not free (e.g., the so-called "primitive" peoples) are men in the full sense. It is not by "thinking about" them but by being "related to" them that we discover concrete men—though even the inadequacies of abstract thinking can prompt us to seek such relatedness.

[35] It would require another study to show that reasoning in the sense in which it here begins to be understood cannot be separated from effective action (economic, social, political). Cf. Herbert Marcuse, *Reason and Revolution* (New York: Oxford University Press, 1941). Suffice it to remark here that the concept of active reason is not a Marxist monopoly.

itself as having the kind of universality desired. Sentiment, too, can readily parade in the garb of reason. In short, there can be any number of attempts to universalize private opinion—and each attempt must manifest its inadequacy (the negative process) if there is to be progress toward true universality. The solution is not to be found in the abstract community of human nature (practical experience discredits this); [36] nor is it to be found in a merely empirical observation of what men *de facto* think and do. It comes, rather, in the recognition that the rational is purposeful activity and that purpose is meaningful only if it is concretely the purpose for which all exist. In the order of mere vital nature, where activity is unconsciously and thoroughly determined, this is not too difficult to see; the purpose of the things of nature is what in fact through their activity they do become. On the level of spiritual activity, however, the difficulty is almost insurmountable because it involves steering a middle course between what actually *is* done (pure empiricism) and what simply *should be* done (pure idealism), a course which can be successfully steered only if both are reconciled in a purpose prescribed by a reason which is at once superior to any individual reason and yet not separable from individual reason when it truly functions as reason.[37]

The answer to this dilemma Hegel finds in his concept of spirit, and it is precisely here that it is most difficult to follow him, not in the sense of understanding what he says (though that is difficult enough), but in the sense of going along with him. He has seen that all efforts to make individual thinking a valid paradigm for all thinking have failed. What is left, then, is that the thinking of all should be the paradigm for individual thinking, which it can be if the thinking of the individual can be concretely identified with the thinking of all. What thinks in this way, Hegel tells us, is spirit, and consciousness is raised to this level of thinking by going through all the stages we have observed—and then some.[38] As an illustration of spirit he

---

[36] Man, according to Hegel, is not by nature good (any more than he is by nature free) —though he might conceivably be by nature "innocent." Man must *become* good, and this involves a negation of mere nature, just as does becoming *rational*.

[37] Here those who would make of Hegel an atheist run up against a hurdle over which they much too facilely leap. One can, of course, say that for Hegel the supreme principle is *Geist*, and that *Geist* is not God. But since *Geist* is clearly not reducible to *mind* or to any function or sum total of functions of the individual, and since it can be treated as an abstraction only if one does violence to the texts, it seems clear enough that, negatively at least, Hegel's conception of *Geist* would be equally unacceptable to an atheist as God would be. Feuerbach, Marx, and Engels at least had the good sense to see this.

[38] The whole discussion of religion, which in fact repeats the overall progress of spirit through history, is integral to this "science of experience." See chap. 5 of this volume, "Human Autonomy and Religious Affirmation in Hegel."

takes what is frequently (more frequently in his day) called the spirit
of a people, a way of thinking which belongs to each because first of
all it belongs to all. On this level, however, there is an element of
unconsciousness in the unity of thinking which has been achieved.[39]
But if the same degree of unity which is observed on this level can be
consciously achieved on another level, then we are a lot closer to what
we are seeking. Hegel feels that this kind of unity can be achieved,
not in a people, but in a state which is truly a state (the qualification,
of course, makes it somewhat abstractly ideal). But the point is that
Hegel is seeking a situation in which community of thought is the
guarantee of its validity rather than one in which the validity of
thought is the guarantee of its community, a conception of democracy
which escaped even Rousseau—and certainly Marx—requiring as it
does a confidence in the people which few share.[40] The situation may
be unjustifiably utopian in its conception, but there is no question
that, *if* achieved, it would be far more concrete than its opposite. To
a great extent we do, in fact, attribute a greater validity to a community of experience than we do to isolated experience. If there are
ways in which the experiences of each can be consciously related to
the experiences of each other and of all, there is hope that the interrelatedness of all experience (rooted in the genuineness of total human
interrelatedness) will have a validity which merely individual experience can never have.[41]

Universal experience, of course, will be just as meaningless as individual experience if it does not have a content. But Hegel's claim is
that it does have a content, a content which we shall grasp if we follow him conscientiously through the successive stages he has described
for us, a description, we might say, which constitutes a run-down of
all the forms which experience (and thinking) has taken in the course
of its long history. Not only is it difficult to conceive of a basic human

---

39 Much of Hegel's "unhistorical" swinging backward and forward can be explained
by his search for illustrations of steps in the process. Here he goes back to the Greeks,
though chronologically he had already passed far beyond them.

40 It is the rare philosopher indeed who says, as Hegel does, that the people as a whole
cannot be fooled: "When the general question is asked, *whether it is permissible to deceive a people* [Frederick the Great], the answer must in fact be that the question is
pointless, since in this it is impossible to deceive a people" (*Phän.* 392).
This, of course, applies specifically to faith, but in another place Hegel accords even a
certain speculative infallibility to an *organized* common thinking: "To Jacobi's remark
that the systems are an organized non-knowing we need only add that non-knowing—the
cognition of individuals—becomes knowing by the very fact that it is organized" ("Diff."
24–25).

41 Thus, the whole question of "intersubjectivity" is not an afterthought for Hegel (as
it seems to be for Husserl, who feels the need of concretizing a universal subjectivity
which is clearly abstract). Intersubjective relatedness is integral to the process of human
experience becoming reason.

attitude which is not presented here (however metaphorically), but no one of them is held up merely as a curiosity; each is seen as a contribution to the onward march.[42] As Hegel presents these forms, they seem to tumble over each other in rich confusion (scarcely systematically) and leave us with one big headache. If we really read the *Phenomenology*, however, we can say that we have seen everything; it will be up to us to make something of what we have seen.[43] It may be that we shall not make of it what Hegel did—the triumphant march toward rationality and self-determination—but, one way or another, the whole will do something to our way of philosophizing; one is never the same after a careful reading of Hegel. But one should not read him at all if one is unwilling that philosophy be a risk. Philosophy as Hegel conceives it is hard work—if one insists on always being in charge, it is impossible work (cf. *Phän.* 57).

[42] Most of the forms of spirit which Hegel describes have names which have been taken from historical movements, e.g., Stoicism, Skepticism, Enlightenment. They are not, however, to be confined to these time-conditioned phenomena; each is a form which appears again and again.

[43] To speak of the "forms of consciousness" without treating "religious consciousness," wherein the object of which the human spirit is conscious is absolute Spirit, which then becomes the object of *thought* in its fullest sense in "absolute knowing," is of course to telescope Hegel's account unconscionably. But since this culmination of developing consciousness is treated at considerable length in chaps. 5 to 9 of this volume, it seems unnecessary to enter into detail here. For a fuller exposition of the overall movement of Hegel's *Phenomenology*, see the present author's *A Reading of Hegel's* PHENOMENOLOGY OF SPIRIT (New York: Fordham University Press, 1976).

2

Phenomenology: Hegel and Husserl

AT A TIME when the philosophy of Hegel is awakening renewed interest among scholars both on the European continent and in the Anglo-Saxon world it would seem not only desirable but even imperative to institute a comparison between one of the most influential movements of our own age, the phenomenological movement, and that part of Hegel's philosophical endeavor for which he is, perhaps, best known, his *Phenomenology of Spirit*. The comparison is of interest, of course, not simply because in both instances the same term, "phenomenology," is employed, but, more significantly, because in both the same sort of appeal is made to human consciousness, to experience, as the key to philosophical knowledge. It would, assuredly, be claiming too much to say that the two types of phenomenology greatly resemble each other in their approach to experience, but it is to be hoped that, even in their differences, they can be seen as somehow complementing—or, perhaps, illuminating—each other.

In allowing these two types of phenomenology to confront each other it would undoubtedly be of major interest to see Hegel's endeavor against the background of the outstanding figures of the contemporary phenomenological movement, both those who have to some extent been influenced by Hegel, such as Merleau-Ponty, Sartre, even Heidegger and, perhaps, Ricoeur, and also those who have been influenced either not at all or only negatively by Hegel, such as Husserl, Scheler, Schütz, and Gurvitsch. But since such an undertaking could be carried out only within the framework of an extended monograph, we shall confine ourselves here to the more modest task of coming to terms with the meanings which Hegel and the most illustrious of "contemporary" phenomenologists, Husserl, give to the undertaking called "phenomenology."

In view of the fact that both Hegel and Husserl make common cause against both the skeptical phenomenalism of Hume and what both consider to be the "empty formalism" of Kant's response to Hume, it can seem strange that Husserl, in the vast corpus of his published and unpublished writings, should for the most part have ignored Hegel and, in the few notices he does give to Hegel, should

An earlier version of this chapter appears in *Beyond Epistemology*, ed. Frederick G. Weiss (The Hague: Nijhoff, 1974), pp. 174–96.

have criticized the latter severely for having retarded the impulse to "scientific" philosophical thinking. One could, of course, put the whole thing down to the difference of temperament in the two men—and this is not without significance—seeing in Hegel the all-embracing universal spirit who will leave no avenue of human knowing, no facet of human experience, untried, and in Husserl the painstaking scientific spirit—the erstwhile mathematician—who will not move forward in the vast uncharted wilderness of philosophical investigation until he has perfected the method which will assure him that what he knows, be it ever so little, he knows "scientifically." It is difficult to escape the impression that Hegel was impatient (he wrote the *Phenomenology of Spirit* in six months) to press within the covers of one book the vast erudition which he had accumulated through years of voracious reading and profound meditation, and that Husserl had the unremitting patience of the experimental scientist, willing to spend years eliminating the influence of those variables which could throw doubt on the results of his investigations. It is just as inconceivable that Hegel could spend a lifetime perfecting techniques which would enable him to pile apodictic certitude upon apodictic certitude in raising the edifice of universal science as it is inconceivable that in investigating consciousness Husserl should range through Greek tragedy and Judaeo-Christian revelation, Stoicism and the Enlightenment, the Ancien Régime and the French Revolution, experimental science and phrenology, or morality, jurisprudence, art, and religion. Hegel and Husserl are alike, it is true, in their contention that no sphere of reality is closed to rational investigation, but they are utterly unlike in that Hegel actually endeavors to come to terms with the totality of reality, while Husserl limits himself to establishing the method which will enable others to achieve a scientific knowledge to which no limits can be assigned.

Tempting as it is, however, to delay on the differences of fundamental attitudes which produced such radically different results, we must take a closer look at the results themselves to see if they reveal similarities as well as differences, to say nothing of complementarities. Before the unpublished manuscripts of Husserl were made available to the scholarly world, it was customary to locate the major difference between Hegel and Husserl in their approach to history. Hegel, we were told, made history—not merely the history of philosophy but also the whole of human history, world history—integral to the process of philosophizing, whereas Husserl philosophized in an historical vacuum. Husserl's 1911 essay, "Philosophy as Rigorous Science," [1] was,

---

[1] "Philosophie als strenge Wissenschaft," *Logos,* 1 (1911), 289–341.

it is true, available, as were the first two parts of *The Crisis of Euro-pean Science and Transcendental Phenomenology*,[2] both of which undertook a somewhat historical investigation of the progress of philosophical thinking. But since the former presented only a some-what truncated record of abortive attempts to make philosophy "scien-tific"—and thus, incidentally, properly speaking, philosophical—and the latter used a relatively brief segment of European intellectual history, from Galileo to Kant, as illustrative of the need for a gen-uinely transcendental phenomenology if philosophy were ever to ful-fill its role of being scientific, little damage was done to the "historical vacuum" thesis. But with the publication of Husserl's *Erste Philoso-phie*, with its "Critical History of Ideas"[3] and the remainder of *Krisis*, and with the availability of other late manuscripts, still un-published, the thesis has had to be re-examined. The result of the re-examination has been to show that for Husserl, even in his late years, world history continues to have no philosophical significance whatever, and the history of philosophy from Plato to Husserl—with notable gaps—records only the vicissitudes of the scientific ideal in philosophy, not the process of philosophizing. The difference between Hegel and Husserl, then, here too remains acute. For Hegel the his-tory of philosophy is integral to the philosophical enterprise; for Hus-serl it serves as illustrative material in his efforts to establish the sci-entific ideal. Hegel took all "significant" philosophers—and they are legion—seriously; Husserl took Plato and Aristotle, Descartes and Leib-niz, Locke, Berkeley, Hume, and Kant seriously.[4] Given his conviction that the *unum necessarium* in philosophy is that it be scientific, it is understandable that he should have taken these men seriously. That he should have ignored the whole neo-Platonic and Scholastic contri-bution, that he should merely mention in passing Bacon and Hobbes, Spinoza, Fichte, and Hegel, that he should have acted as though Rous-seau and Schelling, Marx, Kierkegaard, and Nietzsche, had never existed, is somewhat less understandable. The procedure, however, does permit us to see how he could be so cavalier in his treatment of Hegel, and it points up strikingly the difference between the two phenomenologies.

2 Parts I and II, *Philosophia*, 1 (1936), 77–176 (contained in *Die Krisis der europäischen Wissenschaften und die transzendentale Phänomenologie*, ed. Walter Biemel [The Hague: Nijhoff, 1954]).

3 *Erste Philosophie*: I. *Kritische Ideengeschichte*; II. *Theorie der phänomenologischen Reduktion*, ed. Rudolf Boehm (The Hague: Nijhoff, 1956, 1959).

4 This tendency to accord significance to historical positions only when they manifest a demonstrable relationship to transcendental phenomenology is admirably illustrated in Husserl's preference for empiricism over rationalism, because the former makes clear "the historical tendency toward a thoroughly necessary and true philosophical method, the phenomenological" (*Erste Philosophie*, 1 187).

HUSSERL'S CRITIQUE OF HEGEL

Apart from a remark in Volume I of *Logical Investigations* [5] that Hegel had denied the principle of non-contradiction—a remark which is not documented—and a reference to Hegel's abortive desire in the Preface to the *Phenomenology* [6] to make of philosophy a "foundational science," we find Husserl's complaints against Hegel summarized in "Philosophy as Rigorous Science." Here without further ado he lumps Hegel's philosophy with "romantic philosophy" [7] which either denies the ideal of scientific philosophy, "however much Hegel insists on the absolute validity of his method and his doctrine," [8] or makes it impossible of attainment. In view of Hegel's own vigorous—sometimes almost vicious—criticism of Romanticism this can, of course, seem strange, but it is explained by Husserl's further remarks in the same context. Hegel's "system," he goes on to say, "lacks a critique of reason, which is the foremost prerequisite for being scientific in philosophy." [9] Lest this criticism seem to be written in ignorance of Hegel's own burlesque of Kant's demand that knowledge be validated by a knowledge of the faculty of knowing—like learning to swim before going into the water (GP III 555)—it should be noted that the "critique" which Husserl finds lacking in Hegel is one which guarantees the objectivity of the concepts one employs. [10] To put it in the somewhat more contemporary terms of the philosophy of science: Husserl is accusing Hegel of failing to give an adequate justification of the concepts he forms within a pre-structured "system." In terms of phenomenology this means that Husserl sees in Hegel's dialectical method a means of introducing more into his conclusions than is warranted by the experience to which he appeals.

Paradoxically enough, however, the main thrust of Husserl's objection to Hegel's philosophy is historical. Whatever Hegel's scientific intentions may have been, the results of his efforts, according to Husserl, were "either to weaken or to adulterate the impulse toward the constitution of rigorous philosophical science," [11] an impulse which Husserl had seen at work from Plato to Kant and for which in his own day he looked in vain. Although Hegel called what he was doing "science," with the progress of the natural sciences it was more and more discredited, and its place was taken either by a "naturalism"

---

[5] *Logische Untersuchungen*, 3 vols. 2nd rev. ed. (Halle: Niemeyer, 1913), I 141.
[6] *Krisis*, pp. 204–205.
[7] "Philosophie als strenge Wissenschaft," 292–93.
[8] Ibid., 292.
[9] Ibid., 293.
[10] *Formale und transzendentale Logik* (Halle: Niemeyer, 1929), p. 160.
[11] "Philosophie als strenge Wissenschaft," 293.

coming out of the eighteenth century, which sought to turn philosophy into a positive (exact) science, or by a skepticism which would turn philosophy into a *Weltanschauung* laying no claim to being strictly scientific at all. By the same token, Hegel's "historical relativism," which recognized no philosophy as valid once and for all time, simply did away with the need of one absolutely valid scientific philosophy and opened the door to one *Weltanschauung* after another, each of which is relatively justified for its own time.[12]

This last objection is particularly interesting because it goes right to the heart of the difference between Hegel and Husserl in their conceptions of what philosophy is. As Husserl sees it, philosophy is a sort of Platonic idea which, even though it may take centuries or millennia to realize, is eternally one and the same, unchangeable. If it is realized in his own day with the transcendental phenomenological method, that is nothing but the realization of the ideal which has always been the same [13]—what philosophers have thought down through the centuries makes no difference whatever for the ideal.[14] For Hegel, on the contrary, philosophy is concrete thought, concrete philosophizing. There is no antecedent ideal; it comes into being in the historical process of its development. This is not to say that each individual philosophy is valid for its own age, only to lose its validity in a succeeding age. Rather it is to say that philosophy is a living reality whose life is the process, and which is scientific to the extent that it is inseparable from its process. Individual philosophies are not philosophy; they are "moments" in the development of philosophy, which is one, not because it is an ideal to be realized, but because it is constantly in the process of becoming, corresponding to a reality which is constantly in the process of becoming (EGP 118–34). Husserl can look at history and find there only abortive attempts to achieve the antecedent ideal which is achieved only with the elaboration of a method which makes "scientific" philosophizing a possibility. Hegel can look at history and find there a philosophy constantly on the march, which is in danger of becoming unscientific only if it stops marching. Thus it is that Hegel's much-controverted contention that philosophy ends with himself must, it would seem, be taken figuratively, in the same way as his remark "If one is to begin philosophizing, one must first be a Spinozist" (GP III 376). Just as the latter remark does not mean that philosophy is complete with Spinoza, so the former does not

---

12 Ibid.

13 What bothered Husserl perhaps most about Hegel was that he produced a reaction which became a refusal of any and all transcendental philosophy (cf. *Krisis*, pp. 196, 199, 201).

14 Cf. note 4.

mean that there will be no philosophizing after Hegel. The meaning is simply that it is impossible to go back beyond Spinoza or beyond Hegel—and still do philosophy! Husserl's contention, on the other hand, that philosophy begins with transcendental phenomenology, in the sense that what preceded it was not philosophy—only an impulse to become philosophy—must, it would seem, be taken quite literally.[15]

Given such an enormous difference between two conceptions of what philosophy is, or of what philosophy does, it may seem strange to speak of significant similarities in the two types of endeavor. It should seem less strange, however, if we recognize that even where the differences are most pronounced they are not necessarily contradictions. Husserl is primarily concerned with the rigor, the apodicticity, of philosophical knowing, convinced that once this has been secured no limit can be put on what is to be known. Hegel's primary concern is with what philosophical knowing knows, and he is confident that faithfulness to the content of consciousness will result, not only in a universal knowledge, but also in a method which makes universal knowledge available. Husserl will make the validity of the method, antecedently assured, the criterion for the objectivity of the knowledge attained. Hegel will make the unbroken chain of objectivity in knowing the self-regulating guarantee that the method it progressively reveals delivers the truth of reality. What both are convinced of, however, is that genuine philosophical knowing has a content and that the progressive appropriation of this content is a goal which man can justifiably set for himself. It makes little sense to say with Kojève [16] that the method of philosophical "meditation" is the same for both Hegel and Husserl—what they meditate on is simply too different— but it does make sense to say that they are pursuing similar goals by different paths and that both recognize the need of avoiding the pitfalls inherited from previous philosophers, whether from Descartes or Locke, Hume or Kant.

If one were to draw up a table of the similarities and differences between the philosophies of Hegel and Husserl, it might well be that the differences would outnumber the similarities—or at least outweigh them in significance. At the same time, however, one would be forced to recognize that the differences are genuinely intelligible—and illuminating—only if seen in the light of the similarities. At the risk of becoming prolix, then, it might be well to examine both similarities and differences, in the hope that they will both illumine each other

---

15 "Philosophie als strenge Wissenschaft," 290–91.

16 Alexandre Kojève, *Introduction à la lecture de Hegel*, 4th ed. (Paris: Gallimard, 1947), p. 447.

and throw light on the larger enterprise which might be called the phenomenological endeavor.

Although it would be a mistake to call either Hegel or Husserl a "rationalist," in any narrow sense of that term, it is clear from the beginning that both are very much alike in their extraordinary confidence—itself non-rational perhaps—in the autonomy of human reason and in its capacity to come to terms with reality. Neither will, in theory at least, put any limits to reason's field of competence—above all not limit it to determining the rules of its own functioning. "Infinity," then, is characteristic of reason. But here, immediately, a difference is discernible. For Hegel a capacity for the infinite bespeaks an infinity on the side of reason which is more than potential, but this it can be only if it is ultimately identifiable with concrete infinite reason, infinite or "absolute" Spirit.[17] For Husserl human reason is faced with an infinity of rational tasks, and it is equal to those tasks, in the sense that no task is outside the competence of rational investigation—provided all investigations are rational in the sense in which he means rational.[18]

By the same token, then, both Hegel and Husserl seek an adequate guarantee of rationality in human thinking, and both see the need of a philosophical science if this is to be achieved. What each means by "science," however, particularly when applied to philosophy, is quite different. Hegel sees science in the unbroken character of the chain of implications issuing from an indubitable beginning, whether it be the beginning of experience in the *Phenomenology of Spirit* or the initial affirmation of being in the *Science of Logic*—to begin is to begin a process, and the necessity of the process is science.[19] Husserl, on the other hand, has submitted the very notion of science to a phenomenological analysis and has come up with an eidetic intuition of the "essence" of science. Philosophy will be science if it conforms to this essence.[20] Like Hegel, of course, Husserl recognizes that the *manner* in which philosophy is scientific will not be the same as the

[17] For detailed documentation on this, see chap. 7 of this volume, "Hegel on Proofs for God's Existence," as well as chap. 8, "Hegel's Critique of Kant's Theology," and chap. 9, "Hegel on the Identity of Content in Religion and Philosophy."

[18] Quentin Lauer, s.j., *Edmund Husserl: Phenomenology and the Crisis of Philosophy* (New York: Harper & Row, 1965), pp. 163–64.

[19] In both the Preface and the Introduction to the *Phenomenology of Spirit* Hegel makes abundantly clear what this means.

[20] Cf., for example, the First Cartesian Meditation; "Philosophie als strenge Wissenschaft," 289–91. This ideal, toward which history tends, is called the *Grundforderung der Apodiktizität* (*Krisis*, p. 274).

manner in which the "exact" sciences are scientific—its subject matter does not permit that—but it will be equally scientific.[21] Thus, both Hegel and Husserl agree that without phenomenology, the study of consciousness as the unique locus of givenness, there can be no science. But here a striking difference enters in: for Husserl phenomenology *is* the science of philosophy, because it is at once the unique and the universal method of philosophical investigation; whereas for Hegel phenomenology is, properly speaking, a preparation for philosophy (corresponding, in a sense, to Kant's *Critique of Pure Reason*)[22] because it is the progressive revelation that reason is in truth spirit, whose progressive self-revelation is philosophy. Thus, although for both Hegel and Husserl the implications of phenomena are manifested in a reflection on consciousness, Hegel will draw out those implications in rich profusion—in a logic which necessarily passes beyond the "essence" which reflection reveals, in a philosophy of nature which studies spirit's external self-manifestation, and in a philosophy of spirit which knows spirit itself in the workings of the human spirit—while Husserl will get very little beyond the discovery that the "transcendental subjectivity" which the epoché and reductions have revealed is the "*a priori* source" of all objectivity. Whether the phenomenologist opts for the method of Husserl—with its conceptual rigor—or that of Hegel—with its socio-historical ramifications—he cannot fail to contrast the tremendous issues of total human experience which crowd the pages of Hegel's writings with the painfully detailed "clarifications" of the individual phenomenologist's somewhat banal experiences which emerge from Husserl's voluminous life work. The difference here may very well be due, once more, to the fundamental divergence in approaching the rational problematic. Both Hegel and Husserl agree that reason is consciousness functioning at its peak and that philosophy is reason's highest accomplishment. In Husserl's view, however, this bespeaks a constantly renewed effort to raise consciousness to the level of reason as it confronts each and every task, which means beginning over and over again. Hegel, on the other hand, sees a need of tracing consciousness from its incipient, immediate, abstract form through all the stages of concretion to its perfection in reason (the work of phenomenology) so that then philosophy can begin. Because there is no need to go through the procedure again and again, once reason has begun to philosophize it can keep moving.

21 *Ideen zu einer reinen Phänomenologie und phänomenologischen Philosophie*. I. *Allgemeine Einführung in die reine Phänomenologie*, ed. Walter Biemel (The Hague: Nijhoff, 1950). II. *Phänomenologische Untersuchungen zur Konstitution*, ed. Marly Biemel (The Hague: Nijhoff, 1952), I, nos. 73–75.

22 Hegel, it is true, does not institute a "critique of reason," but in the *Phenomenology* he seeks to trace the process which becomes reason and thus to assure rationality.

The danger that the Hegelian mode of philosophizing may become slipshod is greater, of course, but it has advantages which are too obvious to enumerate. It is one thing to elaborate a method for the investigation of consciousness, another to investigate it. Husserl spends so much time on the former task that he has little opportunity for the latter; Hegel gets on with the show—and the show is most interesting.

RATIONALIZING EXPERIENCE

Perhaps one of the most vigorous reactions to Kant among his immediate followers, a reaction which is shared by Husserl and his followers, was a rejection of the Kantian "dualism" of sense and intellect and its attendant postulation of the non-phenomenal "thing-in-itself." By separating sense and intellect, it was felt, Kant put reason in the position of supplying a rational form for experience but of being unable to rationalize the content of experience. Thus the very heart of reality, that which was somehow "behind" its appearances to consciousness, became for philosophical reasoning simply an "unknown X," and the *a priori* forms of sense, understanding, and reason were left with only a phenomenal content. Both Hegel and Husserl are quick to dispose of this unknown and unknowable reality, and both for the reason that an unknowable reality would not be real; a "thing-in-itself" simply would not be a *thing*. Both, then, will rationalize experience in such a way that reason can be "conscious of being all reality." In order to do this, however, Husserl will appeal to an eidetic intuition of the very "essence" of reason, whose function it is to "constitute" its objects in the mode of necessity—thus permitting an *a priori* constitution even of the contents of experience.[23] An experience so rationalized will have its own "logic," and this will be discoverable in an intentional analysis of transcendental subjectivity, which is the *a priori* source of any and all content for consciousness. Given any conscious act, say the perception of a tree, Husserl will be able so to analyze the act that he will know not only the essence of the perception but also the essence of the tree which is its object. What is important, then, is not the individual act of perceiving nor the individual tree perceived, but the essential contained in the act, i.e., what perceiving a tree *must be* and what a perceived tree *must be*. In all this one has the lingering suspicion that Husserl is concerned neither with trees nor with the perceiving of trees but only with what one must *mean* when one speaks of trees or of the perceiving of trees.[24]

[23] *Formale und transzendentale Logik* has "rational constitution" as its principal theme. Cf. *Ideen* I, nos. 144, 149.

[24] The intentional constitution of essences and the constitution of meaning are scarcely to be distinguished—especially if there are *necessary* meanings.

In any event, it is here that the difference between Husserl's and Hegel's approach becomes glaringly apparent. Apart from the fact that Hegel devotes little time—and that only at the very beginning of the *Phenomenology*—to such experiences as that of a tree, or of color, shape, geometric figure, and the like—all of which are constants in the Husserlian gallery of experiences—he is even less concerned with "essences," be they of conscious acts or their objects. In the dialectic of "Force and Understanding," it is true, he speaks of a search for hidden essences, but only as a stage along the way, a stage which must be superseded if phenomenology is to get anywhere. It is true, too, that in the *Logic* "The Doctrine of Essence" constitutes approximately one-third of the whole work, but here too the movement is such that it must go beyond essences (or, perhaps, meanings) if it is to get to reality, which is reason's concern. The point is that in no sense does Hegel feel that he has reconciled experience and reason by discovering the abstract essences either of experience or of what is experienced. For him experience will be rationalized if he can trace the whole process from its minimal beginnings in sensation to its maximal grasp (*Begriff*/concept) in absolute knowing and show that they are inseparable because no step along the way has been left out. Hegel is very little interested in what the act of consciousness must be if it is to be valid; he is very much concerned with what the total process of consciousness is—if the process is really total, it will be self-validating.

It could be argued, of course—and perhaps it should—that Husserl has the advantage over Hegel in all this of being much more carefully consistent in his use of language and of concepts—if, indeed, it is true that absolute terminological rigor promotes rather than stultifies philosophical discourse. Aside from the fact that Husserl does not always—he cannot—submit his own terminology and conceptual structures to the painstaking analysis which he advocates, it is true that it is easier—if slightly less rewarding—to follow his meaning than it is to follow Hegel's. It may also be true that if philosophical importance is measured by the validity of our cognition and not by its significance, Husserl again has the edge. It is not true, however, that Hegel is less rigorous in describing a movement whose scope is so vast than is Husserl in detailing an analysis whose scope is so limited.

PHILOSOPHICAL SCIENCE

This brings us back to the task of describing similarities in the Hegelian and Husserlian positions, similarities which both illumine and are illumined by manifest dissimilarities. In his own day Hegel was unremitting in his opposition to the non-rational intuitionism of the

Romantics, convinced as he was not only that philosophy could not be unscientific but also that it constitutes the highest form of science—not in the sense that its certitudes were the most certain but in the sense that its truths, which could be genuinely known, were the most significant for man. Husserl, as we know, shared Hegel's conviction regarding the scientific character of philosophy—he saw it as essential to philosophy that it be scientific, such that an unscientific, romantic philosophy simply would not be philosophy. Nor is the meaning which each gives to the term "science"—*Wissenschaft*—so very different; it signifies the purity of the knowledge in question, as opposed to mere opinion or conjecture, and it calls for strict methodical procedures in its acquisition. The difference between them, then, lies less in the kind of knowledge each aims at than in the emphasis they put on the manner of approaching it. If, says Husserl, philosophy is the highest form of rational endeavor—a supposition which, for him, does not seem to require any discussion—then it cannot be inferior to any other form of rational endeavor, certainly not inferior in rationality. At the same time Husserl is convinced that the positive sciences have achieved a very high degree of rationality: they are "sciences" in the strict sense of the term. Philosophy, then, cannot be less scientific in its area of competence, the area of universal "essential" knowledge, than are the particular sciences in their limited areas of competence. Philosophy must, in fact, be in a sense *more* scientific than the other sciences since one of its tasks is the validation of those concepts which the particular sciences employ but which they themselves are unable to validate.[25] If, then, other disciplines are to be authentically scientific, the concepts they employ must be susceptible of thoroughgoing verification in a higher discipline called philosophy. Thus, for Husserl, the very essence of philosophy is revealed in the necessity of an ultimate guarantee of scientific knowledge as such. If philosophy is not scientific, there is no science.[26]

Hegel, as we have seen, will not yield to Husserl one bit in his demand that philosophy be scientific—the knowledge it affords is knowledge in the strictest possible sense of that term; it is "absolute knowing." In his approach to "philosophical science," however, Hegel will not take his cue from the scientific character of the positive sciences or of any other discipline. He will see in the sciences, it is true, as well as in morality, jurisprudence, art, religion, and history, so many manifestations—in addition to philosophy—of reason's operation in the world of man (EGP 298). He will even seek to integrate all these in the universal whole which is his "System," without which science is

25 See *Erste Philosophie*, I 13.
26 "Philosophie als strenge Wissenschaft," 298.

meaningless, but his approach will be to follow the self-development
of consciousness as it progressively manifests and corrects its own de-
ficiencies until it eventually becomes absolute (i.e., unconditioned)
knowing—and this last will be the culmination of the scientific process,
philosophy. Hegel will, it is true, be guided in his quest by his antecedent conviction that man is most truly human when he is most truly
rational, that whatever is specifically human in man's endeavor has
the mark of rationality on it, but he will let rationality reveal itself in
the process, not decide ahead of time what it *must* be. Ultimately
Hegel, like Husserl, will say that reason is the autonomous source of
its own "absolute knowing," but this is a discovery he will make in the
course of tracing the development of consciousness, and he will devote
more than two-thirds of his *Phenomenology of Spirit* to articulating
the implications of this discovery. The result will be a reason which
bears little more than a family resemblance to the reason analyzed by
Husserl.

It seems scarcely necessary to describe in detail—for those who are
not totally ignorant of Hegel's philosophizing[27]—his approach to
knowing through an objective consciousness which does not make
sense, even to itself, until it becomes self-consciousness, a self-consciousness which does not really grasp the self of which it is conscious
until it becomes reason, a reason which runs the risk of bogging down
in its own particularity if it does not move on to identify itself with
the truly universal spirit, the ultimate source of all being and all
truth. All this is too well known already, and any attempt to describe
it, short of rewriting the entire *Phenomenology*, runs the risk of trivializing it. To go back over certain facets of the development, however,
may help us to see why the results of the Hegelian phenomenology
differ so much from those of the Husserlian.

Husserl, we know, was permanently suspicious of Hegel's dialectical
method, both because he considered it an arbitrary construction of
questionable implications and because he saw it as an imposition from
without not demanded by the contents "given" in consciousness. It is
difficult, of course, to answer either of these objections—Husserl was
not the first to raise them—but it is Hegel's contention that if we
follow him faithfully—facing "the labor of the negative" (*Phän.* 20)—
we shall *see* that every implication is inevitable—hence "given"—once
we accept the initial position, which cannot but be accepted. It is also
Hegel's contention, not that the method is imposed from without, but
that it is merely a description of the process through which consciousness goes in discovering its own inadequacies, negating these inadequacies, and thus reaffirming itself at progressively higher levels. Like

27 See chap. 1 of this volume, "The Phenomenon of Reason."

Husserl, Hegel is concerned with the assurance that reason be adequately rational in its functioning. Unlike Husserl, however, he refuses to believe that the apodictic certainty of its knowledge will guarantee its rational adequacy. It is not the certainty of knowledge which constitutes its rationality; rather it is its grasp of reality in its total interrelatedness. Husserl can institute a phenomenology which piles up—and even relates—bits of certain knowledge; and given enough time—and enough phenomenologists—it will get around to investigating society and history, law and morality, art and religion. In this view phenomenology is phenomenology antecedent to any concrete investigation it undertakes; it is a sort of blueprint for future investigations. For Hegel phenomenology is a "science of the experience of consciousness," and it is not complete as phenomenology until it somehow embraces the totality of consciousness—which is why, after beginning as a "science of the experience of consciousness," it realizes itself only as a "phenomenology of spirit." Hegel is determined, then, that his philosophy be rooted in experience, but not merely in his own experience—even as paradigmatic—nor, for that matter, in the experiences of philosophers, privileged as those experiences may be, but in the whole of human experience. It may, of course, be questioned just how successful even Hegel's *Phenomenology* can be in coming to terms with the totality of human experience, but its attempt to do so is a testimony to Hegel's conviction that to attempt less is to condemn reason to being inadequately rational.[28]

SELF-CONSCIOUS REASON

If, then, we take as a sort of least common denominator of any phenomenology, whether it be Hegel's or Husserl's or that of any of the latter's followers, that it will appeal to no data except the data of consciousness, that it will not seek to go "behind" experience to what is not experienced for an explanation of experience, we are still faced with a tremendous difference between the experiences to which Hegel and Husserl appeal. This manifests itself most strikingly perhaps in the approach each takes to consciousness of self. Like Kant, who saw in the original transcendental unity of apperception the basic condition of all consciousness, both Hegel and Husserl see all consciousness as mere empty abstraction if it is not ultimately identified with consciousness of self; consciousness can find its guarantee only within itself, not outside itself, where nothing is to be *found*—to find it would be to find it in consciousness. For Husserl it is not consciousness which discovers within itself the need to become self-consciousness; rather

---

28 What has always fascinated readers of the *Phenomenology*, even those who disagree with it, is the extraordinarily broad range of experiences it seeks to integrate into the process of experience.

it is the philosopher who sees that the necessity of apodictic certainty
—if his philosophy is to be science—dictates that he seek apodictic
evidence where alone it can be found, in the original source of all
objectivity, transcendental subjectivity.[29] It is not too easy to say what
this transcendental subjectivity is since it is neither the individual
subjectivity of the philosopher (although it does seem capable of being multiplied)[30] nor the concrete totality of subjectivity, since his
method, at least at this level, does not give him access to that.[31] One
is tempted to surmise that the exercise of the epoché and the reductions has permitted Husserl to eliminate whatever is idiosyncratic to
individual subjectivity and has thus provided him with a sort of subjectivity as such—which can stand for any and all subjectivity. Such
a subjectivity can well manifest the necessary laws of subjective constitution and thus provide a guarantee for what is subjectively constituted. It can at the same time be sure that no other individual subjectivity—if there be such—can see things differently and be right.

That Hegel, in his search for a subject which will ultimately find in
the consciousness of itself the consciousness of all reality, does not come
up with such a "transcendental subjectivity" is due largely to the
point of view from which he approaches the whole question. He has
begun his study of consciousness with the simplest, most direct, most
immediate form of objective consciousness, sensation. Sensation alone
proves to be inadequate to its own sense object and must introduce
the mediation of reflection in a perception which somehow fixes the
object as a thing. This in turn can find no satisfaction in the abstract
"thingness" of its object and so turns to understanding for an explanation of what appears to it. Understanding proves to be the last
step in objective consciousness, since it is forced to look outside
consciousness for an explanation of what is in consciousness. The next
step resembles what we find in Husserl's procedure. Consciousness
realizes that by continuing to look outward it has gone down a dead-
end street which promises no further satisfaction in that direction.
Unlike Husserl, however, Hegel does not immediately turn inward—
seeking means to purify the inward view—he seeks a relation to the
objective which will mediate the return to the subjective, and this he
finds in appetition; it is appetition which begins to mediate the consciousness of self as the subject of consciousness. It is in following the
development of this sort of consciousness that Hegel realizes that the
self will never find itself merely by itself; a condition for the discovery

29 Cf. First Cartesian Meditation; *Ideen,* I 72–73; *Formale und transzendentale Logik,*
p. 237.
30 Cf. *Erste Philosophie,* I 93–101, 141–48.
31 We get a hint of this in the notion of pure "Ich-Pol" (*Krisis,* pp. 188–90).

of self becomes the discovery of a community of selves, and the voyage of discovery is already a tortuous one; not until the end of the *Phenomenology* will the self find its true self.

It is true, of course, that Husserl too institutes an elaborate procedure—both negative and positive in its elements—for arriving at a pure transcendental subject which will be the guarantee of all knowledge, and the knowledge of which can be called an "absolute knowing." The difference, however, is enormous, which could have been expected, in view of the goal which each has in view. Because Husserl is more concerned with the apodictic certitude of the knowledge he can attain than he is with the extent of that knowledge, his aim is to find in self-consciousness the guarantee of any knowledge, however trivial it may be. Since Hegel's aim is the attainment of knowledge which is truly knowledge only if it is total, he cannot be satisfied with anything less than absolute Spirit's absolute knowledge of itself, a knowledge which cannot stop short of the interrelatedness of all knowing and of all that is known. Thus it is that, even though both men recognize that the investigation of a subjectivity which would be merely individual can produce only abstract results and that the mere universalization of such a subject will not concretize its original abstractness, Husserl will recognize the need of coming to terms with intersubjectivity only after he has completely laid the foundation for genuine subjective analysis, and Hegel will insist that a self outside the framework of mutually interrelated selves is meaningless and can guarantee nothing, not even itself. It is all very well to speak of the autonomy of reason, as both Hegel and Husserl do; for Hegel this autonomy is to be won in dialectical struggle—embracing the whole socio-historical dimension of man—not simply discovered in a process of eliminating whatever would make for contingency and, hence, uncertainty in cognition.[32]

Husserl, as we have said, recognizes that an absolutely valid knowledge makes sense only if it is known to be absolutely valid for any possible subject. This could simply mean that it does not make sense to speak of a knowledge which would be valid for one subject and not for another—only if reason is genuinely one does it make sense to speak of knowledge at all. If that is all it means, however, it would be enough to institute a method to validate absolutely one's own knowledge, since by definition such a knowledge has to be universal.

[32] There is, of course, the danger of undue negative emphasis if one looks only to Husserl's "epoché" as the suspension of any "position" which would make for contingency. The "reductions" are not negative but positive; they make it possible for transcendental subjectivity to reveal the riches contained in its self-consciousness. Still, it is only if the negative function of eliminating contingency is constantly operative that positive discovery in subjectivity can attain to any kind of certainty at all.

The point is, and Husserl saw this clearly, that unless there is some way of determining that others do *de facto* know in this way, "absolute" knowing can be only abstractly universal. Husserl, therefore, finds himself forced to say that the laws of intentional constitution which he has established are operative in all subjects and that there are other subjects. Without going into the intricate details of intersubjective constitution, which occupied Husserl's thoughts for many years —without ever giving him complete satisfaction [33]—it seems safe to say that the constitution of other subjects is simply the extension of self-constitution and that the essential in any subjectivity has already been discovered in the discovery of subjectivity as such. It is not an intersubjective investigation which is what is essential to subjectivity; rather it is the subjective (solipsistic) [34] investigation which reveals what is essential and, therefore, true of any subject whatever.

Hegel's procedure is entirely different. For him intersubjectivity is no special problem, not because it is not a problem, but because it is not distinct from the problem of self-consciousness itself. To attempt to separate the consciousness of self from the consciousness of other selves and then to seek in the former an explanation of the latter would be, for Hegel, to involve oneself in a Humpty Dumpty situation, trying to put together what never should have been put apart. A community of selves, for all of whom knowledge must be the same if it is to be truly knowledge, is for Hegel not an afterthought dictated by the need of concretizing the universality of knowledge. The community of selves is a prerequisite for any meaningful self-realization. From the initial confrontation of master consciousness and slave consciousness, through the gradual development of slave consciousness to a consciousness of being free, down to the ultimate realization that the only framework within which self-consciousness can be legitimately achieved is the totality of consciousness called "spirit," consciousness in isolation, whether as individual or "essential" consciousness, has no place in Hegel's *Phenomenology*. One can readily see why history has such monumental importance for Hegel, whereas for Husserl it is only incidental to the philosophical enterprise that the impulse toward scientific philosophy has a "history." Because he is convinced that development is integral to the very intelligibility of that which develops Hegel is incapable of *doing* philosophy in any but an historical perspective, and the history he considers is always a concatenation of real events, whether the subject under consideration be consciousness, morality, law, art, religion, or philosophy itself. The one exception to this within his "System" is logic, which, because it is concerned with

33 Cf. Fifth Cartesian Meditation; *Ideen*, II.
34 Cf. Fourth Cartesian Meditation, no. 41; *Erste Philosophie*, II 65–66, 174.

logical implications apart from temporal dimensions—"the presentation of God as he is in his eternal essence before the creation of nature or of a single finite spirit" (WL I 31)—can be, if not completely
ahistorical, at least not historically conditioned. This, too, may serve
to illustrate the difference between Husserl's and Hegel's views of the
philosophical enterprise. In view of the emphasis which both put on
the content of thought—as opposed to merely the activity of thinking—
it is no surprise that both seek to institute a new logic which will be
adequate to the content of thought, to the being which reveals itself
in thought. For Hegel this will mean a dialectical logic capable of doing justice to the processual character of the being which reveals itself.
For Husserl it will mean a transcendental logic, which will establish
the laws for the intentional constitution for all content of thought.

For Hegel, then, phenomenology will bring consciousness to the
level of absolute knowing, which is then capable of looking into itself
and discovering all that pure thought reveals. Logic is justified because it has been preceded by a phenomenology. For Husserl the logic
and the phenomenology are not to be distinguished; both are transcendental, both are constitutive of their own content. When the phenomenological method has been perfected to the point where the
"laws" of transcendental constitution have been firmly established, phenomenology *is* logic, transcendental logic.[35] For this very reason there
is a risk, in instituting a comparison between the Hegelian and the
Husserlian phenomenologies, of falsifying the issue. Because it is an introduction to philosophizing and not philosophy itself, Hegel's *Phenomenology* leaves untouched some of the questions raised by Husserl;
Hegel takes them up only later in the *Logic*. Thus the whole question
of the cognition of essence constitutes both the culmination of Hegel's
"Objective Logic" and the transition to "Subjective Logic" or "The
Doctrine of Concept." Here we see both that the knowledge of essence
is not the goal of the Hegelian enterprise and that much of his teaching on subjective knowledge, corresponding to Husserl's transcendental subjectivity, belongs to the *Logic* and not to the *Phenomenology*. If, however, we were to make a comparison not between
phenomenologies but between the whole philosophical endeavor of the
one and the other, we should run the risk of being unfair to Husserl.
In the interests of perfecting a method which would ensure scientific
rigor in philosophical thinking, Husserl deliberately limited his investigations to the kind of considerations which would illustrate the fe-
cundity of the method, and left to others, who would employ the

[35] What *Formale und transzendentale Logik* seeks to do is to justify an ultimate confidence in the "constitutive" function of transcendental subjectivity—provided it adhere
to the "logical" rules established for it (cf. p. 14).

method he perfected, the larger issues which abound in Hegel's system. To put the whole question of the difference between the two men somewhat succinctly—and, perhaps, too simply—both sought to rationalize being thoroughly: Husserl by narrowing the notion of being to that which can be intentionally constituted in reason, Hegel by broadening the concept of reason so that it embraced the totality of human experience integrally interrelated. It is the difference between a concern for what reason can reveal and a concern that it be reason which is doing the revealing.

COMPLEMENTARITY OF THE TWO APPROACHES

If this long comparison of Hegel and Husserl is to be fruitful for our own philosophical thinking and not trail off in a sterile catalogue of similarities and differences, we are now faced with the task of indicating, however briefly, the ways in which the two approaches can complement and thus, perhaps, fructify each other. When we look at the two men we can admire at one and the same time the infinite patience of a Husserl, who is willing to spend a lifetime laying the methodological foundations without which, he is convinced, it is senseless even to dream of a philosophical science, and the majestic impatience of a Hegel, who simply refuses so to linger over the foundations that the philosophical edifice remains incomplete. Our own impatience with Husserl, as he returns again and again to the task of determining conclusively the essence of the various modalities of consciousness, may be tempered as we realize that the rapidity with which Hegel—particularly in the early sections of the *Phenomenology*—takes us from sensation to perception to understanding leaves us with the uncomfortable feeling that we do not quite grasp what is happening. There is much to be said for Hegel's refusal to leave any facet of human experience unexplored—which does not permit him to linger—but this could, and perhaps should, be tempered by a painstaking effort to reconstruct the most basic of experiences. It is not out of the question to see that what Hegel, as well as Husserl, is doing is engaging in a kind of re-constitution of naïve experience. It might, in fact, not be amiss to say that a more conscious theory of intentional constitution could have made Hegel more aware of just what he was doing. Even if we are to look upon the Husserlian method of intentional constitution as primarily geared to ensuring consistency of *meaning*, we might also say that a more meticulous care in the determination of meaning could make Hegel somewhat less difficult to follow. At the same time it should be noticed that had Husserl put less emphasis on the question "What must experience be," and more on the further question

"What does experience reveal," his writings might be both more readable and more fruitful.

Husserl realizes, as well as does Hegel, that the fruitfulness of the phenomenological method lies in its ability to spell out the implications of original experience. We can, however, ask whether the Husserlian method might have proved even more fruitful had he been willing to recognize that the implications which are not immediately available *in* experience but mediated through thought as it *thinks* experience are integral to the total process of experience. Here it is, perhaps, that the suspicion arises that Husserl's insistence on the certainty of the philosopher in *seeing* is an obstacle to his grasping the significance of *what* he sees. The detailed (and repeated) efforts of Husserl to ensure that nothing goes wrong might well give way to a more fruitful confidence in the self-corrective character of experience and thought if we are faithful to their inner dialectic. There is, it is true, no substitute for methodological rigor, but exclusive insistence on method is found to leave philosophy standing still.

From the methodological point of view one cannot help being struck by a certain similarity between Hegel and Husserl in their insistence that philosophy can be legitimate only if it is willing to come to terms with its own beginnings. Hegel, it is true, will not return to the beginning again and again, as Husserl insists one must do if one is not to wander off into uncertainty, but it does not seem farfetched to say that we can detect in Hegel's method something resembling the Husserlian epoché and something resembling the reductions. When Hegel insists on beginning his *Phenomenology*—his voyage through the process of experience—with the simplest of experiences, thus eliminating both what might be foreign to experience and what could be considered too quick a leap into thought, it takes no great stretch of the imagination to liken this to an epoché. By the same token, Hegel's sedulous sticking to the ordered series of implications growing out of this original experience could be looked upon as not unlike the method of reductions. Had Hegel himself made us more aware of such elements in his methodology—if indeed he himself was aware of them— our own task in following him might have been an easier one. In any event, it is not out of the question that we could be helped in doing a sort of Hegelian phenomenology by such a consciousness of what is implied in sticking to experience.

It is scarcely subject to question that no one prior to Husserl, including Hegel, ever made such gigantic—and detailed—efforts to analyze thoroughly the reality of consciousness, the essential *ways* in which we can be conscious. One of the reasons which impel Husserl to do this is his determination not to go, in the process of "objective"

analysis, beyond the evidence afforded by consciousness. Nor is it always clear, even to those who have read Hegel most carefully, that
Hegel does not sometimes advance beyond this sort of evidence—or
at least it is not always clear that he shows adequately that he does
not. Perhaps it is too much to ask that Hegel should show a Husserlian concern for this sort of analysis, but it should not be out of place
to point out that such a concern need neither alter nor compromise
the Hegelian enterprise. At the same time it should not be unfair to
ask whether Husserl's unshakable confidence in the universality of his
method, i.e., as the unique method which will provide the results he
desires, does not prevent him from seeing that the universality of the
method is of little value if no appeal is made to the universality of
experience. One can, perhaps, see some justification for Husserl's limitation of the historical problematic to the tracing, among a carefully
selected list of philosophers, of the impetus to scientific philosophizing,
which is satisfied only when transcendental phenomenology appears
on the scene. One is still entitled to ask whether an intuition into
the requisites for philosophizing which does not in any way take into
account the actual philosophizing which has gone on—even among the
selected few who are considered—is not at best arbitrary. A discovery
of the essence of rational thinking which ignores what rational thinking has been doing for twenty-six centuries—or which denies that it
has been rational thinking—would seem to rule out a very important
testimony to the activity of thinking spirit. One might find in the
Hegelian effort to tie philosophical thinking in with the activity of
infinite reason (spirit) a concretely universal point of view for which
Husserl has no substitute. It is not, of course, clear how Husserl could
permit this to be done without altering or compromising the "purity"
of his own endeavor, but one can wonder how "universal" that endeavor can ever become if it is not thus concretized. In this connection it might not be amiss to point out that a phenomenological theology—Husserlian style—is scarcely conceivable, since God does not
"appear," [36] whereas for Hegel, although God may not appear as an
object, he quite definitely does manifest himself in the very activity of
thinking spirit, with the result that, for Hegel, a philosophy which
stops short of God is but a truncated philosophy.[37]

It has been suggested earlier that Husserl's "constitutive phenomenology" will be particularly significant if we see its primary function
as that of constituting "meanings." There is no doubt that it can be
employed to clarify what we "mean" when we speak. What it claims

36 Cf. *Ideen*, I 121–22.

37 See note 17 and, for additional development of this theme, Quentin Lauer, s.j.,
Hegel's Idea of Philosophy (New York: Fordham University Press, 1971), pp. 55–61.

to do, however, is to tell us not only what we *do* mean but also what we *must* mean when we speak, and since Plato's time it seems to have been rather clear that the establishment of "essential" meanings is not likely to be successful—let alone make sense—in a non-dialectical framework of investigation. Here it is that the Husserlian phenomenology might have its perspectives broadened by an infusion of Hegel's dialectical method. To be even more specific it might be suggested that the Husserlian notion of "subjective constitution" could be rendered more intelligible if it were seen in the framework of an Hegelian subject–object dialectic.

By itself, of course, the dialectical method cannot be a guarantee of the faithfulness of the phenomenological investigation. In fact, if all it is is a method, it can guarantee nothing at all. But if it is, as Hegel contends it is, the method dictated by the movement of consciousness itself, then faithfulness in the examination of actual phenomena will result in a method which is dialectical. Here then is the place to ask whether Hegel or Husserl really examines consciousness more effectively. Husserl begins with an ideal of apodictic certitude,[38] which can be achieved only if the philosophical investigation sticks to the data of consciousness. This passes over to a determination of what the philosopher would necessarily discover if he examined consciousness, i.e., what is essential to an "act" of consciousness of this or that kind. There is, however, a question as to whether the antecedent ideal of apodictic certitude does not prove an obstacle to actual examination of consciousness, since any "act" which is examined will, by the fact that it is actual, also be contingent. Hegel, on the other hand, is not bothered by contingency, above all not by the contingency of any act of consciousness. He is not bothered by contingency because he is convinced that in the overall framework of the process of consciousness it is no obstacle at all to rationality; and he is not bothered by the contingency of any act of consciousness because he never examines an act in isolation from the process. Thus, while both men are determined to establish the rationality of consciousness, Husserl will do this for "acts" of consciousness, precisely as acts, while Hegel will do it for the whole process, by tracing its movement from beginning to end and showing that its implications are inescapable. There are times, of course, when Hegel's conclusions would be more plausible if he commanded a methodology which made more rigorous claims on our assent. But there are also times when we should find the results arrived at by Husserl more convincing if he could show us how they fit into an overall process which is concrete consciousness. Perhaps what we

[38] No amount of phenomenological investigation, it would seem, can reveal just why this kind of certitude is a prime value—for life.

should ask of Hegel is that he take more methodological pains to show us where he is going and how he gets there, while asking of Husserl to show us that he is going anywhere at all, and that it is worthwhile going there.

3

H. S. Harris'

Hegel's Development: Toward the Sunlight, 1770–1801:

A Review

ALTHOUGH IT IS REASONABLE to suppose, with regard to any great thinker, that his formative years were decisive for determining the direction his thinking ultimately took, it is rare for the intellectual historian to have at hand adequate evidence for the reconstruction of that early development. From this point of view, as has been abundantly demonstrated by such authors as Rosenkranz, Haym, Dilthey, Asveld, Häring, and Lukács, the case of Hegel is clearly an exception. Thanks to Hegel's own practice, begun in his early school years and continued throughout his life, of keeping a detailed record of his studies, we have a rich source of information regarding the development of his interests and the maturing of his thought. Like his scholarly predecessors—and perhaps even more successfully—Henry Harris has made excellent use of this vast manuscript material in presenting us with an absorbingly interesting account of these early years of development, which were dominated by Hegel's consciousness of a vocation to be a professional scholar and educator who would hold up to his own people the ideal of a religion of truly virtuous living and thus bring about a social metamorphosis. Harris manifests an extraordinary scholarly sensitivity to the work of his predecessors in this area, but at the same time he bases his own account primarily on a meticulous reading of everything which survives from the pen of Hegel during the period preceding his career as a university professor, which began at Jena in 1801. We see passing in review the excerpts and essays of the Stuttgart period, the program sketched out during the years at Tübingen and crystallized in the "Tübingen Fragment," culminating in the theological and political writings belonging to the years spent in Berne and Frankfurt.

In masterly fashion Harris has shown the essential unity of a pro-

An earlier version of this chapter appears in *Studi Internazionale di Filosofia*, 5 (1973), 270–72.

gram, the fundamental lines of which are already drawn in the "Tübingen Fragment" (which, together with four other previously untranslated manuscripts from this period, is translated in an appendix). What comes out of all this is the account of an extraordinarily consistent development, which begins with the enunciation of a religious ideal, whose elaboration requires the articulation of political ideas, and issues in Hegel's discovery of his vocation as a philosopher. The book might well have been entitled "The Becoming of a Philosopher"—only as a philosopher could Hegel attain the goal he had set for himself from the beginning, and only by following the development can we come to terms with the philosopher he became. When we do this we shall find verified the author's words: "One of the most remarkable things about the development of Hegel's philosophy is that ideas mature in a sort of steady succession and, once matured, remain fairly stable even while other ideas are developing around and above them" (p. 390). Many of the ideas which are familiar to us from Hegel's later writings had already matured during these early years.

The subtitle of Harris' book, "Toward the Sunlight," finds its source in a letter which Hegel wrote to Schelling on April 16, 1795, proclaiming his vision of the task before them: "strive toward the sun . . . that the salvation of the human race may come to fruition." The idea as Hegel presented it at that time was not, Harris tells us, properly philosophical but rather religious–aesthetic (p. xxi). It becomes philosophical only when Hegel realizes, at the beginning of his academic career, that the "salvation of the human race" is to be achieved neither by a religious attitude unsupported by knowledge nor by a merely theoretical knowledge out of touch with life, but only by a real knowledge issuing from a reason (*Vernunft*) which has broken the bonds of the abstract formalism of understanding (*Verstand*). If this is to be accomplished, "What is *objectively* known must be made *subjectively* effective" (p. xxii). To achieve this goal was Hegel's ideal from the start; only gradually did he become convinced that he could achieve the goal only as a philosopher. Thus, the discovery of philosophy came, so to speak, as a sequel to the failure of his initial quest (cf. p. xv).

It is important to emphasize that Hegel's awareness of his vocation as philosopher came to him only gradually. It explains, perhaps, why he ultimately conceived the role of philosopher as much more than that of a technician in handling concepts. The sun toward which he was striving was the sun of philosophical wisdom, but it was necessary to pass through the shadows to arrive there, and "The present book is the story of his sojourn among the shadows and the picture-makers" (p. xxxii). From another point of view, however, Hegel's activity could from the very start be considered philosophical, since it was "an attempt to clarify for himself his own social role as an enlightened scholar and future teacher" (p. 30). One piece of equipment he brought with him to this task was an insatiable intellectual curiosity which made him not only an omnivorous student but also one who thoroughly enjoyed every intellectual challenge he met. Of this he gave evidence even as a school boy. Behind him he left what would lighten the task of his intellectual biographer, the systematic record of his studies of which Harris has made such good use.

His first interest was religion, not, however, religion as simply a given, but as something out of which he could make sense, something which would have meaning for man, the human conceived of not as a static essence but as a dynamic nature. What Hegel sought, then, was a religion which would satisfy three inescapable needs of man. It had, first of all, to satisfy at least minimally the requirements of practical reason, to ensure that a life lived according to such a religion would be one of moral virtue. This requirement he saw satisfied in the Jewish religion. Secondly, however, a religion cannot be adequate if it satisfies only the demands of morality; " 'Fancy, heart, and sensibility must not on this account go empty away' " (p. 145). Hegel was satisfied that the Catholic religion met this second demand. The third requirement, which he felt had been met only in Greek religion, was that " 'all the needs of life, and the public activities of the state, must be tied in with it' " (ibid.). What was needed, however, was neither a return to Greek religion (despite Hegel's conviction as to the superiority of Greek culture) nor, properly speaking, the invention of a new religion; rather it was to realize a Christianity which would synthesize all the requirements enumerated. Thus, the goal Hegel set for himself was that of enabling his own society to regain possession of the Greek ideal, not by going back, but by going forward from the situation of civilized corruption in which it found itself to one of cultivated integrity. His own hope in the re-integrative power of reason convinced him that this could take place, but only a reason which grasped how the corruption had taken place could accomplish what he sought.

The problem, as Hegel saw it, lay in the distinction—or opposition—between the unity of objective religion and the diversity of subjective religious response. If the objective unity is secured by the "positivity" of authoritative formulation (as, for example, in a creed or in church laws), the way it has been in Catholicism, Hegel is convinced that only a dead formalism can be the result. This is not to mean that either objectivity or authority is to be eliminated; it does mean that the objectivity must be in accord with a rational standard, not merely a standard of abstract conventionalized conceptions. It also means that the authority in question must be the authority of reason and not merely that of positive, fixed legislation. Here, then, as in poetry and in philosophy, the appeal must be to experience and not merely to established usage. The problem, of course, was to preserve "the living concreteness of original direct experience" and at the same time maintain a "rational standard of objectivity" (p. 87). Small wonder that the concrete unity of Hegel's philosophical system should find its beginning here.

Christianity, then, as the young Hegel saw it, had become "positive" in a sense which made it inadequate to satisfy the religious needs of men. In Catholicism, forgetful that the only effective way of pleasing God was living a virtuous life, authoritative commands and prohibitions had replaced the moral demands of concrete reason. In Protestantism, reflective criticism had inhibited the impulses of the heart, while the needs of life and the public activities of the State are ignored by Christianity as a whole, which has become a merely private religion failing to integrate the whole of life in society. What, in short, has happened is that the organization of Christianity along official lines has turned God into an object of contemplation instead of an ideal of the will. What is needed is a program of religious reform which will be dictated by reason; not, however, by the exclusively moral reason of Kant but by a reason which takes into account the demands of experience, of the heart, and of the senses—and this within the framework of a large modern state.

Thus, as Hegel sees it, it is religion which must meet the demands of life, not life which must meet the demands of religion, and it is reason as an innate human capacity for the concrete which can tell what the demands of life are. At this stage in his career, despite his emphasis on the demands of reason, Hegel finds religion superior to philosophy, because, although like philosophy it is a product of reason, it is not merely a form of thought, but, more significantly, a form of life. As an illustration of this we can take what Hegel says regarding reverence before the divine. From the point of view of thought we act reverently because we see reverence as what we *ought* to manifest. From the religious point of view, on the other hand, we act reverently in the presence of the divine, because this *expresses* what we feel.

The original question which Hegel had asked himself was: " 'How far is the Christian religion qualified to serve as a folk-religion' " (religion of a people) (p. 415). This led him, then, to a study of the State and of the function of religion within it. As we know, the later Hegel saw the State as the ultimate locus of human rationality, of rational living. At this early stage that view is not lacking, but the focus is on the role which religion plays in the betterment of human living. The question, then, concerns what religion does to make the State the locus of rationality, and this turns into a question as to the relation of State and Church. The State, as Hegel sees it, needs the Church (or churches) precisely because the State cannot do anything which will directly cause its citizens to behave morally. Consistently enough, however, this also means that the State cannot require of its citizens that they belong to a church or impose civic penalties for not belonging to one. Thus we have the paradox of a Hegel who, on the one hand, holds for a separation of Church and State, and, on the other, calls for an integration of religious and political life scarcely seen since the time of ancient Greece, where the integration was achieved without conscious reflection—except, perhaps, in the "city" of Plato. It may or may not be a paradox that, as Harris tells us, Hegel arrived at this on the eve of his move to Jena, where, as a philosopher, he ceased looking for Plato's "city" and turned instead to the Idea (p. 477).

Only in a very summary way can any review indicate the value of the book Henry Harris has written for us. It is more than just a book whose scholarly erudition enables us to view critically the work of a Rosenkranz, a Dilthey, or a Häring. It is more than a scholarly account and interpretation of a crucial period in Hegel's development. It is a work which lays a solid foundation for an understanding of what Hegel later sought to accomplish. It is a work to which we must return again and again as we attempt to grapple with Hegel's determination to follow the Idea wherever it leads him. When we do return, we shall continue to be disconcerted, it is true, by the number of misprints—particularly in the rendition of German—but we shall still be grateful for the unremitting labor which has produced a book which is at once invaluable because of its content and absorbing because of the way in which it is written.

4

Hegel as Historian of Philosophy

ALTHOUGH HEGEL'S *Lectures on the History of Philosophy* have long provided a source of trenchant quotations illustrating his philosophical views, and despite the fact that more than one author has pointed out that the best way to begin studying Hegel is with these lectures, rarely do we find any study of just what he is trying to do in treating the history of philosophy and how he goes about doing it. That Hegel himself attached great importance to the history of philosophy is attested to by the fact that he repeated the course so often, revising it, particularly the introductory lectures, again and again.[1] Nevertheless, we should look in vain were we to seek in the three posthumously published volumes of the *History of Philosophy* a scholarly presentation or interpretation of past philosophical positions. Hegel was not the sort of historian who gives a disinterested account of exactly what each philosopher said.[2] His task, as he conceived it, was rather to show that the development of pure thought so elaborately worked out in his *Science of Logic* has its exact counterpart in the empirically verifiable development of philosophy from the first faltering steps of Thales to the elaboration of Hegel's own system. If the *Phenomenology of Spirit*, an "historical" account of the development of consciousness—not of philosophy—can be looked on as Hegel's introduction to his *Logic*, so too can the *History of Philosophy* be considered a different sort of introduction to the same *Logic*—not exhibiting the development of consciousness to the point where pure speculative thinking can begin but presenting an historical account of the development of speculative thinking itself.[3]

An earlier version of this chapter appears in *Hegel and the History of Philosophy*, edd. Joseph J. O'Malley, Keith W. Algozin, and Frederick G. Weiss (The Hague: Nijhoff, 1974), pp. 21–46.

[1] We are in the unfortunate position of possessing a critical edition only of the *Introduction* (EGP), which assembles all the extant notes for Hegel's introductory lectures to his course on the history of philosophy. For a critical edition of the rest we must wait, and, in the meantime, rely on Michelet's presentation which is found in Volumes XVII–XIX of the *Sämtliche Werke* (GP). What we have, then, may be quite unreliable, but a comparison of Michelet's edition of the introductory lectures with the others indicates a substantial identity of content which might justify concluding that the same is true of the remaining lectures.

[2] Cf. EGP 134–35 for Hegel's thoughts on a "disinterested" presentation of the history of philosophy.

[3] Thus, the *Phenomenology* and the *History of Philosophy* are not "historical" in the same way.

One of the criticisms frequently leveled against Hegel's treatment of the history of philosophy is that it is arbitrary. Having decided what philosophy is, we are told, Hegel simply makes the "moments" of its development fit into the preconceived scheme of its systematic structure. There may, of course, be a certain amount of truth to the contention that Hegel has antecedently made up his mind that the historical development of philosophical thought will correspond to its logical development. It is not true, however, that his procedure is arbitrary. If philosophy is to have a history at all, in the sense in which Hegel understands history, it must throughout its development be identifiable as one and the same, and if its own logic demands the sort of development Hegel has elaborated in his system, it is quite understandable that he should expect to see the "moments" of that development manifested in the historical process (cf. EGP 132, 274–81). In any event the standpoint from which Hegel surveys the history of philosophy is that of his own *Logic*. Only if we are aware of this can we follow his interpretation of the many philosophies which have been elaborated down through history. By the same token, if we grasp the historical development of philosophy as Hegel presents it, we shall be in a better position to understand the same process as presented in his *Logic*.

Here, then, our task is to follow the development of philosophy as Hegel presents its history. For methodological reasons, it would seem, the best way to do this is to look first at his *Introduction* (its many versions constitute a separate book) in which Hegel tells us what to look for in the history of philosophy. Then we can turn to the conclusion at the end of Volume III to see what Hegel is convinced he has found. Finally we can follow him as he tells the story from beginning to end, in order to determine how he finds what he does find, realizing, of course, that what he *finds* is to a great extent determined by what he *looks for*.

In carrying out this task we must be aware from the outset that history for Hegel is more than the record of a succession of events. Its concern, too, is more than just the events themselves; it is the connection of the events with each other, and here Hegel detects a certain logical necessity, whether the events in question be those of world history or the opinions of philosophers who have contributed to philosophy's growth down through the ages. Where the history in question, then, is that of philosophy, subjective opinions are contingent events and as such are not part of philosophy (EGP 27). They are at best the outward manifestation of an inner development, which is that of the rational idea (EGP 100–101). To such a unified development conflicting positions are not an obstacle; they are the necessary "moments" of a concrete dialectical process (EGP 91). Philosophy, then, has a life of its own; it is one and continuous; its manifestations are varied, and no one of them is identifiable with philosophy itself. In the *Phenomenology* Hegel had sought to show that if we begin with the absolutely minimal manifestation of human consciousness which we call sensation and follow out all its successive implications, we shall inevitably come to the highest form of consciousness, absolute knowing. This absolute knowing is philosophical knowing, the highest function of the highest form of human consciousness. Then, in the *Logic*, Hegel spells out all that philosophical knowing implies. This is the knowing whose process he traces "empirically" in the *History of Philosophy*. In one sense, of course, we can say that there are thought and the process of thought only because there are individuals who think. In another sense, however, thought transcends any and all individuals who engage in the subjective activity of thinking, and so does the process of thought. Philosophy, then, which is thought thinking thought, transcends all philosophers and all particular philosophies, and this is its profound unity throughout all the vicissitudes of its history (EGP 120). Thus, although Hegel's historical investigations are in one sense empirical—the evidence is in the record as given [4]—in another sense he sees a *logical* necessity that the development should be such as he discovers it to be (EGP 278).

THE UNITY OF PHILOSOPHY

One can, of course, speak of the unity of philosophy in an abstract, formal way, the way one speaks of the unity of a class concept—all philosophies are united under the one heading, philosophy. But this is not the sense in which Hegel intends the unity of philosophy. He speaks rather of a concrete unity, to which multiplicity and diversity are essential since they constitute the kind of unity in question, "the unity of differentiated determinations" (EGP 30). The history of philosophy reveals the concrescence of these determinations and is, thus, identical with philosophy itself, since philosophy is a process and not a static unity, a process of unification (EGP 120). It is logically necessary that rational thinking should be developmental (EGP 278), and historical investigation shows that the process has, in fact, been rational (EGP 122; cf. EGP 35). What is more, it shows that the historical development corresponds with the logical (EGP 34).

Quite obviously there is a sense in which thinking—even philosophical thinking—is something which a subject does. For Hegel, however, this in no way means that thinking is a merely subjective activity; no

---

4 Cf. EGP 252–53, where Hegel speaks of the *works* of philosophers as the events of philosophy's history.

merely subjective activity can claim for itself objective validity, and yet it is true of genuinely rational thinking that it validates itself— nothing else could. This is what Hegel means when he says of thought that it is free, autonomous; it need not go outside itself for its justification, its determination. Yet this autonomy is not automatic; it is to be won in a long process of development, of overcoming the multiple forces to which it is in bondage—a process eloquently described in the *Phenomenology*.

The point of all this is that only in rational thinking can man come to grips with reality as it is, and this he can do only if he makes thought itself the object of investigation. Philosophy is precisely thought occupied with itself (EGP 83). When it is occupied with the inevitable implications of thinking as such, the investigation is logical. When it is occupied with the *de facto* process it has gone through in time, the investigation is historical (EGP 82). In both types of investigation the task is to find out what reason says: in the logical, to find out what reason *must* say; in the historical, to find out what reason *has* said. "In the history of philosophy, however, there is question only of reason, to the extent that it has been expressed in the form of thought" (EGP 204). But to say that thought is rational is to say that it is free, in the sense of its not being in the service of something other than thought, whether it be a reality outside thought or a position established by authority, tradition, or custom (cf. EGP 218).

It is not, of course, the function of history to validate the very idea of philosophical thinking; that is a logical task (EGP 93). Still, given the idea, the historian of philosophy can eliminate from his account what he sees to be not philosophically significant, either because it is not truly independent thought or because it constitutes no advance in the process of thought (EGP 24, 124). More than that, the fact that someone called a "philosopher" has expressed this or that thought does not make that thought integral to the history of philosophy. Only to the extent that past thought remains somehow integral to our own thinking is it properly historical (EGP 6; cf. EGP 133). Philosophy's past is significant only to the extent that it continues to be part of its present (EGP 12–13); nor are the thoughts of others interesting simply as such, but only to the extent that they constitute "moments" in the ongoing process of philosophy (EGP 281). As presented, the "principles" of a philosophy may be one-sided and therefore to be abandoned, but they can at the same time be integrated into the more comprehensive unity of Philosophy itself. "Thus it is essential to the history of philosophy that one-sided principles are made into 'moments,' concrete elements, and retained in a sort of knot" (EGP 132). In one sense, no philosophy properly so called is ever refuted, since it is an essential "moment" of the one Philosophy; in another sense, all are refuted, because they are lifted to a plane of different significance by being integrated into the whole (EGP 128). It is for this reason that at any given time philosophy is the result of its whole past (EGP 70, 118-19, 126-27), and since the process of development is a process of concretion, an earlier philosophy will be more abstract and a later one more concrete (EGP 66). This does not mean that Philosophy itself changes in the course of time, only that it goes more deeply into itself and becomes more profoundly what it is (EGP 32). The process of philosophy is a necessary one, and each historical step in its development is proper to the time in which it appears (EGP 125), and although no particular philosophy can advance beyond its time (EGP 144), Philosophy itself is not limited to any time (EGP 149). Philosophy is its history, the whole of it; "Thus philosophy is developing system; so, too, is the history of philosophy, and this is the main point, the fundamental concept which this treatment of that history will present" (EGP 33).

After all this one might ask why Hegel bothers doing the history of philosophy at all, since he knows what he is going to find before he does it. His *Logic*, after all, has traced the process of thought without any appeal to its historical development. Although it is not easy to gainsay the charge of arbitrariness in the way Hegel finds historically verified the steps which the *Logic* has revealed to be necessary, it should be remembered that he looks upon his own system as the result of a long process of historical development. There simply would be no *Logic* had the process which extends from Thales to Hegel himself not taken place. It was, in fact, his insight into the concreteness of becoming over against the abstractness of mere being which revealed to him the need of a dynamic logic to supplement the abstract formal logic bequeathed to the West by Aristotle. Philosophy's coming-to-be is its history, but philosophy's coming-to-be is philosophy itself, and thus philosophy and the history of philosophy are identical (EGP 120). We can understand, then, Hegel's contention that the history of philosophy cannot be written without a system as a point of view from which to look at it (EGP 261-62). What he does, so to speak, is to show historically how the system comes to be what it is. This, incidentally, need not conflict with Hegel's further contention that each philosopher is to be interpreted on the basis of what he has said and not in the light of later developments of thought— although there might be reason to question whether Hegel has always remained faithful to his own rule, so convinced is he that the system reveals what its "moments" have to mean. Aside from his reliance on secondary sources for everything he has to say about Oriental philos-

ophy and for most of what he has to say about medieval philosophy—
and his failure even to mention Lucretius as a source for a knowledge
of Epicureanism—he does manifest a tendency to make the words of
philosophers fit into the Procrustean bed of *his* system.

Since, however, Hegel's concern is to show the system in the process
of coming to be, and since he is convinced that it is not simply *his*
system but philosophy itself which is in question, his procedure, arbitrary as it may seem, is at least understandable. For this reason we
can, before watching Hegel trace the process down through the centuries, turn to the conclusions he draws from what he has observed.
These conclusions will, it is hoped, throw a sort of retrospective light
on the whole process as he sees it.

THE OVERALL VIEW

The task Hegel had set himself at the outset of his course of lectures
was that of observing philosophical thought, beginning with its first
abstract attempts to find in reason the explanation of reality and pro-
ceeding to the systematic realization that, concretely, reason finds all
reality in itself. It has taken this thought a long time to come to know
itself as it now does:

> The world spirit has now come to this point. The latest philosophy is the
> result of all former ones; nothing has been lost, all principles have been re-
> tained. This concrete idea is the result of spirit's efforts over almost 2500
> years (Thales was born in 640 B.C.)—the result of its most earnest endeavor,
> that of becoming objective to itself, of knowing itself: *Tantae molis erat, se
> ipsam cognoscere mentem* [GP III 685].

What has happened is that the task announced at the beginning of
the *Logic*, of presenting God "as he is in his eternal essence before the
creation of nature and of a single finite spirit" (WL I 31), has now
been accomplished again through the medium of history. To say that
philosophy is the process of spirit's coming to know itself is to say that
it is the process of the human spirit's coming to know God as God
knows himself, and this is to say of philosophy that it is "necessarily
one philosophy in the process of developing. The revelation of God
as he knows himself" (GP III 686).

This "one philosophy" has become what it now is by going through
a series of stages, by successively discovering the contradiction in each
of its positions, and by rediscovering its own unity in the reconciliation of each contradiction. Five steps on that ladder of development
were cleared during the period of Greek philosophy from Thales to
the neo-Platonists, a period of approximately a thousand years. No
further steps were made until the dawn of modern philosophy, a
thousand years later, and for modern philosophy three more steps

were needed (GP III 686–89). All of which permits us to understand, in retrospect, why Hegel devoted two-thirds of his course (apart from the *Introduction*) to Greek philosophy and only one-third to medieval and modern philosophy combined. In any event, the overall process is one in which philosophy again and again manifests itself as one in the midst of diversity, because spirit comes to know itself as one and the same throughout the whole process of its thinking. "To know opposition in unity and unity in opposition, this is absolute knowing; and science is this: to know this unity in its entire development through itself [by knowing itself]" (GP III 689).

What has been learned, then, in this course on the history of philosophy is that there is only one philosophy, that its process reveals the logical necessity of its various stages, that each later stage contains all that is significant in the stages which preceded it, and that thus there can be only forward movement in philosophy, no regression.

> The overall result of the history of philosophy is: (1) that throughout the whole of time there is only one philosophy, and its simultaneous differences constitute the necessary aspects of the one principle; (2) that the sequence of philosophical systems is not a contingent one but one which manifests necessary progress in the development of this science; (3) that at a given time the most recent philosophy is the result of this development, and truth is then in the highest form which the self-consciousness of spirit has of itself. The most recent philosophy, therefore, contains those which preceded it, embraces all levels, is the product and result of all those which went before. One cannot now be a Platonist; one must raise oneself (*a*) above the trivialities of particular opinions, thoughts, objections, difficulties, (*b*) above one's own vanity, as though one had thought in a specially significant way. For to catch hold of the inner substantial spirit is the position of the individual; within the whole, individuals are as though blind; the inner spirit drives them [GP III 690–91].

Philosophy, of course, could not begin—nor, *a fortiori*, could its history begin—did we not have the conviction that the truth is attainable and that the human mind has the capacity to attain to it. In Hegel's own words, "The first condition for philosophy is that we have assurance of truth and faith in the power of the spirit" (EGP 5–6), or, to continue in a more eloquent vein:

> Man, because he is spirit, should and must deem himself worthy of the highest. He cannot think too highly of the greatness and the power of his spirit, and, given this belief, nothing will be so difficult and hard as not to reveal itself to him. The being of the universe, at first hidden and concealed, has no power which can offer resistance to the courageous pursuit of knowledge; it has to lay itself open before the seeker—to set before his eyes, and give for his enjoyment, its riches and depths [EGP 6].

This faith, however, is a long-continuing one, and only as the power of the mind unfolds itself through the successive efforts of individual philosophers, is it possible to see what riches it does, in fact, reveal. It is this "unfolding" (*Entwicklung*) which Hegel traces in his *History of Philosophy*, beginning with the first independent application of mind to the mysteries of the universe and only after 2500 years coming to the realization that there is no other way to plumb these mysteries than by plunging into the depths of reason itself, where all has been contained since the beginning. The final goal, perhaps only asymptotically approachable, is to see the totality of reality as God sees it; i.e., as God sees himself—and this Hegel comes to grips with in his *Logic*.

DETAILED ELABORATION

In attempting to see how Hegel goes about tracing philosophy's development one could, of course, simply paraphrase the three volumes of his *History of Philosophy*—a not unrewarding task, perhaps, but a somewhat problematic addition to Hegel's own words. A more manageable and, in the long run, more instructive approach is to take some of the key developments which Hegel detects in philosophy's history and to show how he traces these developments from their abstract beginnings to their concrete fulfillment. Not to make the list too long we can, perhaps, confine ourselves to those salient developments whereby mind becomes progressively aware of its capacity to come to terms with the totality of reality. (1) The first of these is to be found in the progressively more autonomous character of thought, mind's progressive realization that it need make no appeal outside itself for the justification of its affirmations. (2) Secondly, there is the growing realization that what thought *affirms* to be so is more really so than what the senses *take* to be so. (3) Closely allied to this last is the progressive identification of those seeming opposites, thought and being, which is realized only in the gradual dialectical reconciliation of opposites, accomplished in "speculative" thought. (4) A thought which develops in this way is conditioned by the progressive realization that the primary category of both being and thought is subject, not substance. (5) Finally, the mere subjectivity of individual thinking is as arbitrary as is mere opinion if it is not fleshed out by identification with the universality of thought itself. Each of these developments, it will be seen, culminates in a systematic completeness which is to be found only in Hegel's *Logic*.

Freedom of Philosophical Thought. In his *Introduction* Hegel tells us that philosophy begins where thought begins to be free, and this it can do only where men themselves (the philosophers) are free (EGP 225–27). He thus links freedom of thought with political freedom, both to justify his refusal to accord any philosophical significance to

Oriental philosophy and to situate the beginning of philosophy in the Greek city-state. One may well question the accuracy of Hegel's interpretation of Oriental philosophy—or of Oriental political life, for that matter—but his decision to seek the sources of contemporary Western philosophical thinking only in the West is at least understandable. In any event Hegel is convinced that only free men can philosophize (GP I 183–84), and that the contribution made by the Greeks to the legacy left by the East was precisely the freedom which makes philosophy possible (GP I 188). The important point here, of course, is that thought itself be free, which it begins to be when with the Eleatics it moves away from its dependence on imaginative representation and becomes "for itself" (GP I 300). Herein, says Hegel, we find the dialectical character of thought (GP I 296). But freedom is a meaningless concept if individuals as such are not free, and it is in Athens, with the Sophists, that the subjective freedom of individuals begins to emerge, that individuals are first encouraged to think for themselves (GP I 400–402). The principle here is that the individual is free "to admit validity only to that which he himself clearly sees, to what he finds in his own reason" (GP II 20). With the Sophists, however, the subjective freedom of ratiocination (*das räsonnierende Denken*) is minimal, and it is only with Socrates that the individual is called upon to take responsibility for his own thinking, i.e., producing his own thoughts (GP II 20):

> With regard to the Socratic principle, the first characteristic of thought, an important one, although as yet merely formal, is that consciousness produces from itself what is true, and, therefore, has as its function to produce precisely this. This is the principle of subjective freedom, i.e., that consciousness is directed upon itself [GP II 71].

Although Hegel has much to say about Plato and his contributions to the development of thought, he does not distinguish him from Socrates on the question of subjective freedom. Still, he does make much of the dialectic of the *Parmenides*, in Hegel's mind the greatest of Plato's dialogues. That he should have found so little on this point in Plato may well be due to the fact that he misses the point of Plato's use of myth (cf. EGP 54–55), which he considers to be only a pedagogical instrument, on which thought no longer has to depend, once the concept is sufficiently advanced (GP II 189). It is Aristotle who brings the concept forward to this point. With Aristotle, then, thought is free because it does not depend on the presence of its object, neither on its physical presence in sensation nor on its imaginative presence in representation (GP II 377).

To understand what Hegel has to say about freedom of thought in the interval between Aristotle and the emergence of the subjective principle at the beginning of the modern period, we should do well to turn to his treatment, in the *Phenomenology*, of Stoicism, Skepticism, and the Unhappy Consciousness. The last, which is a religious rather than a philosophical consciousness, in that it relinquishes freedom in favor of a principle which is *beyond* reason, characterizes, for Hegel, the whole of the Middle Ages and permits him to devote very little time to the medieval period. It is interesting to note, in this connection, that he sees subjective freedom reintroduced not in the philosophical but in the religious sphere with Luther's insistence on freedom of spirit, according to which reason is responsible to itself alone, not to any external authority (GP III 255). Modern philosophical thinking, with its insistence that thought depends on thought alone, begins, properly speaking, with Descartes. It is Descartes who affirms explicitly that what we recognize as true is the product of our own free thinking, in the sense that the evidence for the truth is to be found in consciousness itself (GP III 338). Although Hegel has a good deal to say about the period between Descartes and Kant, with regard to the freedom of thinking he sees very little advance during this time over the principle enunciated by Descartes. With Kant, however, a significant change takes place; he it is who asserts the autonomy of mind with the utmost vigor. "What is true in Kantian philosophy is its grasp of thinking as concrete in itself, self-determining. Thus freedom is recognized" (GP III 552). Kant, however, comes in for more criticism than, perhaps, any other philosopher whom Hegel treats.[5] The reason for this may be found in Hegel's very notion of criticism: Kant was "so near and yet so far," and the task of criticism is not to refute but to show how a philosopher's own principles demand to be developed (WL II 217–18). For Kant theoretical reason is not genuinely independent since it produces only the form of thought and is dependent on sensual intuition for its content (GP III 588–89). Only practical reason is thoroughly self-determining, i.e., free (GP III 590–91). Fichte, who is more "speculative" than Kant, makes more of a case for freedom in the self-development of the absolute concept, the Ego (GP III 615; cf. GP III 618), but the freedom in question is still rather formal, since it consists in a progressive determination of the object by the subject, not a self-development of the concept itself (GP III 637). With Schelling, on the other hand, all knowing is produced by the interior activity of the subject (GP III 653), but the mode is that of intellectual intuition (GP III 654), not the "logical" development which pure thought demands (GP III 662).

The Objectivity of Thought. If all Hegel could say about thought was that it is free, he would indeed be saying very little. It is far more important for thought to be true than for it to be free, unless, of course,

5 See chap. 8 of this volume, "Hegel's Critique of Kant's Theology."

a condition for its being true is that it be free. Of this latter Hegel was convinced,[6] but he was also well aware of the difference between a condition and a guarantee. At the same time he was convinced, both logically and historically, that thought more surely grasps the way things are the more it rids itself of dependence on what is not thought. In short, he was convinced that mind can grasp reality in a way in which no other forms of consciousness can, and that purity of thought made for objectivity in a way in which sense intuition cannot. This is but another way of saying that what reason says is true, no matter what other kind of evidence may seem to be against it. Thus, right from the beginning of his treatment of the history of thought, Hegel will emphasize any movement he detects away from the sensible to the intelligible. This is evidenced in his interpretation of the material principles of the Ionians, which, he says, are objects of thought, not of sense perception. By the same token, we have seen, the Eleatics are concerned with concepts rather than with imaginative representations of reality (GP I 296). Parmenides recognizes true being in thought, not in the sensible (GP I 312), and Zeno is the "master of dialectic" because he occupies himself with pure thought (GP I 318). So true is this that Hegel will not recognize any sort of *solvitur ambulando* as an answer to *reasons* for denying motion—reasons can be refuted only with reasons, not with evidence of the senses (GP I 330). Heraclitus, too, speaks of what reason demands: "Now, Heraclitus understands the Absolute itself as this process of thought, as dialectic itself" (GP I 344). Hegel, in fact, finds in Heraclitus nothing to which he himself cannot subscribe—and that in his *Logic*! (GP I 344)—not only because Heraclitus saw that the truth of being is in becoming (GP I 348–49), but because he saw that only universalized consciousness is true (GP I 367–68). In the proper sense of the term, then, philosophy begins with Heraclitus: "The beginning of philosophy's existence dates from him [Heraclitus]—it is the enduring idea which remains the same in all philosophers up to the present, just as it was the idea of Plato and Aristotle" (GP I 362). Even Leucippus conceived of atoms as objects of thought, in no way sensible, i.e., as ideal objects (GP I 385), and Anaxagoras, with his concept of νοῦς—which Hegel somewhat arbitrarily interprets as teleological (GP I 411–13)—took a big step toward making pure thought the basic principle of philosophy (GP I 397; cf. GP I 408).

It is, of course, the Platonic εἶδος which contains the recognition that reality is truly grasped in thought alone (GP II 218–19), with the result that the most real (το ὄντως ὄν) is seen to be the ideal (GP II 224). It

---

[6] To put this another way: Hegel was convinced that only when thought is fully autonomous is it truly thought and, thus, true thought.

is for this reason that, in Hegel's eyes, Plato is the first to make philosophy scientific: "With Plato philosophical science as science begins" (GP II 169). Plato, again, is the first to make it explicit that not the sensible existent but only the universal determined in itself is true (GP II 199) and that this universal is not simply a thought present in the thinker but is the very truth (substance) of being (GP II 200). Along this line Hegel, in opposition to his contemporaries, looks upon Aristotle as the genuine successor of Plato (GP II 301) and not as an "empiricist" in the commonly accepted meaning of that term (GP II 311–312). Aristotle, too, finds the truth of being in the concept, and he is empirical only to the extent that he finds the concept in what he observes (GP II 312–13; cf. GP II 340–41). Only by a complete misunderstanding of the *tabula rasa* doctrine can interpreters make Aristotle say anything different; the writing on the blank page does not come from without but is the thinking activity of the mind itself (GP II 386–87).

With Plato and Aristotle the primacy of the intellectual over the sensible was so well established that it suffered only minor setbacks in succeeding ages. What remained to be done, however, according to Hegel, was that thought become the universal principle in such a way that it would embrace the totality of reality, which is but another way of saying that philosophy was to become "system." For Hegel philosophy becomes that only with his own system, even though it was already implicit in Aristotle's thought. Why it should have remained merely implicit for so long or why philosophy had to wait for Hegel before achieving the unity toward which it had been moving all along, Hegel does not explain. In any event it was not until Spinoza posited substance, the *causa sui*, as the one unifying principle, that philosophy again took up where Aristotle left off (GP III 372). Spinoza represents, so to speak, a new beginning of philosophy, in the sense that modern philosophy must proceed from the Spinozistic point of view: "In this regard it should in general be remarked that thinking had to adopt the standpoint of Spinozism; this is the essential beginning of all philosophizing" (GP III 376). Still, even though absolute substance is the true principle, it is not the completely true principle; it must also act, and this it does as substance which is also subject, i.e., as spirit (GP III 377). In this process Locke and Hume, with their emphasis on the sensible, constitute negative moments to be overcome (cf. GP III 417–18, 495), whereas Leibniz saw that not sensible but intelligible being is essential truth (GP III 449), even though his intellectual world is left undeveloped, because his principle is absolute multiplicity and not absolute unity (GP III 470). Kant sought to overcome the empiricist emphasis on sensibility by appealing to the self-validation of the intelligible (GP III 558), whereas Fichte and Schelling sought to over-come the absolute multiplicity of Leibniz by insisting on the unity of the absolute subject (cf. GP III 627–28, 683). All three (Kant, Fichte, Schelling), however, failed to achieve a concrete unity of the whole, because for each the ultimate unifying principle was merely formal (cf. GP III 554–55, 637, 681). This, however, brings us to another facet of the developmental process, the progressive identification of being and thought, which Hegel calls "concretization."

The Identity of Thought and Being. In his *Logic* Hegel tells us that the science of logic (philosophy) must begin with what thought first thinks, and this is being. Only gradually does it come to the realiza-tion that what thought thinks is itself and that, therefore, the thought thinking and the being thought are identical. The same he will find progressively revealed in the history of philosophical thinking. Osten-sibly not only are being and thought not identical, they are opposites: thinking stands over against that which is thought. In the dialectical thinking which Hegel espouses, however, it is precisely the function of thought both to engender and to reconcile opposition, as mind progressively recognizes that dialectical opposites must be said of each other if they are to be true and not merely remain one-sided abstrac-tions. To return to the *Logic*: to think being and only being is to think an abstraction which must be complemented by its opposite, non-being. Both being and non-being as opposed to each other are abstractions and demand concretization in becoming. By the same token, to think whatever is implied in the unity of being and non-be-ing (the whole "Doctrine of Being") is to think of it as it is *in* thought, i.e., as opposed to its *mere* being (the "Doctrine of Essence"). But to think the content of thought as somehow other than thought is to remain at another level of abstraction which is to be completed (con-cretized) in the realization that to think at all is to think thought (the "Doctrine of the Concept"). If philosophy, then, can be characterized, as we saw before, as "thought occupied with itself" (EGP 83), the his-tory of philosophy will manifest the gradual realization that to think at all is to think thought and to seek to know anything at all is to look for it in thought. To do this is to be genuinely "speculative," a qual-ity which characterizes philosophical thinking more and more as its concepts engender their opposites. Philosophical thinking is essentially speculative, in the sense that from the very beginning it is in the process of becoming speculative (cf. GP I 204, 213). It is not until Parmenides, however, that the sort of opposition which characterizes speculative thinking becomes explicit—even though Parmenides him-self was not conscious that this was taking place: "Thus, with Parmenides the opposition of being and non-being is manifested more determinately, but still without consciousness" (GP 1 308). Zeno makes even more explicit this movement of pure thought (GP 1 318, 320, 325–26). In Hegel's view, then, Zeno does not really deny movement; he simply seeks to show how it must be *conceived* (GP 1 334). The most clearly speculative thinker among the pre-Socratics, however, is Heraclitus, and the difficulty we find in understanding him arises precisely from this (GP 1 348). He it is who recognizes that being and non-being are mere abstractions, concretized only in becoming (GP 1 348–49). What is beginning to become apparent here is that only where there is opposition can there be harmony (GP 1 352–53), but the turning point in philosophy, where thought and being genuinely harmonize with each other, comes with Socrates (GP II 122–23): "In Socrates there arose the consciousness that whatever is is mediated through thought" (GP II 45), i.e., it is only *through* thought that being can be *said* of anything. The true greatness of Plato lies in the conscious way his thinking brings together the opposed determinations of the being it thinks (GP II 237).

Characteristic of Platonic philosophy is its orientation to the intellectual, the suprasensible world, the lifting of consciousness into the spiritual realm; such that the intellectual took on the form of the suprasensible, the spiritual, which is proper to thought (GP II 236). As a result the intellectual in this form becomes important for consciousness, enters into consciousness, and consciousness finds firm footing on this ground (GP II 170). Το ὄντως ὄν —"what in truth is in and for itself" (GP II 211) is for Plato the ideal (GP II 224). Aristotle makes this even more explicit by affirming the identity of concept and the substance of what is conceived: "Objects are subjectively thought by me; and then my thought is the concept of the thing, and this is the substance of the thing" (GP II 333). This is but another way of saying that the "substantial" (enduring) truth of reality is to be found in thought, not elsewhere. Aristotle's "ontology," then, is on the same level as Hegel's "logic" (GP II 319), and Aristotle's logic is suited for the sort of science which is a function of finite understanding, not to Aristotle's own speculative philosophy (GP II 413–15). This speculative philosophy of Aristotle culminates in the doctrine of the "unmoved mover," the νόησις νοήσεως, of the *Metaphysics*, Book Lamba, which Hegel interprets as Aristotle's affirmation of the primacy of thought (GP II 328–30; cf. GP II 391), which alone permits philosophy to perform its most significant function of reconciling the finite and the infinite, i.e., the infinitizing of a being which in itself is merely finite: "That which alone is great in philosophy is the joining of the infinite and the finite" (GP II 516).

In all this, philosophy is gradually becoming aware that what is immediately present to consciousness is not true being; only what is present through the mediation of thought is true being. The immediate, as Hegel shows us abundantly in the *Phenomenology*, is inevitably bound up in contradiction, which only speculative thinking can resolve. Step by step post-Aristotelian philosophy became conscious of this. Stoicism, which is in general a mere formalism (GP II 454–55), did have the realization that immediate thinking does not yield the true; only a thinking which corresponds to the *logos* does, i.e., rational (speculative) thinking (GP II 447). The mediation which rational thinking effects, however, is precisely the negation of the immediacy with which reality initially presents itself to consciousness. What is important to recognize, of course, is that this sort of negation is just as positive as is affirmation; it is that which determines the merely affirmative to be what it in truth is. Hegel credits Philo with having seen this: "Philo had the correct insight that the opposite of being is just as positive as is being" (GP III 25). To recognize this is to think "speculatively," something which Hegel also finds in Proclus (GP III 72); it is another way of saying that what the mind necessarily thinks in thinking reality is true of reality. This, again, he finds in Plotinus (GP III 53–54), and, strangely enough, he finds more of it in Catholic thought inherited from the Middle Ages than he does in Protestant thought (GP III 259). Not until Descartes, however, is the principle made explicit that only in consulting thought do we find what can be truly said of reality: "What is thought correctly and clearly is so. Thus is expressed that in thought man experiences what actually is true of things" (GP III 354). Unfortunately, the thought of which Descartes speaks is abstract, unable to concretize itself, and, therefore, in need of experience to concretize it (GP III 364). Spinoza, on the other hand, in recognizing that all determination is negation, a function of thought, saw thought as self-determining and, therefore, self-concretizing (GP III 374–75). This permits him to unify all reality under the heading of absolute substance, a unity of opposing moments (GP III 372). Significantly this absolute substance is *causa sui*, i.e., has itself as its effect, and only thought does this (GP III 379). The diametric opposition of this is to be found in Locke, who will judge the validity of thought not from its content but only from the manner of its derivation (GP III 424). This, says Hegel, misses the point entirely: "It is entirely different to ask: Is what is in us true? Whence it comes does not answer the question at all" (GP III 428). What deceives the empiricists—and here Newton is the paradigm—is their conviction that they are dealing with things, when in truth they are dealing with concepts (GP III 447). What must be recognized is that the product of thinking is not only the form of thought but also its content (GP III 481), and this is the realization with which the *Phenomenology* has made us familiar: that reason is the consciousness of being itself all reality (GP III 484). As Kant appears on the scene—Hume is historically important chiefly as providing the starting point for Kant (GP III 493) —then philosophy is on the threshold of assuming its essential task, to *grasp* (*begreifen*) the unity of thought and being: "The task of philosophy is determined to the point of making its object the very unity of thinking and being, which is its fundamental idea, and of grasping (*begreifen*) this idea, i.e., catching hold of the most interior necessity, the concept" (GP III 535).

Although Kant's contribution to the accomplishment of this task was enormous, Hegel is convinced that Kant's concern with the faculty of knowing rather than with what is known (GP III 555) led him to conceive of thinking as a process of *unifying* the manifold presented to it, in which the manifold and the form of unity supplied by the mind remain external to each other. Thus the true *unity* of being and thought is not yet achieved (GP III 558). Because, for Kant, reason is not constitutive but only regulative of knowing (GP III 560), it is dependent on an experience exterior to the concept in order to give the concept a content (GP III 561). The result is that Kant does not succeed in reconciling the contradictions which a reality in process manifests in thought; he simply attributes the contradictions to the inadequacy of finite reason (GP III 583). As we saw before, Fichte represents for Hegel an advance over Kant, in that his thought is more speculative; it calls for a self-development of the absolute concept (GP III 615), permitting a unity of all thought and all being (GP III 619). Still, since Fichte has the Ego progressively determine its objects in the process of thinking, he does not manage to bridge the gap between being and thought (GP III 637). Schelling does take a step in the right direction by completely spiritualizing nature, thus making the whole of nature present in thought (GP III 651). For Schelling "the truth of nature, nature in itself, is an intellectual world" (GP III 683). Thus, he presents a thinking whose content is more concrete, but he falls short of making the whole process one in which the concept need not go outside itself (GP III 683). To show how this complete unity of reality is achieved in the concept is not the task of Hegel's historical treatment of philosophy. This is the work of Hegel's own *Logic*. The history he presents, however, does make clearer what the *Logic* is trying to do. Similarly, the process of thought as subjective activity demands a progressive realization of just what subject is. This Hegel attempts in his *Phenomenology*, but again it is the *History* which helps to clarify what the *Phenomenology* seeks to do.

The Movement Toward Subjectivity. Much of what has already been said regarding the historical development of philosophical thought obviates the necessity of a detailed exposition of Hegel's treatment of the question of subjectivity. In general it can be said that modern philosophy (beginning with Descartes) distinguishes itself from the philosophy which preceded it by its emphasis on the thinking subject rather than on the object of thought. Hegel, however, traces the gradual orientation of thought toward the thinking subject back to the ancient world; he in fact makes the increasing emphasis on subjectivity a condition for progress in philosophy.

He finds this movement manifested as early as the Sophists who, in their concern for teaching, were aware that learning is a development which takes place in a thinking subject.

> To the turning back [on itself] of thinking, which is a consciousness that it is the subject who does the thinking, is linked another side, i.e., that the subject, therefore, has as its task to attain for itself an essential absolute content [GP II 4; cf. GP II 3–5].

To be aware that an object is necessarily an object for a subject is to recognize that somehow the criterion for the objectivity of thought is to be sought in subjectivity. Thus, the dictum of Protagoras that "Man is the measure of all things" can make eminent good sense if it is speaking of man *as rational* (GP II 30). In fact, all further progress in philosophy hinges on a realization that the goal of thinking is to be thoroughly rational (GP II 31). It is Socrates, then, who summarizes all previous thought by turning explicit attention to the subject whose thinking contains all being (GP II 42–43). Plato goes even farther, in his awareness that being is available only in the mind (GP II 203). "The source whence we become conscious of the divine is the same as it was for Socrates. Man's own mind is this source; it contains in itself precisely the essential" (GP II 202). Representations (*Vorstellungen*) of things come from without, but not the thoughts wherein they are universalized; these come from an acting subject, they are not the product of things acting on a subject (GP II 204). Nevertheless, Plato's ideas were not adequately subjective; he came on the scene too early for that: "This lack of subjectivity is a lack in the Greek ethical idea itself" (GP II 294). Aristotle did not improve matters along this line, but he did contribute in his logic an account of the subjective activity called thinking (GP II 411). The Stoics and Skeptics, on the other hand, as we have already seen, pushed subjectivity so far that objectivity was lost. "The Skeptics went all the way in their view of the subjectivity of all knowing; they universally substituted for being in knowledge the expression of illusion" (GP II 538).

Not until the advent of the neo-Platonists did the development we

have been observing reach the point of a consciousness that only in
mind does the world of reality express itself (GP III 4). Here, then, the
identity of the being of which we are conscious and the self of which
we are conscious begins to take its place in philosophy: "More philosophically and more conceptually articulated [begriffener], however,
the unity of self-consciousness and being emerges in the Alexandrian
school" (GP III 31). For some strange reason Hegel does not seem to
have been aware of St. Augustine's contribution to philosophy's consciousness of its own subjective character—despite the Augustinian
overtones of so much of Hegel's own thought—and so he makes a lyric
leap from the subjectivity of the neo-Platonists to the subjectivity of
Luther, who turned men's minds drastically to that which came from
within themselves (GP III 256–57). Luther's question, of course, was
the question of faith, but his realization that the content of faith is
constituted as what it is in being believed (GP III 260–61) paved the
way for the emphasis on subjectivity which characterizes philosophy
from Descartes to Fichte. In this connection it is interesting to note
how much attention Hegel gives to Jakob Böhme, primarily a mysti-
cal thinker, whom Hegel calls "the first German philosopher," whose
principle was the Protestant one: "to place the intellectual world in
one's own inner self [Gemüth] and to observe, know, and feel in one's
own self-consciousness whatever was otherwise outside" (GP III 300).
It is with Descartes, however, that consciousness has within itself all
it needs in order to philosophize: "With him [Descartes] we enter,
properly speaking, into an independent philosophy, which knows that
it comes independently from reason and that self-consciousness is an
essential moment of the true" (GP III 328). Philosophical thought can
now justify itself (cf. GP III 331), and it is thinking in its universality
which reveals the Ego as nothing else does (GP III 342–43). Hegel sees
no further advance along the lines of subjectivity until the advent of
Kant, whose "Copernican Revolution" is the most deliberate and
emphatic turn to subjectivity yet witnessed. There is genuine knowledge only where there is necessity and universality, and the source of
necessity and universality is the subject alone (GP III 554–55). But,
unfortunately, in turning to the subject Kant finds only the subject
(GP III 554), not universal reason which is responsible for the very
objectivity of its content: "The Kantian Ego, however, does not, properly speaking, attain reason, but again remains the individual self-
consciousness as such, which is over against the universal" (GP III 571).
Fichte, on the other hand, is more thoroughgoing in seeking to derive
the categories of being from consciousness of the self—a derivation
which still separates consciousness of self and consciousness of reality
(GP III 627–28). With Schelling, finally, the correspondence of nature

and spirit is complete; the "absolute unity of contradictions" (GP III 659) has been achieved. There has been a complete reconciliation of the empirical and the conceptual (GP III 681), and there is a recognition that the concrete unity must be grasped as process (GP III 646). Still, Schelling fails to work out the process logically (GP III 662), and so, as Hegel tells us in the *Phenomenology*, the unity is one of indistinction, like "the dark night in which all the cows are black" (*Phän.* 19). That subjectivity should have proved inadequate to its task all down the line was inevitable, precisely because individual, finite subjectivity is necessarily inadequate; and the process of universalizing the individual in a more than formal, abstract way had, again, to wait for the finishing touches supplied by Hegel's *Phenomenology*, then to be elaborated in his *Logic*. This reconciliation of the individual and the universal, however, also has its history, which consists in the gradual realization that, although each thinker is an individual, and each thought is individually produced, still thought is thought only to the extent that its content is universal—with all that ultimately implies.

Synthesis of Individual and Universal. The process of thought's progressive universalization, strangely enough, could not get under way until the Greeks began to recognize the importance of the individual (GP I 192). Until then the individual was swallowed up in the *an sich* universality of nature, and this could not be remedied until spirit began to dominate nature (GP I 190). The shift is illustrated in the passage from the abstract, impersonal gods of the Orient to the individually personal gods of the Greeks (GP I 152). If thinking is not individual, it is not really thinking. If, on the other hand, it is merely individual, it gets nowhere; it must be the thinking of spirit: initially the spirit of a people (GP I 291–92), ultimately the universal spirit which embraces all men (GP III 691–92).

The first significant step in this process comes when Socrates affirms his own individuality at its highest (GP II 54–55). His δαιμόνιον which forbids him to acquiesce to the merely common opinion is precisely the affirmation of individuality in the midst of universality; it was Socrates who knew what he as an individual had to do in a given situation, no matter what the Athenians in general thought (GP II 95). Essentially, then, the charge brought against him at his trial was correct; his god was not the god (or gods) of the Athenian people (GP II 106–107, 109–10). By appealing to his own conscience against the conscience of the people he was affirming a merely individual principle which had yet to become truly universal (GP II 115–17). The process of fleshing out this principle, then, begins with Plato and his

realization that thinking is not merely a property of the soul but its
very substance and that thus the soul partakes of the universality
which belongs to thinking (GP II 208). The immortality of which he
speaks in the *Phaedo* simply bespeaks the essence of the soul, i.e., the
universality of thought, which cannot be confined to finite time (GP
II 212–13). The truth of being reveals itself in thought, and so thought
is the work of the universal, not of the individual (cf. GP II 200).

Aristotle once more stresses the significance of the individual (GP
II 302), who is subsumed, however, under the universality of reason
(GP II 410). Thinking, which for Plato was abstract, has with Aristotle become concrete, but not yet so systematic as to recognize the
multiplicity of interrelationships which constitute reality (GP II 420–
21).[7] Here again, throughout the vicissitudes of philosophy's development from Aristotle on, Aristotle remains unsurpassed, as one thinker
after another stresses now the individual, now the universal, constantly failing to reconcile the two adequately. What gradually becomes clear, however, in the long period between Aristotle and Spinoza, who, as we have seen, is the first to take up where Aristotle left
off, is that a reconciliation of individual and universal will be possible
only if philosophy is oriented to a genuine knowledge of God: "Only
philosophy is science regarding God" (GP III 151). Philosophy, then,
must become theology if it is to achieve its destiny as philosophy:
"because philosophy is the knowledge of absolute being, i.e., is theology" (GP III 154). The theme, which had been announced in the
Introduction to the *History of Philosophy*, echoed as it is in the
Phenomenology, the *Logic*, the *Lectures on the Philosophy of Religion*, and the *Lectures on the Proofs for God's Existence*, is here
reiterated in the context of the historical development of Aristotle's
basic insight that God himself is thought thinking itself. For Hegel,
religion and philosophy have the same identical content, the Absolute;
religion under the form of representation, philosophy under the form
most proper to the Absolute, i.e., thought.[8] Along this line, despite his
multiple misinterpretations of medieval philosophy, Hegel does credit
the Scholastics (particularly St. Anselm) with having recognized the
essential infinity of truth (here again his disregard of Augustine is
puzzling), with presenting this infinite truth as spirit (GP III 200), and
with identifying the absolute which philosophy *knows* with the God
who is theology's concern. Where the Scholastics went wrong was in
their attempt to *prove* the being of God on the basis of formal logic,

---

7 Cf. J. Glenn Gray, *Hegel and Greek Thought* (New York: Harper Torchbook, 1968),
p. 71.
8 See chap. 9 of this volume, "Hegel on the Identity of Content in Philosophy and
Religion."

rather than to *grasp* (*begreifen*) that being speculatively (cf. GP III 167, 203). When, in the Renaissance, the revival of humanism led to a renewed interest in antiquity (GP III 213–14), the door was opened to an overcoming of the false Aristotelianism of the Scholastics (GP III 215), and a penetration into the God-idea as the true philosophical idea (cf. GP III 317). Once again, Spinoza is the high point in this development, but even he fails to reconcile the singular and the universal, since he sees the individual existent as essentially inferior to the universal of absolute substance (GP III 381–82). His mistake was to begin with definitions (as one justifiably does in mathematics) and fail to probe the reality of thought's content (GP III 384). In doing this Spinoza took his stand on the kind of knowledge available to understanding (finite) rather than reason (infinite) (GP III 378), which prevented him from grasping God as Spirit (GP III 408). Although it is not presented adequately in the *History of Philosophy*, Hegel's critique of Kant on this point is substantially the same as his critique of Spinoza: because Kant confines philosophical knowing to finite understanding, without going on to infinite reason, he cannot come to terms with the Absolute as the object of thought and must have recourse to *belief* in a God whom finite thought cannot grasp.[9] Neither Fichte nor Schelling, even though their thinking is more "speculative" than Kant's, succeeds in bridging the gap between finite thinking and the Absolute which is the infinite content of thought. Fichte's absolute Ego somehow stands off from the developing concept as the content of its thinking (GP III 637), and Schelling has recourse to an "intellectual intuition" which is not, properly speaking, thinking (GP III 654, 662).

CONCLUSION

The conclusion of all this is what we might have expected: philosophy does not show itself adequate to its own task, the thinking of the Absolute, until Hegel's *Logic* identifies the absolute thinking of absolute Spirit with the absolute object of thought, the Idea. If the being which philosophy necessarily thinks is to be grasped adequately, it must be seen as somehow the product of the thought which thinks it. Thinking, however, produces only thought, and, thus, the being which is the object of thinking and the thought which is the product of thinking must be identified. But this cannot be, if thinking is no more than the activity of a finite thinking subject. It is not so much that the individual thinks thought—and, thus, being—as that thought thinks thought and being in (and through) the individual. The peren-

---

9 For an extended discussion of Hegel's criticism of Kant's failure to recognize the infinity of reason, see chap. 8.

nial problem of philosophy has been the universalizing of a reason whose activity takes place in individuals but whose validity transcends the limits of individual reasoning. Whether or not Hegel has solved this problem may be a moot question; that he has drawn an impressive historical picture of the process whereby reason (or Spirit) has progressively transcended the bounds of finitude, thus revealing its infinity, can scarcely be contested.

5

Human Autonomy and Religious Affirmation in Hegel

FROM ONE POINT OF VIEW it could well seem that the religious philosophy of Hegel, whether in its abbreviated presentation in the *Phenomenology of Spirit* or in its more detailed articulation in the *Lectures on the Philosophy of Religion*, presents fewer difficulties for the informed reader than do other aspects of the "System." In it, to be sure, we do not find the convolutions which characterize the overall endeavor of the *Phenomenology*; nor are we confronted with the difficulty of keeping track of an extraordinarily intricate web of dynamic entailment, as we are in the *Science of Logic*. Even the *Aesthetics*, the *Philosophy of History*, the *History of Philosophy*, and the *Philosophy of Right* make more demands on the ingenuity—not to say the credulity—of the reader who would follow where Hegel's thought leads than does his religious philosophy.

From another point of view, however, that religious philosophy presents a seemingly insuperable difficulty, a paradox not readily resolved. How can Hegel present a religious philosophy at all? In the tradition, which began with Descartes, of progressively secularizing philosophical thought, no one is more insistent than Hegel on the autonomy of human reason, an autonomy which systematically denies that human reason is subject to any higher authority at all, not the authority of custom or tradition, certainly, not even the authority of the Church or the State. The very same Hegel, nevertheless, consistently refused to accept that the safeguarding of rational autonomy demanded progressive opposition to basic Christian faith, as did, for example, the triumphal rationalism of the Enlightenment. One could, of course, as Hegel did, repeatedly lecture on the philosophy of religion, without in any way compromising one's conviction that reason is completely autonomous. But could one's whole philosophy be as religious as Hegel's unquestionably is if one is convinced that there simply is no authority superior to reason?

The entire Hegelian endeavor is essentially religious in character. It is unified around one central theme, knowledge of the absolute,

Reprinted from *Freedom and Value*, ed. Robert O. Johann (New York: Fordham University Press, 1976), pp. 87–106.

and the absolute, terminologically at least, is identified with God. More than that, the God with whom philosophy is occupied—or pre-occupied—is identified with the God who is religion's concern. The pathway to knowledge of the absolute is described in the *Phenomenology*; the abstract framework in which the absolute which knowledge knows articulates itself is detailed in the *Logic*; the "empirical" verification of this articulation is put forth in the *History of Philosophy*, the *Aesthetics*, and the *Philosophy of Religion*; and the consequences of all this for the life of reason are enunciated in the *Philosophy of History* and the *Philosophy of Right*. Thus, the rational approach to the divine, which alone is "absolute," is for Hegel not a *part* of philosophy—not even its coping stone—it is the whole of philosophy, which seeks a comprehensive grasp of the whole of reality. Hegel is not saying, of course, that any philosopher, including himself, knows all reality; nor is he saying that any one philosophy, including his own, is adequate to the whole of reality. What Hegel *is* saying is that no knowledge of reality is truly knowledge unless what is known is situated in the framework of the totality, and that that framework is the system which philosophy has been developing into since its inception. What Hegel is also saying, however—along traditional theological lines—is that total knowledge makes sense only if its paradigm is God's absolute knowing, which is absolute precisely because its content is the absolute, i.e., God himself.

As Hegel sees it, then, philosophical thought requires religion if its content is to be adequately philosophical. The human experience which has God as its object is faith, and if thought is to be adequate to experience, its purview must include the faith experience; to ignore faith is to ignore its object and, thus, to condemn oneself to a truncated reflection on experience. Philosophy will be indeed a *knowing* only if what it knows equals what faith believes. It is for this reason that a reader who is not familiar with the Christian religion—even with Christian theology—will find it difficult if not impossible to fathom what Hegel is saying.

None of this proves, of course, that Hegel was a Christian—although he did throughout his life say that he was—but both his language and his logic have their roots in the Christian religion, in Christian theology. What is more, Hegel's motivation in insisting that both religion and philosophy are oriented to the same absolute, such that his view of "scientific" philosophy could be described as "faith seeking understanding," is not the desire to rescue religion, to give it "rational" underpinnings. Rather, it is his desire to rescue philosophy, which would be less than universal science, would be severely limited in its range of inquiry, if the infinite object of religion were beyond its domain. To put it rather simply: short of in some sense knowing all reality, philosophical knowing is not knowing in the full sense of the term; and short of knowing God, philosophy does not know all reality in any sense. Nor is this to say that for Hegel God must be included in what is known if knowing is to be complete; rather, he is saying that to know at all is to know God, that a consciousness which is not a knowing of God is not knowledge, and that to grow in knowledge is to grow in knowledge of God. To put it another way: for Hegel it is inconceivable that philosophical knowing could be *having* bits and pieces of information, which may or may not be related to each other; there simply are no unrelated bits of reality, and reality is truly known only if it is known as totally interrelated. Paradigmatically, such a knowing is divine, and its object too is divine. It is still true that reason is autonomous, subject to no superior authority, for God is Reason, Absolute Reason—or, to anticipate, "Absolute Spirit."

THE ROLE OF RELIGIOUS CONSCIOUSNESS

To show how all of this runs as a guiding thread throughout the entire Hegelian endeavor would carry us too far afield. If, however, it can be shown that the dialectical movement of the *Phenomenology of Spirit* could never come to term if the march of consciousness toward absolute knowing did not include the movement of religious affirmation, we shall be able to see that religious affirmation—whatever that is to mean—cannot be absent from the systematic articulation of philosophical knowing. The *Phenomenology*, after all, is not simply a preliminary exercise which must be gone through before philosophizing can begin; its movement is the constant foundation of all that follows it.

If we are to understand the part which religion plays, according to Hegel's view, in the onward march of consciousness toward thoroughgoing knowledge, we must be aware that from beginning to end the *Phenomenology of Spirit* seeks to describe the progress of *human* spirit. At no point does the spirit whose development is being described become a disembodied consciousness, and it is precisely in the chapter on religious consciousness that this becomes abundantly clear; a disembodied consciousness simply could not be religious, only the human spirit can. What is more, religious consciousness is not presented as merely *one* of the stages in the spirit's advance, the penultimate one. Rather, the phenomenology of religious consciousness recapitulates the whole of the spirit's advance from minimal objective consciousness to self-conscious moral spirit before serving as a transition to the absolute knowing which is a thoroughgoing consciousness of self only because it is at the same time a consciousness of God. If human spirit is to know itself, it must know what it is to be spirit, and to know this is to know the paradigm of all spirit, God.

It is for this reason that the *Phenomenology*, which began as a "Science of the Experience of Consciousness," was forced along the route to recognize itself as a "Phenomenology of Spirit." At the very outset the consciousness which Hegel is examining begins to be aware that it does not belong to a mere realm of nature, where the mode of operation is that of causal efficacy. To be conscious is to act, not to be acted upon, and what this activity produces is precisely itself, consciousness. Explicit awareness may be slow in coming, but from the beginning it is inevitable that an activity which is not a being-acted-upon will recognize itself as spiritual activity. Even slower in coming is the spirit's awareness that it will not be adequate to itself as spirit until its activity is wholly spiritual, which is to say, in no way effected from outside itself. To call this a "consciousness of being all reality" is simply to say that to be conscious of any reality whatsoever is to be the autonomous center of the activity which is consciousness. Gradually this will also be to say that no reality is opaque to consciousness, provided that consciousness is not looked upon as the isolated consciousness of the single individual, and provided that "all reality" is not looked upon as the accumulation of bits and pieces of reality.

Here it is that the necessity of religious consciousness for the Hegelian phenomenological endeavor becomes clear. If the human spirit is completely autonomous in relation to its object, the spirit can, in that way at least, be said to be "absolute." That, however, is not enough for Hegel. Nor is it enough that "spirit" be concretely universalized by extension to *all* human consciousness, in time as well as space. To say that such a concretely universal spirit is "conscious of being all reality" is still to say that the "all" of which it is conscious is only formally, not concretely, universal. Thus, only if spirit's object is "absolute" is spirit itself absolute in the way in which Hegel intends. If the human spirit is essentially finite, as, I take it, Kant and Heidegger would have it, then its sphere of objectivity is also essentially finite. If, on the other hand, as Hegel would have it, the spirit's sphere of objectivity is infinite, then the spirit itself is essentially infinite. It is, then, essential to the integrity of human consciousness that it be religious, that it be consciousness of the absolute, the infinite, who is God. That for Hegel it is also essential to the integrity of human consciousness that the "of God" be taken as a subjective as well as an objective genitive is a further point, which takes consciousness beyond the religious, as Hegel understands it; but to go beyond the religious is not, dialectically, to cease to be religious. As Hegel sees it, the autonomy of the human spirit demands that as self-conscious reason it must be both conscious of infinite reality and aware that this very consciousness is its own consciousness of itself. Only a reality which is spirit can be infinite; only a spirit which is infinite can be adequate to infinite reality; only if the human spirit is in some intelligible sense infinite can it be adequate to infinite reality.

Not even Kant and Heidegger, it would seem, would dispute the last statement. What both would dispute, however, is the one which precedes it. In Kant's view human reason in its speculative knowing—its knowing of what really is as opposed to what ideally ought to be—is limited to a finite field of objectivity. Reason itself is essentially finite, since its function is merely regulative of what is presented in sense intuition and elaborated in the *a priori* categories of understanding. If there be an infinite, it is the object of faith alone, which is discontinuous with reason. Without going into the question of faith, Heidegger, for whom philosophy has nothing to say as to what is of faith, sees human consciousness as authentically human only when it is aware of its own essential finitude and of the finitude of the Being which is its "element." In opposition to Kant Hegel claims that the authentically human is characterized by thought and that, thus, a faith whose object would be beyond thought would not be authentically human. Against Heidegger he would argue that it is simply arbitrary to cling to a phenomenology of merely finite consciousness whose "element" is merely finite Being—and that it is a thoroughgoing phenomenology of human consciousness as spirit which demonstrates precisely this.

In saying this Hegel is not saying that the human spirit, either singly or collectively, is to be identified with God. What he is saying is that a consciousness of self which is not at the same time a consciousness of God is not in the full sense a consciousness of self, because it is not a consciousness of self as spirit in the full sense. Man is not God, but man's self-consciousness is man's God-consciousness. None of this, however, makes any sense if the God of whom man is conscious is some "Being" highest in the scale of being, a "supreme Being," or even an "absolute Being," who would be an object of human knowing only as an abstraction or a projection. Only a God who is "Spirit" is concrete, and for man to be conscious of himself as spirit is to be conscious of the concrete Spirit who is God, the knowledge of whom is a condition for any knowing's truly being knowing.

Against this background it is not difficult to see why for Hegel religious consciousness is an essential stage in the march toward adequate self-consciousness, which is identified with adequate knowing. Unless in the process of its development consciousness becomes religious, the self of which it is consciousness would be only partially a self, not all that the self as spirit is. It is the God who is present to consciousness in religion—however inadequate the form in which he is present—who reveals by his presence just what it is to be spirit, what it is to be activity without passivity, what it is to be truly autonomous. When Hegel says of this autonomous activity of the spirit that it is infinite he means what he says, but we should not be misled into thinking that he means it to be simply non-finite. The term is not negative in that sense at all. Rather, he is saying that the finite spirit is infinite, where "is" denotes neither identification nor attribution but "passing over to" or "becoming identical with," very much in the sense in which Aristotle says that in knowing the knower "becomes" the known. When finite spirit knows infinite Spirit—and only that is knowing in the full sense—it "becomes" the Spirit it knows.

HEGEL'S GOD

When all of this has been said, of course, it could still be argued—as Kojève, Kaufmann, and Findlay do argue—that the "absolute Spirit" of which Hegel speaks need not be God, that it need only be the concretely universalized human spirit, something like the Feuerbachian projection of the perfectly human. If, in fact, all we had to go on were the *Phenomenology of Spirit,* it might be difficult to prove this argument wrong. It is, nevertheless, equally difficult to see how a non-divine absolute would make sense, even if we were to confine ourselves to the *Phenomenology.* Nor is it easy to maintain that Hegel is simply speaking of a concretely universalized human spirit, which neither Feuerbach nor Marx claimed he was doing; they said, rather, that that is all he could legitimately do, and that thus he was wrong in what he did do. If, further, we look at the whole of Hegel's philosophy, such an interpretation seems completely incompatible with his emphasis on the so-called "ontological argument," of which the *Science of Logic* is a prolonged elaboration, and which occupies a central position in the *Lectures on the Philosophy of Religion,* the *Lectures on the Proofs for the Existence of God,* and in the *Introduction* to the *Lectures on the History of Philosophy.*

In any event, whether or not for Hegel religious consciousness bespeaks a consciousness of God, it clearly bespeaks an object which transcends mere finite human spirit. It is clear, too, that in Hegel's view only a "divine" spirit is concretely universal and that only for such a consciousness is there no conflict between the world of reality (objectivity) and the world of spirit (subjectivity), precisely because they are one and the same world. We might say, either a consciousness of divine Spirit or no adequate comprehension of reality. One may opt for the second member of the disjunction, but it is difficult to see how one would be following Hegel in doing so. It is true, of course, that spirit needs the mediation of a world of reality in order to know itself as spirit—hence the "System"—but the world of reality will make spirit known to itself only if the world itself is a revelation of Spirit. The human spirit can see itself as the autonomous source of the world (all reality) it knows only if it *re-creates* a world which the divine Spirit *creates*.

Up to this point, it might well seem, religious thinkers could find Hegel's exposition congenial to their own thinking. In fact, however, many religious thinkers, with Kierkegaard in the lead, have been quick to point out that Hegel goes too far. It is all very well, they say, to contend that a consciousness which does not ultimately have God as its object is a truncated consciousness and that it is religious consciousness which expressly makes God the ultimate content of consciousness. Still, the argument continues, to go further with Hegel and to insist that even religious consciousness is not adequate to its object, that to believe in God and to worship him is not enough, since he also must be *known* by autonomous, self-conscious reason, is to downgrade religion and to rationalize God. The reaction is understandable but perhaps not justifiable. First of all, Hegel is speaking of the *phenomenon* of religious consciousness, i.e., in any of the forms in which it has yet manifested itself. In all of these, Hegel finds, although the God who is the object of religion is the Absolute, ultimately—in Christian religion—Absolute Spirit, still the form under which he is present to religious consciousness is the form of "representation," which *stands for* God but is not the very *presence* of God in thought. God, then, can be present in thought only if thought itself is absolute, if it is "absolute knowing," which would seem to be saying that religion is swallowed up in what Hegel considers to be philosophical thought. This, however, would be true only if faith ceased to be faith once it had achieved a rational grasp of its own content; and it might furthermore well be true that rational thought could not have God as its content, the way it does throughout Hegel's *Logic*, if it did not constantly have faith as its underpinning. If this be the case, then philosophical knowing neither swallows up nor cancels out religious consciousness; it simply transforms religion into an explicit consciousness of its own implications. In any event what Hegel has to say about developing religious consciousness and of its necessity in the story of developing spirit will make a great deal of sense against the backdrop of the present interpretation.

From another point of view it might be argued, with Feuerbach, that the ultimate logic of Hegel's position demands a humanizing of the divine, reducing God to the only kind of object he can be if he is to be the object of human thought. But, again, it could be argued with equal, if not greater, cogency that Hegel's position involves a divinizing of the human in that it insists that a human consciousness of self which falls short of being a consciousness of God is not consciousness of the integral self. Not until we have gone through the history of religious consciousness as Hegel presents it, with its culmination in "absolute knowing," will it be possible to choose between the alternative interpretations.

THE PROGRESS OF RELIGIOUS CONSCIOUSNESS

In an effort to follow Hegel, then, as he engages in a phenomenology of religious consciousness, we can say in a general sort of way that a religious human consciousness consists in an awareness of a divine being (whatever "divine" will ultimately mean) which transcends both man and man's world and is, thus, "absolute." Initially this awareness is minimal, no more than a sort of intuitive affirmation of a vague being, out there, which is dependent on nothing and on which all depends, an all-pervasive presence—"the Absolute." Now, just as the whole *Phenomenology* consists in a progressive and tortuous concretization in thought of an originally indeterminate minimal consciousness, and just as the *Logic* presents the progressive thinking determination of an originally purely abstract being, so the phenomenology of religious consciousness consists in a progressive elaboration of the implications contained in the initial awareness of "the Absolute."

The process, as Hegel describes it, might aptly be designated an *ascensio mentis in Deum*, wherein the ascent of individual man recapitulates the slow ascent of social man through history. Roughly the process is divided into three stages: religion of nature, religion of art, and religion of revelation.

(*a*) Religion of Nature: Nature, which stands over against man and embodies a force which is sometimes benign sometimes hostile, reveals to man a more than nature itself. This it does with a minimum of intervention on the part of the human spirit, with a minimum of thought. The God (or gods) of this stage is simply a felt need if man is to cope with nature, an absolute to be invoked or placated. We can call it the Absolute as "force."

(*b*) Religion of Art: The activity of human spirit takes over as man transcends nature by consciously—and self-consciously—producing works of art which reveal at once a more than themselves and a more in man's consciousness of the Absolute. In the work of art there is a divine presence, but it is put there by man. The God of this stage can be called the Absolute as "beauty."

(*c*) Religion of Revelation: Man has gradually become aware that his God is Spirit, one who previously spoke to man through nature, then through the products of man's own creative activity, and now speaks to man in a language which the mind of man can grasp. At this stage the divine Spirit is truly present to man. Spirit speaks to spirit, and not through sensible or imaginary embodiments. The Absolute here is recognized as Spirit—who "speaks."

Even in this last stage, however, the divine Spirit is present to man only in the "word" which Spirit speaks. The word, it is true, is the most spiritual of all instruments, but it is still only an instrument. Only when the divine Word "becomes flesh" is the divine Spirit truly present among men; and only when the "Word become flesh" dies can the divine Spirit be present in the spirit of man. It is thus that Hegel interprets those words of the Fourth Gospel "The Spirit shall teach you all truth"; the Spirit will not merely speak *to* man, he will speak *in* man. Thus the "absolute knowing" in which Hegel's *Phenomenology* culminates (to be explicated in the subsequent "System") is the actual presence of the divine Spirit in man which follows upon the death of the *individual* God-man.

To expand these broad outlines to include the details of the process as Hegel presents it would be to rewrite the *Lectures on the Philosophy of Religion* or, at the very least, the long seventh chapter of the *Phenomenology*. Suffice it to say that Hegel does touch all the bases in going from the vague image of "Light" which characterizes Zoroastrianism to the purified "religion of the spirit" which he considers German Lutheranism to be. What is important to note is that Hegel sees the process of developing religious consciousness (both individual and historical) as an organic continuum with its own logic, parallel to the overall continuous process of consciousness journeying by its own efforts from minimal sensation to "absolute knowing." It is important, too, to note that for Hegel consciousness will never reach the goal of the overall journey if it does not make the religious journey. Only if the God of whom man is conscious is progressively spiritualized will man progressively recognize the true spirituality of his own consciousness. The human consciousness which is conscious of itself as thoroughly spiritual in its activity is by the same token conscious of its own autonomy, since to be spiritual is to be not acted upon. In relation to the world of objectivity over against man, this means that he actively makes it his own—"appropriates" it—re-creates it.

HIGHLIGHTS OF THE MOVEMENT

To appreciate the role which Hegel assigns to religious consciousness in this process of spiritualization we can, without reproducing all the details, consider the highlights of man's progressive awareness of the

divine. It should be noted at the outset, however, that Hegel does not
see the movement as one from individual to corporate consciousness;
it is integral to religious consciousness that it be from the beginning
corporate. It should be noted, too, that its forward movement is constituted by an "appropriation" at each successive level of what is "represented" at the immediately preceding level. This "appropriation" is
the active "doing" of self-consciousness in its progressive awareness of
selfness. Primitive man represents to himself a divine power "out
there," a divinity which, the more primitive the representation, the
more its "attributes" are what they are because they are "attributed"
to it by man. Thus, the god who is made known to man in the works
of nature is, so to speak, a "natural" being, a "first cause," a "force,"
a "supreme being," the source of nature's workings. When man's
spirit begins to intervene in the process by creating the work of art
which embodies man's god, then the god himself begins to be revealed
as spirit. The revelation of the god as spirit and the revelation of
man's own spirituality run a parallel course, both moving from vague-
ness to concreteness. As the art work becomes less and less a material
thing "out there" and becomes more and more the "acting out" of
religious mystery, the human performer becomes more and more
aware of his own importance as the "god-bearer" and, thus, of the
presence of divinity in human artistic activity, which is at the same
time religious activity.

Up to this point, Hegel contends, it is inevitable that man should
represent divinity to himself as a plurality of individual gods, a plurality which, again, is progressively united in the vague community
of divine being through the medium of self-conscious poetic expression—an artistic activity suffused with spirit. The poetic expression of
divinity-consciousness reaches its high point in Greek tragedy. There
can be no doubt that Hegel sees the progress of art from the primitive
to the sophisticated as a developing spiritualization of artistic activity.
There can be little doubt, although he does not say so expressly, that
he sees all poetry (perhaps all art) as in its original development essentially religious, i.e., as the progressively more self-conscious expression of a *people's* religious awareness.

However high Hegel's esteem of Greek tragedy as an art form, he
does recognize it as a point of no return in religious consciousness.
Like Plato he sees the legendary gods of tragedy (inherited from Greek
mythology) as essentially non-gods with their all-too-human foibles. It
was necessary, then, that these gods be cut down to size in comedy,
revealed as what they were, substitutes for the unified divinity of the
Absolute who is Spirit. It is the very irreverence of comedy, then,
which ushers in the sublime ideals of "the beautiful," "the true," "the

good" celebrated by Socrates and Plato, given an identifiable divine form in the "thought thinking thought" of Aristotle's *Metaphysics*, his "divine science." With this, the way to religious–philosophical monotheism is opened. Once more the paths of a God becoming spiritualized and of man becoming conscious of his own spirit run parallel. Ultimately, only a God who himself is totally spirit could satisfy the demands of a human consciousness gradually becoming more fully aware of its own spirituality. To such a God the Greek spirit could not attain. As Hegel sees it, only a God who actively, self-consciously reveals himself to man as Spirit can satisfy man's spirit. For such a God the Greek spirit, with an infusion of Judaic revelation, was ready; Christian history could begin; God could reveal himself to man and thus reveal to man what man himself is. Even God, however, could not do this merely through the instrumentality of human words; only through a revelation which is incarnation could God do it. Thus, for Hegel, it is necessary that there be the leap to Christian religion, to Christian revelation, a revelation of what it is for God to be man and, therefore, of what it is for the human to become divine, of what it is for man to be truly man, the "god-bearer," truly spirit.

HEGEL'S "THEOLOGY"

When Hegel reaches the Christian religion, which he considers to be the culmination of the progressive development of religious consciousness, affording the highest degree of self-consciousness which religion as such can, he is impelled to interpret it in such a way that it elucidates all that any religion can regarding the reality of human consciousness as "spirit." For Hegel Christian religion is "absolute religion," in the sense that religious consciousness simply cannot go beyond it: there is no religious "beyond." If there is a consciousness of the absolute beyond Christian religious consciousness, it must be, so to speak, a suprareligious consciousness. Before going into the question of such a suprareligious consciousness, however, Hegel seeks to interpret "spiritually" five major themes of Christian revelation, with a view to showing that the "mysteries" in question when properly—"spiritually"—understood constitute a revelation of consciousness as spirit and of self-consciousness as a consciousness of being spirit (of what it is to be spirit). In the context of Hegel's elaboration it would seem that "spiritual interpretation" is roughly equivalent to "demythologization," in which the language of the revelation is stripped of its inevitable metaphorical character in order to uncover its true meaning. The five mysteries which Hegel has chosen to interpret thus are Incarnation, Trinity, Creation, the Fall, and Redemption.

Hegel has quite obviously chosen well. It might, of course, be argued that the themes of Creation and Fall—even of some sort of Redemption—are not uniquely Christian. If, however, the mysteries as interpreted are meaningful only in an incarnational context, as Hegel claims they are, then all five themes are uniquely Christian. The Incarnation is, clearly, the central mystery of Christianity, not only in the sense that from it Christianity derives both its name and its character, but also in the sense that the other four are intelligible from a Christian point of view only as making possible an explication of Incarnation. The trinity of "Persons" in God is necessary if God's entry into human history is to be possible at all. Creation is necessary if there is to be a human history into which God can enter. The movement away from God in the Fall is necessary if there is to be a reason for Incarnation. Redemption is necessary if Incarnation is to be an effective presence of God in human history.

Incarnation. In Christian religious consciousness the Incarnation is a uniquely concrete union of the divine and the human in the individual God-man, whom history calls Jesus and whom Christians call the Christ. According to Hegel Jesus Christ is the most totally human of all humans precisely because he is divine, the model of the integrally human, because only the man who is more than merely natural man is integrally human, spiritual. Gone, says Hegel, is the fragmented divinity of the Greek pantheon whose only unified intelligibility is the abstract unity of divine "substance," a sort of "class" to which all the "gods" belong—or from which, perhaps, all are derived. This sort of substantial unity bespeaks no unity of self-consciousness either on the side of divinity or on the side of a humanity related to the divine. The incarnation of the God-man, Jesus Christ, reconciles divine substance and human self-consciousness. In Jesus the divine substance "empties" itself (the Pauline κένωσις) becoming a concrete human self and thus revealing a concrete selfhood in God. It is thus that Jesus reveals *that* God is Spirit—not merely substance or "supreme being"— and reveals too *what* it is for man to be essentially spirit. As Hegel sees it, however, precisely because in Jesus Christ God is sensibly present in bodily form, Jesus is not yet fully *who* he is; his body must die that his Spirit may live in the Christian community.

Trinity. The God of the philosophers, whether of Plato, Aristotle, or Plotinus, whether the deistic God of the Enlightenment—or even the God of Kant, Jacobi, and Fichte, to whom philosophical thought cannot attain—is no more than an abstract "supreme being." The concrete God of Christianity is a trinity of "Persons," revealed, not in the Incarnation alone, but in the Incarnation and the descent of the Spirit consequent on the death of the God-man. Because the Spirit is present in and to the human spirit—in the community—the en-spirited community can see the man Jesus as the human revelation of the divine. The divinity revealed in and through Jesus is triune: the divinity *in itself*, the Father; the divinity in the individual Jesus, the Son; the divinity in the believing *community*, the Spirit. Herein there is a reconciliation of transcendence and immanence only because the transcendent Father is immanent in the Son, whose Spirit is immanent in the community, extended in both space and time. To grasp conceptually *(begreifen)* the divine reality, human consciousness finds that its awareness of God is of a God articulated into a related triplicity (Trinity). To articulate this triplicity in language, the Christian community employs names to designate the members of the triplicity. Thus, the names—Father, Son, Spirit—are metaphors based on human relationships. The distinctions of persons are meaningful only if they are at the same time grasped as non-distinctions in a reality of dynamic movement, self-movement, with which only "speculative thought" can ultimately come to grips. When religion, even "absolute" religion, gives names to the "persons" of this trinity, it is articulating this self-movement, which is Spirit—God as Spirit. The "moments" of this spiritual movement, says Hegel in an effort to transcend the metaphors of "names," are "being," "knowledge," and "love," united in the dynamic unity of self-comprehension which he calls "concept," thus foreshadowing the dynamic unity of totally interrelated reality and totally interrelated conceptual thought.

Having given his "spiritual" interpretation of the Incarnation as the movement of God's supreme self-revelation, a movement which extends through the whole earthly life of the God-man culminating in his physical death and resurrection whereby the Spirit comes to dwell in and animate the community, Hegel has been able to interpret the Trinity as self-movement in the interior life of God. This, then, enables him further to interpret a series of figurative terms which occur in Christian theological speculation in the language of the "concept" understood as a movement of "concrescence." "Creation," "Fall," and "Redemption" are themselves figurative terms, and in their explication theology employs other figurative terms which demand interpretation.

Creation. If the term "create" is taken to mean "make out of nothing," a making which is, as ordinarily understood, in the mode of causal efficacy, Hegel contends, then it is a "representational" (metaphorical) term designating God's spiritual activity in relation to the

world's coming-to-be. This divine activity Hegel sees as a "knowing"—
with its distinctively Hegelian overtones of "conceiving," which is
comprehending by concretely putting together. The *Phenomenology*
has sought to establish that all knowing is a knowing of self. Thus
even God's knowing is a knowing of himself, and his knowing of the
world is the explicitation of that self-knowledge in conceiving and
thus bringing into being a world as the outward expression of God's
own being. If human knowing is to be truly a knowing, then, it must
be analogous to divine knowing, such that man in knowing his world
knows himself and in knowing himself knows his world in a manner
parallel to God's "creating." Creation, then, is the work of reason
knowing, bringing into being and putting together what it knows.
The world is the creation of divine Reason and is, thus, rational, revealing both in its spatial dimensions (nature) and in its temporal
dimensions (history) reason as its source. By the same token the world
grasped in human knowing is the re-creation of the world in human
reason; the primordial unity of divine creation having been fragmented by the abstractive activity of scientific understanding is put
together again by the creative (re-creative) activity of reason. Thus,
human re-creative reason whereby the human reason knows itself is a
sharing in the divine Reason whereby God knows himself.

The Fall. If it is true to say that the phenomenon of the human is
a sharing in the divine, then it would seem reasonable to say also that
human failure to express the divine is a falling away from that which
makes the human to be integrally human. This, however, is not the
way Hegel interprets the biblical account of the Fall. Rather, he sees
the creation of man as initially man's mere being in the world and
man's "innocence" as no more than his lack of responsibility for that
world. Becoming responsible, then, is the movement which explicates
creation; negatively expressed: it is the loss of "innocence." It is worth
noting that the German term for "in-nocence" (*Schuldlosigkeit*) is
literally translated "faultlessness," a state which is proper to *nature*,
not to *spirit*. Thus, if man is to pass from nature to spirit, nature
must, so to speak, be "faulted"; fault becomes a condition for the
movement from being *innocent* to being *good*. In this context the
"tree of knowledge of good and evil" becomes the symbol of that
knowledge which puts an end to innocence; the "fruit" which the first
couple, as comprising all humanity, pluck and eat is the symbol of that
self-knowledge which is the beginning of responsibility for a world of
reality as known; and the "Angel of Light" (Lucifer) who opens the
eyes of humanity's first couple symbolizes the awakening of consciousness which will ultimately culminate in the authentic life of spirit. It

is all one movement, but at the same time it is but the first faltering steps of a larger overall movement. Thus, the Fall itself is the first step toward reconciliation; to know good as good and evil as evil is to be on the road to reconciliation, and the *felix culpa* is truly "happy" because it sets the scene for "redemption."

Redemption. Looked at from the side of God, "creation" is not an instantaneous act but a movement wherein man, who has come into being in a world of reality which is over against him and unknown by him, makes that world of reality his own by progressively sharing in the divine creative activity. Looked at from the side of man, that same process can be looked at as the one overall movement of "redemption." Here, once more, "incarnation" becomes central; incarnation *is* redemption. The abstract being of a God who is seen only as "Creator" is in time expressed in the concreteness of a human self-consciousness. Creation, then, is the beginning of externalization of an otherwise abstract God, and incarnation is the further concretization of a God who takes upon himself human self-consciousness in order that man may take to himself concrete God-consciousness and thus be redeemed. Incarnation, however—and thus creation, too—is not complete until the individual God-man dies physically in order to rise spiritually in the community which is to live his life.

Whether or not this Hegelian systematization of salvation history, in which all events are "moments" of one connected movement, can prove fruitful in coming to terms with religious mystery we can leave to the theologians—or historians of theology. That, despite its sometimes quite obviously fanciful exegesis, it tells us a great deal about Hegel's conception of the progressive "spiritualization" of human reality is unmistakable. It is also clear that Hegel means to be taken seriously when he articulates the moments of this process "religiously." How religious all this really is is disputed by many—on both sides of the religious divide. Secularists like Marx and Feuerbach see the whole thing as illegitimate precisely because Hegel takes God and the divinization of man seriously. Secularists like Kojève, Kaufmann, and Findlay legitimize Hegel's account by seeing in it the complete secularization of what is only metaphorically called "religious consciousness." Religionists—and their name is legion—tend to condemn Hegel because he has destroyed religion altogether. No one, however, denies that Hegel has provided us with a fascinating, grandiose, and in some ways compelling panoramic vision of human development.

Without denying a certain cogency to the "secularist" interpretation of Hegel's account—at least of the one contained in the *Phenomenology*—we can turn now to the two principal objections raised by

religionists. The first, which was raised by Kierkegaard, is quite simply that the account is too systematically coherent. By it Hegel has
so rationalized religion—and Christianity in particular—that it has
ceased to be religion at all; a faith which has been transformed into
rational knowledge is no longer faith. A first answer to this objection
might be to give the account all over again. It is scarcely "rational"
in the narrow sense implied by Kierkegaard—Hegel is not a "rationalist" in that sense at all. Mysteries do not cease to be mysteries, nor
does faith cease to be faith, in a systematic framework of intercon-
nection wherein both belief and what is believed have significance
only in relation to the ongoing development of the human spirit.

A somewhat more sophisticated answer to the same objection might
be to point out that Hegel was neither the first nor the last to avow
that *fides* must seek *intellectum* if it is to be adequate as *fides*. It is
also true, of course, that Kierkegaard was neither the first nor the last
to insist that faith must avoid doing precisely that. The point is that
Hegel has quite firmly inserted his philosophical enterprise into the
tradition of Augustine, Anselm, Bonaventure, and Thomas Aquinas,
for none of whom was it a degradation of faith to seek at least a limited understanding. It might be argued that Hegel's fault lay in seeking an *unlimited* understanding, a totally *rational* account, but this
too hangs on the meaning of "rational." What Hegel has done is not
so much to rationalize faith as to broaden the concept of reason so as
to embrace faith. His attempt, then, to articulate faith in rational
terms is an attempt to show it as a continuous dynamic movement
with its own inner logic, a logic which is not different from that of
man's spiritual development, his growth toward rational autonomy.
It is true that in so doing Hegel has given to what are termed the
"mysteries" of faith the inevitability of rational process, but he does
not fail to explain what this means. He first distinguishes between
"mystery" (*mysterion*) and "secret" (*Geheimnis*). Mystery, then, is a
profound truth in which is revealed to man what his relationship to
the divine truly is. Secret, on the other hand, is what is hidden from
man, preventing him from knowing either himself or God. In this
context it is the function of reason to embrace mystery—the mystery
of man in God and God in man. "Rational process," too, is not the
process of formal logical-entailment; rather, it is the process of organic
growth, continuity of movement. The content of religion given in
faith grows to maturity; faith itself grows to maturity; and so do the
"faithful."

The second objection is not completely different from the first, even
though, perhaps, it is more widespread. It is specifically directed
against the place accorded to religion in the *Phenomenology of Spirit,*

but it involves the complaint that the Hegelian "System" has become a substitute for genuine religion. If, it is claimed, religion is the penultimate step in the march of human spirit to the complete possession of itself in "absolute knowing," then religious consciousness is "superseded by," "swallowed up in," absolute knowing. The objection is serious and has its plausibility. It is true, of course, that Hegel does speak of religion as being *aufgehoben* in absolute knowing. It is true, too, that *aufheben* is usually translated by "supersede" (or, sometimes, "transcend"), but Hegel is hardly to be condemned on the basis of an inadequate translation of this key term in the language of dialectic. He himself takes pains to point out that the term *aufheben*, even in ordinary German usage, has three meanings: "cancel," "retain," and "raise up." As a *dialectical* term, he then tells us, it has all three meanings at once, each inextricably bound up with the others. Thus, to say that religion is *aufgehoben* in absolute knowing is to say that the latter "cancels" (or "eliminates"), not religion, but the inadequacy of the "form of representation." At the same time absolute knowing "retains" the same absolute content of religion, such that without the retention of religious consciousness knowing would have no absolute content; nor would it know what it is to be "absolute." Furthermore, absolute knowing "raises" religion to a level of realization of all that religion implies. Because, as Hegel sees it, "thinking" characterizes human spirit at the highest pitch of intensity, then man's relationship to the highest, to God, must be a thinking-relationship. Religion, we might say, is most truly religion when it is thought. It should be pointed out, however, that the "thinking" in question is not merely theoretical. Because, he says, religious consciousness "thinks" God under the guise of "figurative representation" (religious metaphor), it can "unite" itself to God only in a subsequent activity, that of "cult." Absolute knowing, then, by canceling the form of representation can combine the two steps into one; it is at once a "knowing of" and a "dynamic unification with" God. Absolute knowing does not "swallow up" religion; it "completes" religion, makes it to be what religion truly is. If all consciousness is ultimately self-consciousness, then the God-consciousness of religion is ultimately self-consciousness. This is the Hegelian version of Spinoza's *amor intellectualis Dei*, where the "of God" is to be taken as both an objective and a subjective genitive—man knows God, and thus God is the *object* of his knowing; man knows God, and thus the human *subject* is divinized in the knowing.

It might still be objected, of course, that to designate the profoundest relationship of the human spirit to the divine Spirit as "knowing" is a deceptive use of terms. Perhaps it is. Perhaps there is a better term to designate that spiritual activity of man's which is at once most autonomous and most characteristically divine in man. If there be such, I am sure Hegel would raise no objection. Philosophy is not a matter of words—nor is religion.

6

Emil L. Fackenheim's
The Religious Dimension in Hegel's Thought:
A Review

LIKE ARISTOTLE, Hegel is a thinker who invites extensive commentary, if for no other reason than that the wealth of insight his thought provides makes interpretation a means of clarifying the commentator's own thought. After a period of relative eclipse Hegel's thought has seen a revival of interest among philosophers, not only on the European continent, but also in the Anglo-Saxon world. Because that thought is obscure, even at times confusing, interpretations vary, and controversy rages. Out of all this no one expects the definitive interpretation to emerge, but there is always hope that with renewed interest new light will be shed, new avenues of approach will be opened up, and new possibilities of development will be revealed.

To the growing Hegel literature Emil Fackenheim has contributed a book which, although modest in its proportions and deliberately limited in scope, should go a long way toward fulfilling that hope on all three counts. He has sought to bring out not simply what Hegel thought *about* religion—what might be called his philosophy of religion—but, more significantly, the essentially religious character of the whole Hegelian philosophical endeavor. This, of course, has been recognized before. To take but two significant examples: we find it in Heidegger's characterization of Hegel's philosophy as "Onto-theologie" and in Ilyin's monumental *Die Philosophie Hegels als kontemplative Gotteslehre*. Fackenheim's presentation, however, is at once more sympathetic (and more knowledgeable) than Heidegger's and more simple (although no less profound) than Ilyin's. Rarely has an interpreter presented with such clarity the intricacies of Hegel's thought; rarely has anyone succeeded so well in unifying that thought around one central theme, thus going a long way toward making the whole more intelligible.

In a very real sense Hegel is the most modern of modern philosophers. He is heir to a long tradition which, from Francis Bacon and

An earlier version of this chapter appears in *International Philosophical Quarterly*, 8, No. 4 (December 1968), 630–35.

Descartes to his own day, sought to secularize philosophical thought and to make it autonomous as the self-activity of supremely rational consciousness. None of this will Hegel repudiate. He will, it is true, seek to reinstate religion at the very heart of philosophical thinking, but he will do so without compromising the secular grandeur of that thought. He will endeavor to synthesize a faith, which is essentially receptive of the divine, with rational thought, which is autonomous and self-creative. If such a reconciliation succeeds, it cannot be less than monumental. Fackenheim is not sure that Hegel's endeavor was successful; he is sure, however, that we shall never understand Hegel's thought at all if we do not see it as precisely such an endeavor.

To a contemporary mind, which finds Hegel's definitive religious thought (or, worse still, his definitive repudiation of religious thought) in his *Early Theological Writings* and which sees in the *Phenomenology of Spirit* a complete humanization of the divine, Fackenheim's attempt can be little less than foolish. Fackenheim, however, finds the foolishness entirely on the other side. To emphasize the *Early Theological Writings*, which not only are the work of youth but were never intended to be published, and to de-emphasize the published works of Hegel's philosophical maturity, he feels, is simply to violate the fundamental canons of philosophical interpretation. On the other hand, to miss the profoundly religious character of the *Phenomenology of Spirit* is to misread it in the light of one's own prejudices.

The problem which Hegel faces—in the *Phenomenology* and throughout his career—Fackenheim tells us, is that of "the relation between all of human life and an all-comprehensive philosophical thought" (p. 22). This, then, specifies itself "into a problem concerning the relation between *religious* life and philosophic thought" (p. 23). Thus, it is not simply by choice that philosophic thought occupies itself with religion; it requires religion if it is to be philosophic at all, in the sense in which Hegel understands that term. Thought is not thought without a content, and it is religion which supplies this content to philosophy. True, religious "representation" is *aufgehoben* in philosophical "thought," but this says precisely that the former is indispensable to the latter. It is of the utmost importance to recognize that for Hegel "*Reason is not the final form of selfhood in life; that just as Reason is the 'Truth' of self-consciousness so the Truth of Reason is Spirit*" (p. 61). Because man is spirit and not merely reason, his thought is incomplete precisely as thought if it is no more than rational.

Paradoxically enough, Hegel has the utmost confidence in reason. This he can have because for him reason is truly reason only when it is not merely reason. Early in the *Phenomenology* consciousness is presented as coming to the realization that as reason it finds in itself all reality. On the level of mere reason, however, this is but an empty realization; it is without content until as religious consciousness it *receives* a content. This, we might say, is the paradox of Hegel's philosophy—as rational thought it is self-active; as more than rational it is receptive. Not only does the one not contradict the other; thought is receptive in its very self-activity and self-active in its very receptivity. Here, in Fackenheim's words, we seek to fathom "the relation between rational self-activity and religious receptivity to the Divine, and the relation of philosophical self-activity to both" (p. 37, note).

What is operative here is a philosophical thought which can "make radically intelligible what is already actual" (p. 12). Precisely as philosophical Hegel's thought is religious, because it seeks to unite modern secular self-confidence with confidence in an infinite God who has entered the world and redeemed it. Hegel's lifelong endeavor was a search for the absolute; not, however, an absolute outside of and beyond the world but an absolute present in the world. This he found in the Christian revelation of an incarnate God; the task was to make this revelation the content of philosophical thought. "Hegel asserts, with unwavering insistence, that Christianity is the absolutely true content, and that his philosophy both can and must give that content its absolutely true form" (p. 112). Just as thought is not genuinely philosophical until it has been raised to the level of the divine content which has been revealed to it, so revelation is not complete as revelation until the form in which it is made manifest is the form of thought.

There can be no question that a thought such as this constitutes a speculative transformation of Christianity. The point is, however, that Hegel does just this, and he does it in all seriousness; he sees the situation of Christian faith in the modern world as requiring this of both philosophical and theological thought. It is important to note, however, that from beginning to end Hegel's concern is with the actual Christianity of history. What changes as he matures is his conception of the nature of the transformation which is to take place—but it remains transformation and does not become substitution. In his youth Hegel (under the influence of Kant and Fichte) looked for a new philosophical religion which would supersede Christianity. With maturity he became more and more involved with historic Christianity, which philosophy was to take up and make its own. "For the early Hegel, philosophy will produce a new religion on the ruins of the old. For the mature Hegel, philosophy comprehends the old religion, and this latter is not and cannot be ruined" (p. 209).

It should be noted in all this that for Hegel—at least for the mature

Hegel—religion and Christian religion are practically synonymous. This does not mean that he did not recognize the existence or even the validity of other religions—particularly the Jewish—but simply that Christianity as the "absolute religion" stands for religion as such; historically it had superseded all other religions. Thus, to transform Christianity speculatively was to transform religion. Christianity is for him paradigmatic because it manifests in a way no other religion does or can the two essential characteristics of religion in its highest form: it is comprehensive and it is revealed. Here he finds the presence of Spirit which is the ultimate authority for both religion and philosophy. Only in Christianity can be realized the goal of human development, which is the dignity of human freedom, because only in Christianity is this dignity recognized as the dignity of each and all. Thus, Christianity alone is susceptible of the speculative transformation which his philosophy is to bring, since in Christianity alone the divine has become truly human, and only where the divine is truly human (or the human truly divine) can speculative thought be both self-active and receptive.

By the same token, however, only Hegel's own philosophy can do justice to the religious content which Christianity has provided. The progressive secularization of philosophic thought, of which we spoke earlier, was such that it demanded progressive opposition to basic Christian faith. Autonomy of thought and heteronomy of faith simply could not be reconciled. In Hegel's philosophy faith and thought are reconciled, because both have their source in Spirit. "Only the final modern philosophy—Hegel's own—can *recognize* that modern speculative thought presupposes the Christian faith which it was previously bound to oppose, and that the opposition between the two is relative rather than absolute" (p. 166).

The Christian faith in question is, of course, Protestant; not, however, simply because Hegel had a theological preference for Protestant teaching, but because philosophically faith as a present inward experience made more sense to him than a reaching out toward a God who was above and beyond the world. A characteristic of Hegel's thought which is not too often stressed by the commentators is what we might call its "earthiness," its rootedness in experience. For all his "absolute idealism" Hegel was an incorrigible realist—not in any naïve sense of that term, but in his conviction that speculative thought does deliver reality as it is. It is spirit which thinks, and man is incarnate spirit for whom being in the body is essential to even the highest thought, to logic itself. Experience is not simply preparatory to a thought which goes beyond it; experience is a dialectical component of a thought which never goes beyond experience, precisely because to think is to experience in the highest sense of that term. It is for this reason that he can—and must—integrate faith into his thinking; it is part and parcel of total, comprehensive experience. No one perhaps— not even Nietzsche—had greater reverence for Greek thought than did Hegel, and yet it was precisely in the inability of Greek thought to integrate religion that Hegel saw its weakness over against Christianity. Greek philosophy destroyed the religion out of which it took its rise, whereas the philosophy to which Christianity gives rise "culminates in a process which transfigures and reinstates its religious basis" (p. 186).

The thought which integrates both experience and the world which is experienced is for Hegel at once a human task and a divine gift. More than that, the self which constitutes itself as free in the process of thinking experience is a self which is recognized as already actual, precisely because the thought which thinks is paradoxically both an autonomous process and a presence of the divine in man. The ultimate philosophical question concerns the relationship of man and God, but, says Fackenheim, quoting Hegel's *Berliner Schriften* (BS 314), the question must be understood as asking not "how man reaches God," but rather "how God reaches man" (p. 161, note). The mystery of human thought is that its origin is both human and divine, that it is no less human for being divine.

> A thought which *recognizes* the divine Love of Christian faith forever *begins* as faith, humanly receptive of the divine gift; forever *rises above* such human receptivity, by reenacting the divine gift to the human other as a divine self-othering; and forever *reinstates* human faith as a phase in its own rise above humanity. Only a thought of this kind can be divine and yet a possibility for thinkers who are, and remain, human [p. 206].

One might say, as Kierkegaard did, that Hegel's thought is not religious but rather destructive of religion. Such a conclusion, it would seem, follows from a particular conception of what it is to be religious. According to Hegel that which distinguishes man as spiritual being from all beings of lesser stature is thought. This in turn means that those activities which are most characteristically human should be thought activities. Now, the most thoroughly characteristic human activity is that whereby man relates himself to God. Man relates himself to God, then, not through imagination or emotion or sentiment, but through thought, which is to say, man thinks God. This, in Hegel's mind, is not a downgrading but rather an upgrading of the religious relationship. It does not destroy religion but rather reinstates it as most inescapably human. Man, even modern man, is most authentically man when he is religious man. The point is, however, that he cannot be modern, rationally free, man with one side of himself and religious man with another. In Hegel's day secularized thinking saw philosophical thought as the summit of specifically human achievement. Hegel agrees with this, but, unlike his contemporaries, he sees in this supreme achievement of thought a specifically religious achievement. Thought is infinite activity, and infinite activity is activity of the infinite who is God. Religious man thinks God, because in thinking he shares the infinite activity which is God's.

In Hegel's philosophy, then, we find not simply a philosophy of religion (although that, of course, is not absent); we find a thought which is from beginning to end essentially religious. Never, perhaps, has philosophical thought been so thoroughly religious. The reader, of course, may not like this sort of religion (to say nothing of not liking this sort of philosophy); he may even feel that Hegel has watered down religion to accommodate it to his philosophy. What the reader cannot find, and this Fackenheim has demonstrated admirably, is that Hegel has permitted religion to be swallowed up in a purely humanist speculative thought.

7

Hegel on Proofs for God's Existence

WESTERN PHILOSOPHY began as an attempt to replace the cosmogonic myths of ancient Greek religion with a rational explanation of the experienced world. When, however, with Socrates, Plato, and Aristotle, philosophy became more sophisticated and more conscious of its power, the light of reason was turned to an investigation of what had previously been considered to be above and beyond scrutiny. The scientific spirit felt constrained to approach God (or the gods) in the only way worthy of a being endowed with reason; thinkers began to give reasons for their beliefs. From this time forward, with a few exceptions, the rational approach to the divine became an integral part of philosophic investigation.

As we go through the history of philosophy from Plato to modern times, however, we are struck by the variety manifested in these philosophic approaches to God. The explanation of this variety lies not merely in the diversity of philosophical systems but to a great extent in the diversity of religious experiences which philosophy seeks to explain. Many "proofs" have been given for God's existence, but rarely have they been looked upon as a means of "discovering" God. Rather they are considered as rational explanations of attitudes which antedate the proofs. Already accepting God on one ground or another, philosophers have sought to spell out these grounds in terms of detailed reasonings. In so doing they have revealed little about God which religion had not already taught, but they have revealed much about man and his manner of thinking. "Proofs" for God's existence do not lead to God; they describe in rational terms the path which men have taken in going to God.

No philosopher in ancient, modern, or even medieval times has shown more interest in the philosophical approach to God than has Hegel. More than that, however, Hegel could not be satisfied with an investigation which would reveal to him *that* God exists; for him the task of philosophy was to grasp in thought all that religion—particularly the revealed religion of the Judaeo-Christian tradition—by way of faith and religious representation could reveal concerning God. Nowhere does Hegel evidence any concern with "Does God exist?" His concern is "What can we know of God?" or "What is it to know

An earlier version of this chapter appears in *Kantstudien*, 55, No. 4 (1964), 443–65.

God?" Ultimately, the question is reducible to "Is there knowing at all short of knowing God?" or "Is there something divine in knowing?" [1] In the Introduction to his monumental *Science of Logic*, which is unquestionably the keystone of the entire Hegelian system, he speaks of its content as "the presentation of God as he is in his eternal essence before the creation of nature or of a single finite spirit" (WL I 31). It is for this reason that Karl Löwith has referred to the *Logic* as "ein perennierendes Definieren Gottes" and that Martin Heidegger has designated the Hegelian philosophy as an "Onto-theologie." There are those, of course, who, like Kojève,[2] claim that Hegel did not believe in God at all or that his speculations did more to destroy than to establish God, but it is difficult to take such contentions seriously, just as it is to accept the same sort of contentions with regard to Descartes or Spinoza.[3]

What is, perhaps, most remarkable in all this is the fact that Hegel's philosophical concern with and extensive treatment of God should have come in the immediate wake of Kant's apparently irrefutable invalidation of all philosophical "proofs" for the existence of God. On the other hand, nothing gives us a clearer insight into the character of Hegel's philosophizing than his contention—thrown in the teeth of romantics and rationalists alike—that the proper task of philosophy is to *think* the same content of which religion affords only a representation (*Vorstellung*). In this connection it is significant that the form of argumentation to which he devotes the most time and accords the most respect is the so-called "ontological argument," which had been advanced by St. Anselm. According to Kant all arguments for the existence of God are ultimately reducible to the ontological argument and are thus equally invalid. According to Hegel all arguments must ultimately be reduced to the ontological argument and thus share its validity as a description of the human spirit's elevation to God. To understand this would require a complete grasp of the "System" in its entirety and, above all, a minute understanding of the *Logic* whose movement constitutes an extended presentation of the ontological argument. It would in addition require a most accurate understanding of Hegel's severe and sometimes almost violent critique of Kant, which is constantly cropping up in his writings—nowhere more tell-

---

[1] "It is verily . . . the essence of revealed religion to know what God is" (GP III 611; cf. PR II 396). See note 9.

[2] Alexandre Kojève, *Introduction à la lecture de Hegel*, 4th ed. (Paris: Gallimard, 1947).

[3] An example of this sort of thing can be found in Laurence J. Lafleur's Introduction to his translation of Descartes' *Discourse on Method* (New York: Liberal Arts Press, 1954): "The concept of God is also used as a quite unnecessary logical support for Descartes' argument" (p. xix). "It is perhaps not too much to believe that the whole treatment of God in Descartes may be due to policy rather than to philosophy" (p. xx).

ingly than in his introduction to "Subjective Logic" (WL II 213–34).[4] In any event—and paradoxically enough—whether one prefers to look upon Hegel as an atheist or a theist, there is no way of grasping the movement of his philosophizing without carefully studying his treatment of the "proofs" for the existence of God.

FAITH AND THOUGHT

Though no one to date has characterized Hegel's thinking, in terms familiar to the Middle Ages, as *fides quaerens intellectum*, there is a significant sense in which this phrase describes his thinking most accurately.[5] So much so that one contemporary author has referred to Hegel as "the most Christian of thinkers, for while the official defenders of Christianity have usually borrowed their logic and the cast of their thought from Aristotle or from other sources, Hegel alone among thinkers has borrowed the whole cast of his thought from Christianity." [6] A superficial reading of the *Early Theological Writings* might cause some doubts as to the Christian roots of Hegel's thought, but a more careful examination of these same writings will reveal that this thought takes the Gospel as its point of departure. Hegel has, of course, been accused—particularly by Kierkegaard—of subordinating religion to philosophy, of making religious representation a mere "moment" in the dialectical march to true speculative thinking, but such a criticism fails to recognize that the dialectical *Aufhebung* always signifies for Hegel not only a passing-beyond but also a retention of the "moment" which is *aufgehoben*. It is not that faith disappears when thought takes over, but that faith is realized in its fullness when it becomes thinking faith. If man is characterized—distinguished from lower forms of life—by thought, then what man does will be at its best when it, too, is characterized by thought. According to Löwith,[7] it was on this point that Goethe parted company most violently with Hegel—

---

[4] Cf. chap. 8 of this volume, "Hegel's Critique of Kant's Theology."

[5] Since Hegel himself does not employ the expression as descriptive of his own thought, there need be no discussion as to whether Hegel *means* by it what the Augustinian medieval tradition did. The contention here is that the expression is descriptive of what Hegel *did*, even though it can be argued that the faith which seeks to understand in his case is not to be identified with the faith of Anselm or of the Augustinian tradition. In any event, the use of the expression here is not intended as an interpretation of its use in the medieval tradition.

[6] J. N. Findlay, *Hegel: A Re-examination* (London: Allen & Unwin; New York: Macmillan, 1958), p. 354. One might, of course, have legitimate reserves as to whether Findlay's criteria for calling Hegel a Christian philosopher are valid. The point here, however, is that Hegel's *philosophical* thought finds more nourishment in the Gospel than does the thought of so many presumably "Christian" philosophers—whether or not one judges Hegel to be a Christian.

[7] Karl Löwith, *Von Hegel zu Nietzsche*, 2nd ed. (Stuttgart: Kohlhammer, 1950), pp. 28–31; cf. Goethe, *Gespräche mit Eckermann*, February 4, 1829.

Goethe could see no excuse for introducing Christianity into philosophy itself, or philosophical thinking into Christian belief.

There is no question, then, of thought's taking over, so to speak, and proving what religion can only imaginatively represent. Rather it is a question of philosophy's thinking out a content which faith makes available—it was no less a critic than Feuerbach who saw in Hegel's philosophy no more than religion in another form. If there is to be a Christian philosophy, it cannot be one whose conclusions are forced upon it by an antecedent faith or theology—rather it must be a genuine philosophical reflection on an experience, the Christian experience of God. A philosophy is not Christian because a Christian theology has dictated to it what conclusions it may or may not come to; it is Christian because the experience upon which it reflects (and philosophy must reflect on experience) is a Christian experience. Faith no more disappears in thought than does being; both find their essence in thought. By the same token, just as the truth of being is in thought —which by no means denies that being is true—so, too, the truth of faith is in thought—which does not deny that faith is true, or that it is faith. To put it simply: faith without thought is empty (PR II 365)— we know not what we believe—belief must become progressively aware of a content which is initially only implicit. Faith seeks to understand because without understanding it is not complete as faith. It is not that understanding is merely a desirable consummation of faith; faith is simply not true to itself if it does not seek such an understanding.[8] Though it is seldom remarked, the quest for God is true even of the dialectical movement described in the *Phenomenology of Spirit*. The perfection of the Christian God is such that for him there is a simple identity between what *appears* and what *really is*. The *absolutes Wissen*, toward which the *Phenomenology* moves ineluctably, is one in which this same identity of appearance and reality will (ideally perhaps) be established. If all we had to go on were the *Phenomenology*, all this, of course, would be compatible with the mere hypothesis of divine perfection—nor can it be stated with certainty that the whole is more than an ideal of absolute knowledge—but to interpret the God of the *Logic* or of the *Lectures on the Philosophy of Religion* in such a hypothetical fashion seems to be stretching the esoteric character of Hegel's writing beyond the limits of plausibility.

We must remember how violently opposed Hegel was to the Romantic intuitive approach to religious truth, to God. In both the

---

[8] It should be remarked that "understanding" is not being used here in the technical sense of the *Verstand* which is opposed to *Vernunft* (reason). It is simply the Latin *intellectus* which we translate here as "understanding," in the sense of "intellectual comprehension."

Logic and the *Philosophy of Religion* he returns constantly to the attack against Jacobi and the intuitionists. Religious emotion, he contends, does not lose its purity when raised to the level of thought. On the contrary, just as thought distinguishes man from beast, so too do religion, morality, and law—precisely because these are *realized* in thought (EPW 34). The philosophy of religion is religious philosophy; it is religious reason philosophizing, making the content of religion the content of thought, thus realizing it—*an- und für sich*. At the same time it is important that this content be a content of feeling, too, provided it be not mere feeling.

> Yet not only can there be a true content in our feeling; there *should* and *must* be, or as used to be said, we must have God in our hearts. Heart is, of course, more than feeling; the latter is momentary, accidental, transient. But when I say "I have God in my heart," feeling is being expressed as an enduring, permanent mode of my existence. The heart is what I am, not what I am at the moment, but what I am in general, my character. The form of feeling as a universal, then, signifies the principles or habits of my being, my permanent manner of acting [PR I 144–45].

This is a far cry from a rationalization of either religion or philosophical thought. As Hegel saw it, "In regard to both content and form rationalism is contrary to philosophy" (GP I 112). The artificial faith–reason dichotomy produces a "rationalism" which is anything but genuinely rational. When thus separated, faith is not really faith; nor is reason, reason.

Though Hegel rarely uses the term "grace"—his language is more reminiscent of Spinoza's—he sees man's relation to God as ultimately a thought-relation, which is possible because the divine nature is in man. This is Spinoza's *amor intellectualis Dei*, the love whereby God loves himself in man, but it might also be called "grace" if this latter is understood as the divinizing of human nature. The grace of God is not some gift coming from without and fundamentally foreign to the nature which it transforms. The action of grace is the *return* of man into his own self-contained depths: "The Holy Spirit, then, is the subject's spirit, insofar as the subject has faith" (PR II 337). For Hegel the ultimate reality is not *substance*, as it is for Spinoza, but rather *subject* or *Spirit*, and its manifestation is spiritual activity (WL II 216). If, then, man can think God, he can do so because God thinks God in man. This is not thinking *about* God; it is God expressed—or rather expressing himself—in thought. It would be difficult, of course, to show any direct connection between Hegel and Augustine, but in the way he sees man finding God by entering into his own depths, his thought is certainly reminiscent of Augustine's. Knowledge of God is not something immediate, inevitable, which man cannot escape; it is something which true thinking will inevitably reveal, precisely because true thinking is "godly" thinking.

> The relation of spirit to spirit is a feeling of harmony, their unification. . . . Believing in the divine is possible only because there is the divine in the believer himself, and this divine rediscovers its own nature in what it believes, even if it is not aware that what is found is its own nature. . . . Belief in the divine stems from the divinity of the believer's own nature [TJ 313]. [9]

There may be a sense in which Hegel can speak of "proofs" for God's existence, but he cannot see the conviction of God's existence waiting on these proofs, any more than eating waits on a knowledge of chemistry, or digestion on a knowledge of anatomy and physiology (EPW 35). To "prove" the existence of God is to ascend in thought the existential pathway of acceptance which has preceded philosophical thought. This is not to say that the proof is otiose; it is a concrete working out of what was previously only abstractly grasped. All of which is but another way of describing the movement of the *Logic*, the march of the concept toward objectivity (WL II 354). In this process the least significant of the determinations to be "discovered" is *existence*; Hegel is not, as we said, much concerned with *whether God exists*; he is very much concerned with *what God does*. What God does, however, is God's self-manifestation (God "proves" himself), and this self-manifestation is completed in man, who thinks, and whose thoughts are God's thoughts.

INFINITY OF THOUGHT

In an earlier age it was customary to speak of divine thought according to an analogy with human thought. If thought, which is an obvious perfection, is to be found in man, then *a priori* it is to be found in the summit of all perfection, God. It is highly questionable, thinks Hegel (EPW 64), that in so saying one says anything intelligible. It is to say that God does something, we know not what, which, by analogy with what man does, can be called thinking. But since we do not really understand what this can mean when it is said of God, can we be said to know what we are saying? If, on the other hand, we observe that there is thought, and if we see that a thought which is ultimately merely finite is really no thought at all, we see a character of infinity in all thought. God thinks because God is the source of all thought, just as God is because he is the source of all being. Man's thinking,

---

[9] It is precisely this sort of thing which has led so many interpreters to see Hegel's thought as "pantheistic." It is difficult to see, however, that anyone can avoid an honest effort to resolve the paradox of a finite thinking which has something of the infinite and, therefore, of the divine in it. To say that when man thinks, God thinks in him, is not to say that God is man or that man is God. It is to say that universal "thought," in which true thinking shares, is at once divine and human.

then, is God's thinking, and to say that man thinks is to say that God thinks. Better still, it is to say that spirit thinks, and that spirit thinks and that spirit is, ultimately, only as infinite. In any event it is to find the necessity of what is said of God in God himself, not in human perfections.

The movement, then, is not so much from finite to infinite thought as it is a recognition of the infinite in the finite. Once again, one is reminded of Augustine's contention that truth is infinite, beyond mere finite capacities, and therefore revelatory of the Infinite.[10] For Augustine any truth bespeaks the infinite Truth, which is God; for Hegel any thought bespeaks infinite thought in the infinite Spirit, who is God.

The being of God, then, is revealed primarily in thought, not in nature or in the teleological ordering of finite reality. Thus, the proof of God from thought—the ontological proof—is the primary and only genuinely significant proof of God. Thought is truly thought only if it is infinite thought, and its content is truly being only if it is infinite being. The inadequacy of all proofs, then, whether in their classical formulation or in the Kantian refutation of them, lies in their failure to be truly rational. They are proofs of understanding, which is unaware of its own truth precisely because it is limited to a content of formal concepts, from which no conclusions can be drawn regarding reality.[11] It is true that we cannot *think* God if all we have to think with are finite concepts. Anselm was on the right track when he realized that a content of thought such as God could not be *only* in thought, but he erred in trying to present the argument in the guise of a formal syllogism, inferring, so to speak, one truth from another, better known truth (GP III 166–67; cf. GP III 163–64).[12] This is to make of the proof a *Verstandesschluss*, the kind which belongs to natural science, permitting the mind to cope on a finite level with the conclusion it reaches.

More than one critic has accused Hegel of being a pantheist,[13] seeing in his preference for the ontological argument an identification of the world's finite being with the infinite being of God. To accuse him of this, however, is to miss the distinction he makes between "rational proof" and "proof of understanding." One of the reasons he gives for

---

10 E.g., *In Ps. 119, Sermo* 23.1; *Confessiones* 10.26; *Retractationes* 1.4.13.

11 To see "proof" as a passage from contingent beings or contingent ends to an "unconditioned" is to see thought only in its *Verstandesform* (cf. PR I 129).

12 Hegel also finds fault with Anselm for his assumption that there are two kinds of object of *thought*: those which do, and those which do not, exist.

13 E.g., Franz Grégoire, *Études Hégéliennes: Les Points capitaux du système* (Louvain: Presses Universitaires de Louvain, 1958), Étude III, "Idée absolue et panthéisme," pp. 140–220.

rejecting the latter is that it can lead to pantheism, since to posit an objective ground for God's existence would be to make his infinite being dependent on the finite being of that ground, thus confusing God's infinite being with the finite being of the world (EPW 64; cf. PR II 477–78). If thinking God somehow *depends* on thinking the world, then the being of God somehow depends on the being of the world (EPW 74–75). The result of this is not so much a divinizing of the world as it is a finitizing of God, as an object *over against* the thinking subject, an object among objects (EPW No. 36). And the knowledge which the subject has of such a God consists in nothing more than an accumulation of finite predicates, quantitatively increased and attributed *eminentiori modo* to God (EPW No. 36). In fact, any proof which proceeds by *inferring* the being of the infinite from a consideration of the finite sets the one *over against* the other, which is but another way of saying that each is limited by the other.

As Hegel sees it, the process of truly rational thought is entirely different. It is not a process of "inference" at all; rather it is a "thinking consideration" of the world, wherein "thought is raised above the sensible," thus passing from the finite to the infinite (EPW 75–76). This is recognizing that the finite can be *thought* only when the infinite is thought (PR II 447–48), that the true being of the finite is in the infinite, precisely because true being is intelligible, not sensible— the being of the sensible is in its intelligible being. This means ultimately that the empirical form of the world as experienced is transformed—which is not to say that the world of experience is not, but that the being it has is in God, who alone truly is. Hegel emphasizes this by asking why it is considered reasonable to accept a system which affirms the world and denies God but unreasonable to accept one which affirms God and denies the world. God, he says, is more obvious than the world and is the point of departure for thinking the latter, not vice versa (EPW 76–77).[14]

In the famous dialectic of the finite and the infinite which enjoys such a prominent place in the first volume of the *Logic* (actually it describes the movement of the entire work), Hegel is at pains to show that the finite is not one kind of being simply distinguished from another kind of being, the infinite, such that each would be the simple negation of the other and, thus, its limitation. The finite, it is true, is negative in relation to the infinite, but in the very negativity of the finite the infinite is already implied, and the finite must proceed to the explicit infinite by the negation of its own negation. Thus, the infinite is not merely *inferred* from the finite.

14 Cf. GP III 164: "This proof flows from the concept . . . that God is the universal essence of essences."

It is the nature of the finite itself to go beyond itself, to negate its negation and to become infinite. Thus, the infinite does not stand *over* the finite as something complete for itself, in such a way that the finite would continue to be *under* or *outside* the infinite [WL I 126].

Infinity, then, is not a static absence or denial of limitation; it is the process of passing beyond limitations, the self-determination of the finite to its truth in the totality of being: "The infinite is the finite's affirmative determination, that which it truly is" (WL I 126). There is, of course, distinction between the finite and the infinite, but it is the dialectical distinction of dynamic relationship, where each is only in the passage from one to the other (WL I 125). Because infinity is that short of which nothing truly is or is known, there is infinity to any being or knowing. The very negativity of the finite must be negated if it is to be; but the negative element of the infinite (its opposition to the finite) must also be negated, thus restoring the finite in the process. Result: an infinite finite, a finite whose reality is in the infinite (WL I 136). The reality of which Hegel speaks here is not opposed to ideality; it is, in fact, real by being ideal, and ideality is the "quality of infinity" (WL I 140). In this context, then "the idealism of philosophy consists in nothing other than in not recognizing the finite as truly being" (WL I 145; cf. EPW No. 60).

INFINITY IN FINITUDE

God, then, is not the world, nor is the world God; the world is God's appearing, God's activity of self-manifestation, an appearing which is completed in man. The world, and man in it, are real only to the extent that God is in them, and their true being is in God, which is but another way of saying that the finite is the appearing of the infinite and has its being in the infinite. To know is to know being, and to know being is to know God. God is spirit and thus knows himself; man is spirit and thus knows himself; and in knowing himself man knows God with the knowledge whereby God knows himself. Knowledge is truly knowledge (*absolutes Wissen*) only where appearance and reality are identified. This is divine knowledge. In this sense, then, any knowledge which is truly knowledge is divine knowledge.

Therein is contained more precisely, that it is not so-called human reason with its limitations which knows God but rather the Spirit of God in man. To use the previously mentioned speculative expression, it is God's self-consciousness which knows itself in man's knowledge [PR II 398].

Such thinking is a participation in the activity of infinite Spirit.

God is God only to the extent that he knows himself; his self-knowing is, moreover, his consciousness of self in man, and it is man's knowledge of God which becomes man's knowledge of himself in God [SP III 454].

It is for this reason that every "proof" of God is reducible to the ontological proof; each argues from the necessity of thinking the infinite if we are to *think* the finite. Man knows in thinking, but to think is to think God—only infinite thought is, only the infinite is. It is not "because the finite is, the infinite must be" but "because the finite is not, the infinite is."

> The more precise way of expressing the proposition "If the finite exists, so too the infinite" is . . . the following: "The being of the finite is not merely its own being but also the being of the infinite" [PR II 456].

The movement of thought from finite to infinite is a legitimate movement, because the movement from infinite to finite is a thought movement. Thought, then, is being's own self-mediation, and the fullness of being is in the concept. Being truly is only in the fullness of being, which is to say that being is (and is grasped) only in the concept, which in its fullness is the infinite. This is not to deny reality to the empirical, but to deny it any reality in abstraction from the concept, in which abstraction "the hour of its birth is the hour of its death" (WL I 117). Thus, to know the empirical simply as empirical is not to have science; science, for Hegel as well as for Kant, is necessary knowledge, but necessary knowledge is knowledge of the necessary, the absolute. Thinking is scientific to the extent that it is thinking of the absolute (PR II 479–80), and the absolute is God. To know, then, in the fullest sense of the word is to know God, and whatever *knowing* there is is ultimately knowing God. Where there is the concept, there is God. As Gustav Müller puts it summarizing the sixth lecture on the "Proofs of God's Existence," "The concept is in and for itself the proof of God." [15] Or, as Hegel himself puts it in the *Logic*: the ontological proof is the concept's self-determination to objectivity (WL II 353; cf. GP III 168).

If, of course, the concept were to be looked upon as no more than the formal abstract presence of reality in thought, none of this would be true. Thinking *about* God tells us nothing of God, not even that he exists; it is *abstract* thinking, because God himself is not in the thought. The thinking of God, however, which is God's thinking, is God's manifestation of himself in thought. This is the thought which is being's own self-mediation, wherein the unity of concept and reality is not simply there but must be worked out—and this is the "ontological proof." It is, in fact, the task of the ontological proof to negate the mere subjectivity of the concept; a merely subjective conception is not *the* concept. Where there is question of the true concept,

---

15 Gustav E. Müller, *Hegel: Denkgeschichte eines Lebendigen* (Munich: Francke, 1959), p. 368.

there is proof of God in the very inconceivability of God's not being. "Concept and existence form an identity; in other words, God cannot as concept be conceived of without being" (PR II 549). Kant had said that given the subject, God, being could not be denied of him, but that the subject need not be given—it can be canceled out in thought, with the result that the whole proposition "God is" is also canceled out.[16] Hegel simply denies that the subject can be canceled out.

The foregoing cannot fail to seem thoroughly arbitrary if we do not grasp the import of Hegel's critique of Kant, based on his contention that Kant does not adequately distinguish between "understanding" and "reason." As understanding, Hegel will admit, consciousness is finite; as reason, however, it is infinite, because this is God's consciousness of himself in man. Kant objects to the ontological proof because he looks upon it as a function of individual consciousness, as a "proof of understanding," rather than as a self-concretization of the concept. Kant does this because he has initially made a distinction between thought and being, while identifying concept and representation.[17] This, Hegel feels, is unjustified, particularly where there is question of thinking God. If Kant wants to say that there is no content to being, he may well do so, as long as he remains on the conceptual level of understanding. It is not on this level, however, that the question of God enters in at all. In this sense, of course, there is no more conceptual content to 100 real than to 100 possible Talers! But what justification is there for this abstract consideration of content? If the subject who does the conceiving enters into the consideration, then the real difference in his buying power enters into the very conceiving of the 100 Talers (WL I 72–73). The point is that the concept of 100 Talers simply is not a true concept, precisely because it is isolated, abstract, and, therefore, unreal. If we are to remain on the level of the finite, then the distinction between reality and concept holds; but this is not the level of true thought, it is the level of merely formal conceptualization, which belongs to the "thinking" of the isolated subject.

> This so-called concept of the 100 Talers is a false concept; the form of simple relation to itself does not belong to such a limited, finite content by itself. It is a form which has been constructed and lent to it by subjective understanding; 100 Talers does not constitute something relating itself to itself but merely a changeable and passing something [WL I 73].

We can, if we want, choose to remain on this level of conceptualization when we are considering 100 Talers, but we are simply falsifying the issue if we want to consider God on the same level.

16 Kant, *Kritik der reinen Vernunft*, B622–23.

17 Long before Kant the Scholastics had recognized that no representation could be adequate to God; that, therefore, if concept and representation are identical, there can be no concept of God.

It is the very *definition of finite things* that, in them, concept and being are different, that concept and reality, soul and body, are separable, that they are, therefore, passing and mortal. On the other hand, the abstract definition of God is precisely this: that his concept and his being are *unseparated* and *inseparable* [WL I 75].

If, then, we are able to think God at all, we must think him as existing—this concept *includes* being: "It is this unity of concept and being which constitutes the concept of God" (EPW 78). What is more, to *think* at all is to think God (EPW 78), because to think at all is to rise above the sensible and finite to the infinite (EPW 94–95). Kant, it is true, did see that belief in God is the work of practical reason, but what he did not see is that the concept of reason is spirit, i.e., reason itself realizing freedom. Like the Greeks he saw philosophy as somehow opposed to religion, because he could not see how the content of religion could be *thought* (EPW No. 552). Kant, according to Hegel, insists on seeing the concept as only formal and abstract and, thus, as inadequate to reality (WL II 219–20). This sort of concept is something which understanding *has* (WL II 221); it is that wherein the manifold of a given intuition is united. The unity which this demands, then, is one of consciousness, a "transcendental unity of apperception" (WL II 222). It is as though the content of consciousness, supplied by sensible intuition, were more real than the concept of which it is the content (WL II 225). To such a content the understanding would give a form, which would be the formal concept, in itself not real at all.

> This relationship is looked upon both in the ordinary psychological representation and in the Kantian transcendental philosophy in such a way that the empirical *matter*, the manifold of intuition and representation, is first there for itself, after which the understanding *comes in*, brings unity to it, and *lifts* it to the form of universality through abstraction [WL II 224; cf. EPW No. 9; GP I 53].

Such a concept would be merely subjective, something which consciousness does. It would belong to the spiritual level, it is true, but only as a sort of addition to reality (WL II 223–24).[18] Hegel, on the other hand, sees the concept as objective, precisely because it is the process whereby the abstract comes to concretion in the subject.

> The *conceiving* [*Begreifen*] of an object consists, in fact, in nothing else than that the I makes the object its own, penetrates it, and brings it to its own proper form, i.e., to a *universality* which is immediately *determination*, or to determination which is immediately universality [WL II 222].

[18] With regard to Hegel's critique of Kant, we need not concern ourselves with its accuracy. It is presented here not because it reveals to us the thought of Kant, but because it very clearly reveals the thought of Hegel.

What was exterior, the *appearance* of the object, becomes interior in being posited (WL II 224); the essential in the appearance is present only in the concept; its true reality is not there to start with, it *comes to reality in the concept* (WL II 226). That an object appear to this or that finite subject is, of course, contingent, extrinsic to the essential being of the object. That it appear, however, is not contingent; it is essential to its being *object*. Nor is the object's movement of appearing other than the movement of consciousness in being conscious of the object, in positing it as object.

GOD AND CONCEPT

For Hegel, then, the ontological proof is but another way of describing the whole movement of the *Logic*, wherein are identified the *process* of thought and the *process* of reality whose interrelatedness explains their unity and whose unity is both knowledge and being. Viewed in this way the argument does not consist in a passage from formal concept to reality (as it does for Kant); rather it presents the realization that the fully developed concept *is* reality—the movement which, he says, Anselm unfortunately presented in the guise of a formal syllogism (WL II 353).[19] "The rational *is* real" is but another way of saying that what is in thought fully developed, determined, mediated, *is*. To know God is to know him as existing, not because some sort of inference permits us to link the determination "existing" to the subject "God," but because to think God other than as existing is simply not to know him—not really to think him.

Because Kant sees the entire manifold as a content somehow *outside* the concept, the "reason" of which he speaks turns out to be disappointing; "it becomes the well-known, purely formal, purely regulative *unity* of a *systematic use of the understanding*" (WL II 228), which has no content apart from the sensible manifold (WL II 229). It is true that the *mere* concept is inadequate to the reality it represents, but this inadequacy is not due to the absence of a sensible content; it is rather "that the concept has not yet given itself its *own* reality, produced from itself" (WL II 230). Nor is this reality which the concept gives itself some sort of second-rate reality, inferior to that which belongs to a sensible content, but accepted because by itself the concept can do no better.

19 There is no need to follow Hegel all the way in his interpretation and, above all, in his critique of Anselm. That the criticism, in particular, is unjustified can be seen from Paul Vignaux, *La Pensée au Moyen Âge* (Paris: Colin, 1948), pp. 28–43; the same book was re-edited in 1958 under the title *Philosophie au Moyen Âge*. Cf. Henri Bouillard, s.j., "La Preuve de Dieu dans le *Proslogion* et son interprétation par Karl Barth," *Spicilegium Beccensi*, 1 (1959), 191–207.

Deducing [*die Herleitung*] the real out of it [the concept]—if one wants to call it deducing—consists first of all essentially in this: the concept in its formal abstraction shows itself to be incomplete; through the dialectic which is grounded in itself, it passes over to reality in such a way that it produces this reality from itself and does not fall back again into an already given reality over against itself, taking refuge in something which had shown itself to be inessential in appearance, because, having looked around for something better, it found nothing of the sort [WL II 230].

The determinations of the concept are not the subjective, formal categories of understanding; they are the concept's own self-determination. From the point of view of mere understanding Kant may well be right in trivializing the definition of truth as agreement of cognition with its object.[20] In merely formal concepts no such agreement is to be found (WL II 231). It is true, too, that in a purely formal logic there can be no question of truth; but a purely formal logic does not rise above the level of understanding, whose truth is in reason (cf. WL II 24–31). A reason which did not agree with reality would be false, and, thus, its concept is something else again; the formal concept of understanding must concretize itself in the concept of reason from which reality is inseparable (WL II 243).[21] This process of concretization, however, cannot stop short of God, the concrete being par excellence, the ultimate reality, spirit.

Such a being will not be recognizable in a concept which is not his own doing, in a representation which the subject *has* of him. God is recognizable in what he does, and what he does can be found in the very determinations in which man recognizes him.

God as a living God and still more as absolute Spirit is recognized only in his *activity*. Early in his career man was directed to recognize God in his works; only from these can proceed the determinations which are called God's attributes, just as therein also his being is contained [WL II 354–55].

But if God is looked upon as something which should be experienced, touched, possessed—like 100 Talers—this will be impossible. A philosophy which accepts no contents not presented by the senses, not experienceable in this way, *must* stop short of God.

When a philosophizing does not raise itself to a being above the senses, by the same token, even in the concept it does not relinquish mere abstract thought; and this latter stands over against being [WL II 355].[22]

20 *Kritik der reinen Vernunft*, B83.

21 In all this we are not to understand that there are, so to speak, two distinct kinds of concept, one of understanding and the other of reason. Rather, it is the function of the representation to concretize itself in concept, just as it is the function of understanding to concretize itself in reason.

22 Thus, says Hegel, Kant accepts "finite knowledge as the fixed and ultimate standpoint" (GP III 554).

Other forms of cognition may be content to stop short of the concept; philosophy cannot. It cannot be content to rest in representations; they must become concept (WL II 357). The content of a mere representation tells us nothing of its own reality. Raised to the level of concept, however, it both is and is known in God.

All this might seem to be *an* application, in relation to God, of a process of concretization which is to be found in any passage from the abstract formal concept to the concept which *is* reality. It is not, however, *an* application; it is the paradigm of all thinking, as the process which *is* the process of reality. The ontological proof is not *a* proof which is justified by the *Logic*; it is the description of thought as the concrete march toward God which justifies the *Logic*; Hegel's *Logic* depends for its validity on the validity of the ontological proof.

> Still, in the exposition of the *pure concept* it has further been indicated that this same is the absolute divine concept itself. Thus, in truth there would be no question of a relation of application; rather that logical process would be the immediate presentation of God's self-determination to being [WL II 356].

In the Introduction Hegel had characterized the *Logic* as "the presentation of the divine essence *before* creation." Creation, however, is God's self-manifestation. Logically speaking, all that can be said of God can be said *before* creation, but if we are to recognize God in his activity, then it is in creation that we recognize what the essence of God is. The ontological proof is this recognition, not an inference from the finite world to its infinite creator, but a passage from the essential non-being of that which is merely finite to the essential infinity of being. The thought which thinks infinity is infinite thought, and infinite thought is the thought of God himself. To think truly (in reason) is to discover infinite thought, and to discover infinite thought is to dicover God, i.e., it is to discover God thinking.

> That man knows God is, in accord with the essential community [of God and man], a community of knowing; i.e., man knows God only insofar as God knows himself in man. This knowledge is God's consciousness of self, but at the same time it is God's knowledge of man; and this knowledge of man by God is man's knowledge of God [PR II 496].

Unabashedly Hegel tells us that the ontological proof begins in the concept and that its validity consists precisely in its beginning there. The concept *is* reality, and to start with the concept is to start with reality. In no other way can we get to God. To begin with a reality which, by supposition, would not be God would be to condemn ourselves to stop short at an abstract God, at a Kantian concept, from which neither the existence nor the nature of God could ever be derived.

The form which this mediation takes is that of the ontological proof of God's existence, wherein we begin from the concept. Now, what is the concept of God? It is the most real of all things, to be grasped only affirmatively, determined in itself. The content here has no limitation; it is *all reality*, and only as reality is it without limits, thus leaving over, as previously remarked, only the dead abstract. The possibility of this concept, i.e., its identity without contradiction, has been shown in the form proper to understanding [PR II 213].

RELIGION COMPLETED IN PHILOSOPHY

When speaking of religion in the *Phenomenology*, Hegel tells us that revealed religion is the highest form of religion and that the Christian religion is the highest form of revealed religion (*Phän.* 523–31, 544–45; cf. PR II 193–94). If, further, religion is to be defined as "consciousness of absolute truth" (EPW 432), then the content of the concept with which philosophy has to do is to be found here. Understood in this way, religion, particularly the Christian religion, is not replaced but rather completed by philosophy. One might in fact well ask whether the ontological proof could begin other than in Christian religious belief, precisely because the movement to the philosophical concept can begin only when the content has reached the level of religious perfection where it can be the full content of the philosophical concept.[23] This, of course, would imply that Christianity reaches its own perfection only on the level of philosophy—the objection constantly leveled against Hegel by Kierkegaard.

> Only in Christianity has the completed and *total concept* of God arisen; Christianity alone, therefore, is also the first *true* total formulation, the formulation of the *total* concept of God in all its moments.[24]

This, however, also raises the suspicion, as Dulckeit has remarked, that "logical" reason tells Hegel *a priori* what Christian revelation *must* mean.[25] It is for reason, so to speak, to pass judgment on the representations which revealed religion affords.

> It is, in other words, reason's task to make clear what part of the content of faith *still* consists in mere representations and what representations of faith are already in themselves concepts.[26]

By this standard "the revelation of God in Christ" would require a grounding in the systematic philosophy of Hegel.

[23] Religious writers have for centuries reminded us that the God of philosophy is not the God of Abraham, Isaac, and Jacob. But if the God of Abraham, Isaac, and Jacob is the only God there is, then a God who falls short of this is at best an abstraction, which is all Kant would permit speculative reason to have.

[24] Gerhard Dulckeit, *Die Idee Gottes im Geiste der Philosophie Hegels* (Munich: Rinn, 1947), p. 158.

[25] A suspicion which is confirmed by a careful reading of the *Early Theological Writings*.

[26] Dulckeit, *Die Idee Gottes*, p. 112.

Thus, the doctrine of Christianity, to the extent that it sees Christ as the manifestation of *God*, must also have already found its *logical grounding* in the *systematic developmnet of the concept of God*.[27]

This need not mean, however, that Hegel was making reason or philosophy superior to revelation or religion. It need mean no more than that even the religious man cannot be satisfied with a revelation whose content he has not understood or a religion which he grasps only in representations. If we do not *think* God, can we really be satisfied with what we represent to ourselves as God? Is there not something empty in a religion which does not think out its own content? Is not a "blind" faith something less than human? Religion is completed in thought, without ceasing to be religion, because only in thought can human finitude raise itself to infinity.

> Insofar as it has achieved the universal, thought is unlimited; its end is infinitely pure thought, such that any cloud of finitude has disappeared, because it thinks God; all separation has disappeared, and thus religion, the thinking of God, begins [PR II 225].

This sort of "thinking," Hegel says, not only is a possibility, it is a *duty* for the religious man.

> In the Christian religion God has revealed himself, which means that he has enabled men to know what he is, so that he no longer remains something hidden and mysterious. Along with the possibility of knowing God the duty to do so is imposed on us. God wants no narrow-hearted souls and empty heads for his children; rather he wants those whose spirit is poor in itself but rich in the knowledge of him and who see in this knowledge of God the supreme value [PG 41].

This cannot mean that every man is equally qualified to "think" his faith; it does mean, however, that no man—be he ever so simple—can be satisfied with a mere *unthinking* faith.

It is the work of "proofs" for God's existence to carry on the march from finitude to infinity, which is a way of describing the movement of thought from the abstract to the concrete: "the abstract is finite; the concrete is truth, the infinite object" (PR II 226). They are, then, not really proofs. They are *thinking* a content which is already there, though not yet in the form of thought, the specifically human relationship to this "infinite object," and the "logical element of this transition is contained in those so-called proofs" (PR II 231). God reveals himself, it is true, but thought must think what God reveals if the revelation is to be complete.

> When we say *God*, we speak of him merely as abstract; or when we say God the Father, the Universal, we speak of him only in terms of finite existence. His infinitude consists just in this: that he supersedes this form of abstract

27 Ibid., p. 123.

universality, of immediacy, and in this way difference is posited; but it is just his very nature to supersede also this difference. Thus and only thus is he true reality, truth, infinitude [PR II 232].

Revelation itself is abstract until it is completed in thought. "In the Christian religion it is known that God has revealed himself, and it is the very nature of God to reveal himself, and to reveal is to differentiate" (PR II 552).[28]

In the *Phenomenology* Hegel describes a dialectical movement which goes from the immediacy of sense certainty, through a long and devious route of mediation, up to absolute knowledge. At each stage in the overall dialectic there is a passage from the certitude of immediacy to its truth which is mediated, i.e., given an explicit content. Thus, each stage along the way has its own dialectic, and one of these stages is that of religion, which moves from a first level of immediacy and vague abstractions, through steps of progressive concretion, up to absolute religion, which is religion beginning to *think* its own content. It is with this last and absolute stage that the last part of the *Philosophy of Religion* begins, and it is here that Hegel once more returns to the "proofs" for the existence of God. But because it may not yet be evident to all that a "proof" is but a manner of thinking out the content of religion, Hegel appended to the *Philosophy of Religion* sixteen lectures concerned precisely with the "proofs."[29] In them we find repeated much which we have already seen from the *Logic* and the *Encyclopedia*, but we also find a greater explicitation of all that this "thinking out" implies. Taken all together, these lectures provide a more detailed description of Spirit's process of concretion: "Whatever is spiritual is concrete; in this we have before us the spiritual in its most profound aspect, that is, spirit as the concrete in faith and thought" (PR II 364). This same process is described as a movement toward God, who "is Spirit, only for Spirit, and only for pure Spirit, that is, for thought" (PR II 369). In this context, then, a "proof" is the "elevation of the thinking spirit . . . to God" (PR II 369).[30] The elevation is necessary if spirit is to be spirit; what is needed for a "philosophy of religion" is a description of the process.

The movement begins in faith, the immediate; but where there is a content there must be knowledge, and where there is knowledge there must be thought (cf. PR II 378–79). Thought does not render uncertain the certainty of faith; nor does it reduce the significance of feeling. It does, however, transform the subjectivity of both faith and

---

[28] Cf. PR II 197: "A spirit which is not revealed is not spirit."

[29] For an explanation of the circumstances under which these lectures were composed, see chap. 8, "Hegel's Critique of Kant's Theology," p. 149.

[30] One might ask if the paraphrase of Anselm's well-known definition of prayer is accidental.

feeling into objectivity (cf. PR II 384–90). In this process God is both starting point and end: starting point as already known in faith, end as spiritually grasped in thought. In both ways, however, it is God who communicates himself. "God *is* and gives himself to men by coming into relation with them" (PR II 396). Man knows God, because as spirit he shares God's knowledge of himself (PR II 398; cf. PR II 191–92). What Anselm had seen and what Hegel repeats is that the concept of God contains the very being of God, not because his being can be *inferred* from the concept, but because either God himself is the concrete concept or there is no concept of God at all (PR II 409–10). The function of logic is to show that this concept is truly a concept and that the characteristics of the concept (the attributes of God) exist in the very unity of the concept (PR II 410–11). In this sense the true concept must be the concept of God, containing within itself the determination of being. "The highest conception cannot be in the understanding alone; it is essential that it should exist" (GP III 165–66). Where this is not true, it simply is not the concept which is in question.

> The concept, and still more the absolute concept, the concept in and for itself, the concept of God, is to be taken for itself; and the concept contains being as a determinate characteristic [PR II 542].

If, then, there is a concept of which concrete being is not a characteristic, this is not the concept of God—i.e., it is not concept at all, in the fullest sense of the term. What is only represented is not, nor does it constitute, a genuine content. The content of thinking which is thought itself is such that it determines itself to being; what is not is only an untrue representation (GP III 168). Because men are finite, they have, it is true, many finite concepts. The objectivity and truth of these concepts, however, is not in their finitude but in the infinite concept, which is God (cf. PR II 539–40), the concept which is life, soul, spirit (cf. PR II 543–44). The order of proof, therefore, is not different from the order of being: God is the reason for whatever is; the concept is the reason for whatever is true. We cannot proceed from our finite, abstract conception of God to a knowledge of God's being. "The concept which is only something subjective and is divorced from being is a nullity" (PR II 549). Rather, God himself must manifest himself to us, thus verifying our conception, which in itself is merely subjective; "Insofar as being is separated from the concept, God exists in a merely subjective way in our thought" (PR II 547). This subjective concept can be a point of departure, but its becoming objective cannot be simply our doing. "The concept shows itself eternally in that activity whereby being is posited as identical with itself"

(PR II 551). The manifestation takes place in finite spirit, but it is the doing of infinite spirit. "The consciousness of finite spirit is concrete being, the material for the realization of the concept of God" (PR II 551). Not even the abstract concept of God is our own doing—it is given in revelation—and its working out, its realization, is God's work in us.

> In the sphere of revealed religion what we have first to consider is the abstract concept of God. This free, pure, revealed concept is what forms the basis; its manifestation, its being for another, is its existence, and the region in which this existence shows itself is the finite spirit [PR II 546].

DIVERSITY OF PROOFS

After all this it might well seem that Hegel is not being serious when, in the lectures appended to the *Philosophy of Religion*, he speaks in the plural of "proofs" for God's existence. In the broadened sense in which he speaks of "proof," it would seem that only the ontological is really a proof and that whatever other traditional proofs there are must be reduced to the ontological if they are to be viable at all. There is a sense, of course, in which this is true. To the extent that the other arguments are "proofs of understanding," they are not proofs at all, even in the broadened sense. Only a "proof of reason" is adequate to thinking God, and the so-called ontological proof, the self-developing movement of the concept, is the paradigm for proofs of reason. But because there is a fundamental element of contingency in human thought, there is a plurality of possible starting points in the *ascensio mentis in Deum* which warrants speaking of a plurality of proofs, even though the basic movement of thought in each must ultimately be the same (PR II 414–17). In thought, which progresses from the abstract and finite to the concrete and infinite—or it is not truly thought—there is an experience of God. This experience can be repeated, and in a variety of ways, because it is in continuity with a variety of initial experiences—God manifests himself in a variety of ways.

> In the subject confidence and the intensity of his belief in God are strengthened by the repetition of the spirit's essential elevation to him and through the experience and knowledge of him as wisdom and providence in countless objects, events, and encounters [PR II 415].

God reveals himself in his activity, and he reveals himself to man's thought, but God is not limited to one kind of activity.

Kant had classified all "rational" arguments for the existence of God under three headings: the cosmological (from the centingency of the world), the physico-theological (from teleology), and the ontological (from the concept).[31] The first two terminate necessarily in the concept of an *ens realissimum*, which contains within itself the necessity of its own existence (else it would not be *realissimum*), from which is concluded that the supreme being, who is God, exists. Ultimately, then, every argument derives from the concept of God and is either overtly or covertly identical with the ontological argument. Since, as we have seen, Kant recognizes only the abstract formal concept, each argument involves, for him, an illegitimate leap from the order of thought to the order of being.

For Hegel the abstract, formal concept is a concept at all only to the extent that it is a moment in the true concept's process of concretization. There is, then, no leap; there is a process of self-determination, of concretization. Because on the level of abstraction the concept is finite, it is not unique; there can be and are many concepts. But because no finite concept is true, precisely because it is finite, its truth lies in the infinite, the unique concept. The passage from finite to infinite, then, is not a leap; it is the explicitation of the infinity present in any finite concept. What is more, as Hegel sees it, there is a dialectical necessity which forces the movement from finite to infinite—not the subjective necessity of thinking the infinite (à la Kant), but the inner necessity of dialectical self-realization, according to which concept is not *really* concept unless its content is real.

If one were to argue from the contingency of finite beings or finite ends in the world to an unconditioned, infinite being, who stands over against the finite, the argument *would* involve an illegitimate leap (cf. GP III 583–84). Because Kant saw the argument this way he was correct in rejecting it. But if one recognizes that in *conceiving* the finite being or finite ends of the world of sense one has already gone beyond the world of sense, beyond the finite, and entered into the realm of the infinite, there is no leap at all; in *conceiving* the finite, one has already begun with the infinite. To conceive is an infinite task, which only the infinite can accomplish. The infinite, then, is both the end and the beginning.

> The question is simply this: how to begin to demonstrate that something begins of itself, or, better, how to reconcile that the infinite should at one and the same time proceed from another and in so doing should proceed only from itself [PR II 449–50].

There is a sense in which conceiving God is a passage from the world to God but only because God's relation to the world is God's own activity and finding God is finding him in the world.

---

[31] There is a fourth argument—"from the consent of men"—the suasive force of which Kant will not deny. He will not, however, dignify it with the title "rational argument."

> The relation to the world, then, appears first as a relation to another outside God; still since it is his relation, his activity, then to have the relation in himself is a moment of himself. The connection of God and the world is a determination in himself. In other words, the being-other of the one, duality, the negative, determination in general, is an essential moment, to be thought in God—or, God is concrete in this, exclusive in himself, and thus positing in himself distinctive determinations [GP III 16].

It really makes little difference where we begin; to begin at all is to begin with being (cf. WL I 51–64) and being as such is infinite—there is no stopping short of the infinite in true thought (PR II 454–56).

As Hegel sees it, there is no possibility of beginning with the contingent and moving on from there to the absolutely necessary being, who is God (PR II 476–77). Either God is in thought from the beginning or he is not there at all—which is another way of saying that if God is not in thought, it is not truly thought. Contingent being can be the content of thought only if it is recognized that the being of the contingent is the necessary.

> Not because the contingent is, but, on the contrary, because it is non-being, merely a phenomenon, because its being is not true reality, is there absolute necessity. The latter is the being and truth of the former [PR II 480].

The being of the contingent does not have a value of its own, other than that of the absolutely necessary, so that recognizing the necessary in thinking the contingent is *not* a passage from one form of being to another; it is a movement "from one determination of thought to another" (PR II 482).

> Contingent being is *at the same time* the being of an other, that of absolutely necessary being. . . . The being of the contingent is not its own being, but merely the being of an other, determinately, the being of its own other, the absolutely necessary [PR II 484].

This, in another place, Hegel calls "the peculiar inner necessity of contingency" (PR II 501). Still, he insists, this is not pantheism, because it does not deny that the being of the contingent is in any sense its own; it simply asserts that the being of its own which it does have is a nullity apart from the infinite (PR II 510–12). To *know* contingent being is to know God, because to know is to know God.

To speak, then, of "proofs" (or of a "proof") for the existence of God is not to speak of a way of arriving at God by beginning with what is not God. It is the recognition that God is present from the beginning in all true thought, in all true knowledge. But because this very recognition requires the labor of speculative thinking, it can be said that God is "proved" if thinking is recognized for what it is. Thinking is the ineluctable logical march of the concept to objectivity, and the ultimate objectivity short of which thought cannot stop (and still be thought) is the reality of God (cf. WL II 354). Finite spirit cannot take upon itself the task of proving that there *is* a God; rather God himself shows himself for *what* he is in finite spirit (cf. PR II 398–99). What God reveals to man in thought is as much revelation as what he reveals in Scripture. The two, in fact, are not to be separated, as though they were two distinct sources of divine knowledge. What begins in faith ends in thought, not because thought is different from and higher than faith, but because faith is fulfilled, *as* faith, in thought—and the content of both is God.

8

Hegel's Critique of Kant's Theology

OF ALL THOSE who have undertaken to criticize Kant's philosophy—and their number is legion—none, it would seem, has been more consistently caustic than Hegel. This, despite the fact that Hegel never ceased to acknowledge the greatness of Kant or the debt which he himself owed to Kant. It has, of course, been pointed out more than once that Hegel, particularly in his younger years, based his interpretation of Kant's philosophy on what it had become after being transformed by Fichte.[1] Although there is undoubtedly some truth in this contention—Hegel himself speaks of Fichte as the one who presents Kant's principles in abstract form (WL I 230)—Hegel's criticism is still at its most devastating when he addresses it directly to Kant's own words. It is clear that he at least thinks that he is criticizing Kant, not merely Fichte.

The criticism ranges from minor complaints regarding Kant's use of language to major attacks against what is fundamental to the entire Kantian philosophical endeavor. Hegel refers to Kant's terminology as "barbaric" (GP III 558) and to his method as "psychological" and "empirical" rather than "philosophical" (GP III 559). He sees the whole of Kant's philosophy as a "complete philosophy of the understanding, which dispenses with reason," a good "Introduction to Philosophy" (GP III 610). Kant's philosophy of nature is "thoroughly unsatisfactory (GP III 587) and his paean to the infinity of time and space at the end of the *Critique of Practical Reason* simply sings the praises of endless "boredom" (WL I 226–27). More significantly, Hegel pokes fun at Kant for demanding that knowledge be validated by a knowledge of the faculty of knowing—like learning how to swim before going into the water (GP III 555; cf. *Phän.* 71–73). Kant, Hegel tells us, "describes reason very well, but does so in an empirical manner from which thought is absent and which deprives itself again of its own truth" (GP III 554). "No human being is so mad as is this philosophy," which clings to empty concepts (GP III 585), "sifting empty straw through the empty . . . straw of ordinary logic" (GP III 585–86). There

---

An earlier version of this chapter appears in *God Knowable and Unknowable*, ed. Robert J. Roth, s.j. (New York: Fordham University Press, 1973), pp. 85–105.

1 Walter Bröcker, in the Preface to Ingtraud Görland, *Die Kantkritik des jungen Hegels* (Frankfurt: Klostermann, 1966), p. v.

is no part of Kant's philosophy which escapes Hegel's criticism; his *Critique of Pure Reason* fails to come to terms with genuine reason; his moral philosophy is purely formal and empty; his philosophy of religion is purely subjective, has no object at all.

THE CHARACTER OF HEGEL'S CRITICISM

One wonders at the end of all this what, if anything, is left of Kant's philosophy as Hegel sees it. To answer this question we must seek to understand what Hegel himself means by criticism of a philosophy. As we learn from his most extensive critique of Kant, in the Introduction to the section on "Subjectivity" in the *Science of Logic* (WL II 213–34), it is not the function of criticism to refute what another philosopher has said—above all, not by the application of principles foreign to that philosopher's own thinking. Rather it is to show that this very thinking demands that the philosopher go farther than he did, or that his thinking demands development beyond the point where he left it. Thus, in regard to Spinoza, Hegel attempts to show that what Spinoza said about substance demands in reality the kind of development which it finds in Hegel's own thinking, resulting in a substance which is subject, active, self-determining, free (WL II 216–18). By the same token, although Kant has made a tremendous contribution to the progress of philosophy by his insistence on the autonomy of reason, "for whose authority nothing external is an authority—no authority can be valid except through thought" (GP III 552), Hegel will insist that what Kant has said about reason will not be consistent with itself if it does not get beyond the point of finitude where Kant left it.

There is a sense, then, in which everything which Hegel has to say in criticism of Kant comes together in one point. The "Copernican Revolution," which had freed philosophy from the futility of a "dogmatic" metaphysics by making reason genuinely autonomous and, thus, dependent for its truth on nothing external to itself, had not been sufficiently revolutionary. Kant had persuaded reason to look into itself and not outside itself for all that it was capable of knowing, and then had so reduced this capability of knowing that it had to stop short of being objective, of coming to terms with the absolute, short of which knowing is not truly knowing at all. We can say, then, that Hegel's principal criticism of Kant is theological, in the sense that he finds fault with Kant's thought for not being adequately theological, for not going so far as Hegel's own thought would in coming to grips in thought with God himself. Kant's thought is inadequately philosophical because it is inadequately theological; it stops short of the one object which would make it truly philosophical.

With the publication by Hermann Nohl of *Hegels theologische*

Jugendschriften, it became clear that Hegel's preoccupation with matters theological, which manifests itself so clearly in the *Phenomenology of Spirit*, in the *Science of Logic*, in the *Lectures on the Philosophy of Religion*, and in the *Lectures on the History of Philosophy*, was a preoccupation which dated back to his earliest years. When we read what Hegel had to say in these early manuscripts (presumably he had good reasons for not publishing them), we are immediately struck by two characteristics they manifest: (1) they are strongly influenced by Kant, particularly by his *Religion innerhalb der Grenzen der blossen Vernunft*, with its insistence on the moral foundations of religion; and (2) they already testify to a growing dissatisfaction on the part of Hegel with Kant's approach to the religious problematic. What Hegel was looking for was a religion which would make rational sense, as opposed to a merely "positive" religion based on authority, but he was also looking for a religion whose object—God—would make rational sense and would not be simply the object of a non-rational intuition or a non-rational faith. Hegel's dissatisfaction with the Kantian–Fichtean emphasis on religion as a subjective response, as opposed to theology as a rational investigation of religion's object, comes out more pointedly in two other early writings which he did publish, the *Differenz des Fichteschen und Schellingschen Systems der Philosophie*, published in 1801, and *Glauben und Wissen*, published in 1802. In the first of these Hegel seeks to come to grips with a problem which had plagued both theologians and philosophers from the earliest times: how can human reason, which is a finite capacity, be a capacity for the infinite, i.e., God? Spinoza had solved this problem to his own satisfaction but not to Hegel's; Kant and Fichte had simply shelved the problem by turning God into a moral absolute, infinite in one sense, perhaps, but not a real object for reason. Hegel's solution—although it is not terribly clear at this stage in his career—is that reason is a capacity for the infinite precisely because it itself is not finite, i.e., because in genuinely speculative thinking it passes beyond the finite to the infinite, by recognizing that even the finite object is really known only in a knowing which is infinite ("Diff." 6).

In *Glauben und Wissen*, Hegel voices the fear that reason (philosophy) in vindicating its autonomy from faith (religion) may have cut itself off from the rich content which faith supplies (GW 1). This, he contends, is what "has happened in the philosophies of Kant, Jacobi, and Fichte" (GW 2). The suprasensible has become the suprarational, and the only approach to God left is through faith (GW 2). This sort of philosophy cannot get beyond reason's reflection on itself (GW 10–11), and thus becomes a mere critique of the capacity to know the finite (GW 14). What it comes down to is that rational knowledge is denied, since its only object is the capacity to know, not reality (GW 23). It is true that Kant has given us the "beginning of an idea of reason" (GW 25), but what he did not see was that there is no distinction between what reason truly thinks and what is truly real (GW 37–38); Kant's reason is forbidden to affirm the reality of what it knows.

As Hegel develops his own independent philosophy, it may seem strange to us that the main target in his polemic against Kant should become more and more Kant's philosophy of religion. We shall be able to understand this, however, if we realize that one of the most significant aims in Hegel's own thinking is to overcome the romantic religious intuitionism of a Jacobi or a Schleiermacher. Hegel is convinced that Kant has made a great contribution to the accomplishment of this aim by recognizing the uniqueness of that response which we call religious and which is at the same time rational. In doing this, however, Hegel felt, Kant has so concentrated on the subjective religious response as to deprive the God to whom religion was responding of all objectivity—as though the subjective response were something reason could fathom, since as a subjective response it is finite, whereas the God to whom religion responds, being infinite, is beyond the capacity of reason to grasp. Kant's reason, so to speak, is conscious of its incapacity to grasp any reality outside (or above) itself; Hegel's reason is "conscious of being all reality" (*Phän.* 176) and, thus, is conscious that there is no reality outside (or above) itself for it to grasp. This will have to mean ultimately a dialectical identification of finite and infinite reason, and precisely this identification Hegel will dare to make: "There is but one reason. There is no second, super-human reason. Reason is the divine in man" (EGP 123).

THE STORY OF REASON

This last, however, is the story of Hegel's *Phenomenology of Spirit*, which from this point of view can be looked upon as the Hegelian counterpart of—and answer to—Kant's *Critique of Pure Reason*. The whole point of the *Phenomenology* is to show that philosophical thinking need not—and indeed cannot—be preceded by an investigation of man's capacity to do philosophical thinking. Rather, to begin at the beginning with the mere fact of human consciousness—which Kant, and even Hume before him, will grant as "given"—is already to engage in philosophical thinking. It is not going to be an easy matter, as Hegel tells us in the Preface to the *Phenomenology*, but if we are faithful in following the process of human consciousness, it will lead us from the minimal awareness of mere sensation to the total fullness of "absolute knowing." Along the way it will be revealed that mere objective consciousness, culminating as it does in the abstract conceptualizations of understanding, will not be true to itself if it does not pass beyond itself to self-consciousness, involving a realization that ultimately whatever object consciousness has will be itself. But even this consciousness is incomplete if it does not come to recognize that, despite the fact that there is no source outside itself for its grasp of reality, no reality is closed to it. This recognition comes to it when consciousness becomes reason, which finds all reality in itself. If the reason here spoken of, however, were merely individual, subjective reason, the identification of reason and reality would be simply non-sense; reason must universalize itself, not by abstract generalization, but by identifying itself with the totality of reason, which in the concrete is spirit. It is spirit, then, which is not only an infinite grasp of reality but also a grasp of infinite reality, which it renders present to itself by expressing itself, first in the form of sensible images, *art*, then in the form of internal representations, *religion*, and finally in the form of thought, *philosophy*—the only form which is adequate to the infinite reality which is its content.[2]

In this hasty and, therefore, inadequate rundown of the *Phenomenology*, we can see how far Hegel has moved in 1807 from the Kant who influenced him so strongly in his youth. The explicit criticism of Kant in the *Phenomenology* is not extensive, but the reason (spirit) Hegel speaks of here is a far cry from the reason of either the *Critique of Pure Reason* or the *Critique of Practical Reason*. Nor should it be too difficult to see from this why the major thrust of Hegel's criticism of Kant is focused on the latter's philosophy of religion. From the beginning, as we have seen, Hegel had recognized with Kant that religion must in some sense be the work of reason. But, as he matures, as Emil Fackenheim has pointed out, Hegel takes more and more into account the historical religious realities which Kant had not.[3] It is not merely religious reason (or rational religion) with which Hegel is concerned; it is the God of religion—of concrete religion, and particularly of Christianity—who must be shown to be the same God whom philosophy thinks. A God in whom faith believes but whom thought does not think is an unknown God, adequate to neither religion nor philosophy.[4] Hegel had developed Kantian reason to the point where its function was no longer that of determining regulative

---

[2] This argumentation can be found developed in greater detail in chap. 1 of this volume, "The Phenomenon of Reason," and in chap. 5, "Human Autonomy and Religious Affirmation in Hegel." See also the present writer's *A Reading of Hegel's* PHENOMENOLOGY OF SPIRIT (New York: Fordham University Press, 1976), passim.

[3] Emil L. Fackenheim, *The Religious Dimension in Hegel's Thought* (Bloomington: Indiana University Press, 1967), p. 53.

[4] Cf. Hegel's criticism of the Enlightenment, *Phän.* 187–91.

principles for the use of understanding, but where it was genuinely
capax Dei, an infinite capacity for an infinite object. In so doing Hegel
compels philosophical thought to come to grips with the God he sees
revealed in Jesus Christ.[5] Thus, in Fackenheim's words:

> The Hegelian philosophy radicalizes not only the Kantian autonomous
> reason. It radicalizes, as well, the Kantian and post-Kantian search for an
> existential matrix of philosophical thought. And in this process it is driven
> into a unique philosophical confrontation with historical Christianity.[6]

INFINITE REASON

This brings us back to the Hegelian notion of a criticism which is not
the refutation of a philosophical position but the drawing out of the
implications which that philosophical position left undeveloped. It
was the "confrontation with historical Christianity" which permitted
Hegel to see the non-rationality of a merely finite reason which could
come to terms only with a finite religious response to God and not
with the infinite God to whom religion responds. From the *Logic* on,
Hegel's criticism becomes at once more pointed and more explicitly
directed against Kant. If Kantian reason can examine understanding
and determine regulative principles for its use, then reason must
transcend understanding. In fact, if reason is to transcend understanding at all it must be more than the finite reason to which Kant clings.
By the same token, however, if reason can examine reason it must also
transcend reason, which is to say it must transcend the merely finite
reason which transcends mere understanding.

> Even so, Hegel radicalizes the Kantian reason. This latter remains finite and
> human; for it is an empty self-activity except when united with a sensuous-
> ness which, by itself, is blind. In contrast, the Hegelian *Logic* has "raised"
> rational self-activity to infinity.[7]

In the Preface to the first edition of the *Logic* Hegel agrees with
Kant that it is impossible for the human mind not to be metaphysical.
The conclusion he draws from this, however, is neither that the human mind is bound to deceive itself nor that it must confine its metaphysical investigations to those principles within itself which can be
known without any appeal to experience. Rather, the conclusion is
that a genuine science of metaphysics must be possible and that what
reason finds to be absolutely necessary must necessarily be. Thus, if,
in investigating being, reason ultimately discovers that being must be
infinite, then being is infinite. The whole of the *Logic*, then, becomes
an extended proof that being is infinite—or that infinite being is—

5 See Fackenheim, *Religious Dimension*, p. 231.
6 Ibid., p. 228 (emphasis deleted).
7 Ibid., p. 226.

and, correlative to this, that the reason which knows infinite being is itself infinite. This does not mean that any individual thing which is is infinite or that any individual human reason is infinite; but it does mean that only if infinite being is can finite being make sense at all, only if reason is infinite can finite reason make sense. That the term "infinite" is negative in form is clear enough; the point is, however, that the negation of the finite is the determination whereby the finite is what it is—it negates what is negative in the finite (WL I 127). This sort of infinity could, of course, be quite empty, as it is in Kant's "category of the infinite" (WL I 128), and empty it will continue to be as long as we remain, with Kant, on the level of understanding, which keeps infinite and finite apart, finding no means of going from one to the other (WL I 128). The only infinite this sort of thinking permits is a kind of infinite progress—in time or space—a calculus which always approaches an affirmative infinite, but never arrives (see WL I 131).

What Hegel is looking for is an infinite which makes sense, and he agrees that Kantian reason will never attain to it—only in a union of the finite and the infinite will it make sense (WL I 132), and this union will never be achieved if the point of departure is simply the finite which is to be overcome by passing beyond it (WL I 136). What is needed, then, is not a passage from the finite to the infinite but a recognition that in the finite itself there is an infinite dimension, without which the finite does not make sense as finite (WL I 144–45). Hegel states the same thought pithily in his earlier *Jenenser Logik*: "This alone is the true nature of the finite, to be infinite, to supersede itself in its being" (JL 31). The finite is real enough, and it is really finite—no human being who experiences himself could say otherwise—but it is real only as a "moment" of the infinite (WL I 139). Admittedly, of this, understanding, as the faculty of abstract conceptualization, can make no sense (WL I 137–38), but this is no reason to reject the dialectical unity of finite and infinite; it is reason to go beyond the abstractness of understanding to the concreteness of reason (WL I 139–40). What Kant had done, according to Hegel, was to see a contradiction in this (cf. the "antinomies of pure reason") and then, out of unwarranted "tenderness" in regard to reality, to blame the contradiction on the finitude of reason (WL I 136).

INFINITY OF CONCEPT

In the second volume of the *Logic*, in the introduction to what he calls "Subjective Logic," Hegel returns to the polemic against Kant. Recognizing that all he has said in the first two books of the *Logic* regarding "being" and "essence" is not customarily considered to be logic, Hegel now turns to an analysis of the subjective function of thinking (WL II 211). His task is to show that nothing he has said previously, particularly about the infinity of being, will make sense unless he makes clear that all he has said about "objective reality" is contained in the "concept," the function of subjective reason. What he will attempt to do will be to show that if logic has truth as its goal, it cannot stop short of an affirmation of infinite being, which is God (WL II 212). It is a difficult task, and it is intended to meet Kant head-on. Kant will grant, particularly in his analysis of the traditional proofs for the existence of God, that human reason is inevitably led to think of an "unconditioned," "infinite" being. What he will not admit is that the necessity of thinking that way is any justification for affirming the being of the infinite. What Kant, in effect, is saying is that any attempt to *prove* that God exists is ultimately reducible to the "ontological argument," which involves an illegitimate leap from the order of concept to the order of being. What Hegel will attempt to show is that the passage from concept to being is neither illegitimate nor a "leap," precisely because the truth of being is to be in the concept.[8]

Thus, the movement which Hegel describes in the *Logic* is not one from concept to being, but rather from being to concept as that in which being realizes itself fully as being—as being all that being truly is, i.e., infinite being. In the "Doctrine of Being" (Book I) being is simply posited, and its objective determinations are manifested. In the "Doctrine of Essence" (Book II) what being essentially is is shown to be contained only in reflection. In the "Doctrine of Concept" (Book III) Hegel will attempt to show that "being" and "essence" are dialectical "moments" in the becoming of concept, which is thus their "foundation and truth," "as the identity into which they have been resolved and retained" (WL II 213). The multiplicity of relationships which being manifests, and apart from which being simply is not known, have been shown to be relationships of causality and interaction, the determinations of "substance." Now it will be shown that "the dialectical *movement* of *substance* traced through causality and interaction is, therefore, the immediate *genesis* of the *concept*, whereby its *coming-to-be* is presented" (WL II 214). Just as being, then, had been shown to make sense only in the process of becoming, and essence had been shown to make sense only in the process of reflection, so both will be shown to make sense only in the process of thinking which is the activity of subject—not merely of substance (WL II 216–18)—and this activity is not determined by anything outside subject;

8 For a detailed explanation and documentation of this statement, see chap. 7 of this volume, "Hegel on Proofs for God's Existence."

it is self-determining, i.e., free (WL II 214). What is being said here is that the determinations of reality are to be found nowhere but in the activity which is concept, and that substantial reality manifests itself as what it really is in rational concept, i.e., it necessarily is what it is truly thought to be (see WL II 216).

Hegel recognizes, of course, that the concept has had hard sledding in his day (WL II 220); it has been identified with the empty activity of the individual I (WL II 220–21), and has thus been characterized as what such a subject *does* or *has* (WL II 221). Kant had the merit of seeing through this and of recognizing that the unity which constitutes the essence of the concept is "the *originally-synthetic* unity of *apperception,* as unity of the *I-think,* or of self-consciousness" (WL II 221). In conceiving an object, Kant saw, the subject makes the object its own in such a way that to know the object is to know its own concept, its own self (WL II 222). Kant's problem, however, was that he recognized only a purely formal concept, a sort of intellectual form unifying a manifold of sense and universalizing it (WL II 224) but of itself empty of content, containing no reality (WL II 225). It is obvious that from this point of view "no amount of effort can hammer reality" out of the concept (WL II 223). What Kant has failed to see, thinks Hegel, is that the concept is not something which the subject forms for itself; rather, as self-developing, the concept "gives itself its own reality" (WL II 225). Granted: that without intuition there will be no concept, intuition is not to be separated from concept as a condition of the latter; it is part of the continuous process which is the coming-to-be of the concept (WL II 226).[9] Without the manifold of intuition the concept-process will not get started, it is true, but this does not mean that the concept is so enduringly conditioned by sense that it never gets beyond it. "Synthesis" should not mean the mere putting-together of disparate elements; it is the concept's superseding of the merely intuitive character of its content (WL II 227). What Kant has done, then, is to substitute the formal character of the concepts of understanding for the concrete character of concepts of reason (WL II 227–28). Even though Kant sees the object of thought as the unification of the manifold of intuition in the unity of self-consciousness —hence the objectivity of thought in the identity of concept and reality—he still sees this identity as merely phenomenal, because the content of the concept never ceases to be merely the manifold of intuition (WL II 228–29). The point which Hegel will make here is that the concept is no more separated from reality than is sense intuition; that it is, therefore, justified in its self-determination as real:

9 The whole of the *Phenomenology* is a detailed description of this development.

On this point it has been recalled that this manifold, to the extent that it belongs to intuition as opposed to the concept, has been superseded precisely in the concept, and through the concept the object has been brought back to its non-contingent essentiality. This essentiality is ingredient in the appearance, and for this very reason the appearance is not simply essence-less but is a manifestation of essence. The thoroughly liberated manifestation of the essence, however, is the concept [WL II 229].[10]

The concept is not dependent on reality outside itself, and it is no less real for all that. Thus, the whole point of the third book of the *Logic* is to show "how it [the concept] constructs in itself and from itself the reality which has disappeared in it" (WL II 229). This reality which the concept produces is true reality (WL II 230).

To get back to Kant: Hegel feels that he has simply missed the boat in failing to see the concept as concrete (in which thought and reality "grow together"—*concrescunt*):

Deducing [*die Herleitung*] the real out of it [the concept]—if one wants to call it deducing—consists first of all essentially in this: the concept in its formal abstraction shows itself to be incomplete; through the dialectic which is grounded in itself, it passes over to reality in such a way that it produces this reality from itself and does not fall back again into an already given reality over against itself, taking refuge in something which had shown itself to be the inessential in appearance, because, having looked around for something better, it found nothing of the sort [WL II 230].

As Hegel sees it, then, the rational knowledge of which Kant speaks is simply not rational, precisely because to exclude reality from it is to exclude rationality (WL II 231–32). It is not enough that reason should be autonomous in its formal function of unifying the concepts of understanding, which depend for their content on the manifold of sense; reason must be autonomous in regard to the content which it justifiably gives to itself. What is more, says Hegel, in his notion of "the *a priori* synthesis of the concept" Kant has a principle which should have enabled him to bridge the gap between thought and reality, "but sensible matter, the manifold of intuition, was for him too powerful to permit him to get away from it to a consideration of the concept and the categories *in and for themselves* and to a speculative philosophizing" (WL II 233). Thus, Kant, because he sees the categories as merely subjective forms of self-consciousness, explains them as finite determinations incapable of containing true reality (WL II 234).

GOD AS OBJECT OF REASON

In all this, of course, one might see only a direct critique of Kant's epistemology or of his failure to find room for a genuine metaphysics,

[10] To say that the concept is "thoroughly liberated" is to say that in conceiving (*begreifen*) reason is determined by no alien source.

not a critique of his theological (or anti-theological) argumentation. If we recall, however, that even Kant refers to God as the *ens realissimum*, the reality of all realities, it is not difficult to see that the most significant "reality" he withdraws from man's rational grasp is God (WL I 99; cf. WL II 61). What is more, after the *Logic*, Hegel's critique, particularly in the third volume of the *History of Philosophy* where it becomes most caustic, will concentrate on Kant's inability to see any rational validity in proofs for the existence of God. Kant had said quite clearly with regard to himself: "I had to suspend [*aufheben*] *knowledge* in order to make room for *faith*." [11] Hegel is convinced, not only that this separation of knowledge and faith is illegitimate, but also that the God in whom religious consciousness *believes* is identical with the God whom philosophical consciousness *knows*. Much of his *Introduction* to the *Lectures on the History of Philosophy* is devoted to an exposition of this identity of content in religion and philosophy.[12] Although there is nothing in this *Introduction* which Hegel has not said before, here it becomes abundantly clear that, in the words of Wilhelm Dilthey, Hegel's "theological work as a whole can be adequately summed up as a confrontation with [*Auseinandersetzung mit*] Kant's *Religion Within the Bounds of Reason Alone*." [13] Like Kant, Hegel had as his goal a religion which would make rational sense,[14] but he would not pay the price of impoverishing that rational sense by confining it to finite reason. The reason of which he speaks is but the abstract expression of spirit; "Spirit and reason are the same. We do, it is true, represent reason to ourselves abstractly; but active, knowing reason is spirit" (EGP 175). Spirit, however, is truly spirit only when it knows God (the summit of reality), and in knowing God it is infinitized (EGP 178). Thus, any talk about not *knowing* God sets an unwarranted limit to spirit (EGP 179).

When, then, in the third volume of the *History of Philosophy*, Hegel comes to treat of Kant's philosophy he focuses on the limited character of the reason Kant presents, on its inadequacy precisely as reason if it cannot ascend to a genuine knowledge of God by breaking the bonds of individual subjectivity (GP III 554). Thus, having put an end to the "dogmatism" of a causal metaphysics, Kantian philosophy falls back into a "subjective dogmatism" which cannot get be-

---

[11] Kant, *Kritik der reinen Vernunft*, Preface, B xxx.

[12] See chap. 9 of this volume, "Hegel on the Identity of Content in Religion and Philosophy."

[13] *Werke* IV 61, quoted by H. S. Harris, "The Young Hegel and the Postulates of Practical Reason," *Hegel and the Philosophy of Religion*, ed. Darrell Christensen (The Hague: Nijhoff, 1970), p. 61.

[14] See below, p. 154.

yond the finite determinations of understanding (GP III 554). Hegel interprets understanding here, in Kant's own words, as "the faculty of thinking the object of sensible intuition" (GP III 565).[15] A reason which does not get beyond understanding, says Hegel, is no reason at all; it is no more than "individual self-consciousness" (GP III 571), and even though Kant sees reason as the faculty of the unconditioned, the infinite, he is unwilling to let the infinite be a real *content* of reason (GP III 574). Spirit, however, is not to be identified with a simple subjective reason; it is the totality of concrete reason.

It is not surprising, then, that at this point Hegel turns to a critique of Kant's treatment of "proofs" for the existence of God (see GP III 575, 578–79), something which he will do in much more detail later in his *Lectures on the Proofs for the Existence of God*. Kant agrees that God is an "ideal" corresponding to the Wolffian definition of "the most real Being." The question, however, is whether reason can justifiably ascribe reality to this ideal. This Kant denies. The basis of this denial is the contention that any attempt to ascribe reality to this ideal (to "prove" it) will involve an illegitimate passage from concept to reality, since existence is not a conceptual content at all and cannot, therefore, be derived from the concept (GP III 583–84). This, as Hegel sees it, is but another way of saying that the concept is finite and must remain so (GP III 584). It is here that Hegel becomes sarcastic regarding Kant's example of the "hundred possible Talers." That no amount of *thinking* is going to make them real he agrees; if one wants to have them one must stop thinking and get to work! The trouble is, says Hegel, that Kant has confused "representing" (*vorstellen*) and "thinking" (*denken*). Real thinking does not merely represent its object—as represented, the object is precisely not real—it grasps (*begreifen*) it in its reality, and "concept" (*Begriff*) is this grasping (GP III 585). It is not, then, a question of ascribing a nonconceptual content to the concept; the real *is* the content of the concept. "Thinking, concept, is necessarily this: not to remain subjective but rather [*bass*] to supersede this subjective and to show itself as objective" (GP III 585). What Kant has done is to reduce reason to being "no more than the formal unity for the methodical systematization of understanding's cognition" (GP III 586). When subject and object, thought and reality, are separated in this way they cannot be brought together again (GP III 587).

"PROVING" GOD'S EXISTENCE

If all we had were Hegel's critique of Kant from the *History of Philosophy* we should know that Hegel disagrees with Kant and that he

---

15 The reference is to *Kritik der reinen Vernunft*, A51.

disagrees with him for not doing what, as he told us in the *Introduction*, it is philosophy's task to do. We should not know what is to be done or why Kant can be criticized for not having done it. Since the main thrust of this critique is directed against Kant's philosophy of religion—or lack thereof, i.e., the failure of genuine reason to function religiously—we might expect to see it crop up again in Hegel's *Lectures on the Philosophy of Religion*. But, surprisingly enough, here he leaves Kant very much alone. He does return to the attack, however, in his independent *Lectures on the Proofs for the Existence of God* [16] and in a separate lecture, usually included with *Proofs for the Existence of God*,[17] "On Kant's Critique of the Cosmological Proof."

In introducing this course of lectures Hegel makes a remark which is particularly interesting in the context of what we are examining in this paper. Since he is also lecturing on logic, he says, he has chosen to give another series of lectures on a topic "related [to logic] and constituting a sort of supplement to it, not from the point of view of content but from that of form, since the topic is simply a specialized form of the fundamental determinations of logic" (BDG 1). Clearly, then, Hegel still (in 1829) looks upon the question of God's existence as integral to the logical problematic. An investigation of knowing cannot sidestep the issue of what knowing knows, and in Hegel's view knowing knows nothing if it does not know God. Faith and reason, then, are not separate operations, in the sense that faith could deliver an object which reason could not; they are united in such a way that neither can be without the other—even though pure (independent) thought is a development out of the dependent stage of belief (BDG 8–9). It is by separating the two that contemporaries think they can investigate rationally the subjective function of religion, while leaving God, who is religion's object, entirely outside rational investigation—a philosophy of religion is permitted but not a theology. The result is that "we hear much, endlessly much—or rather, little, endlessly repeated—spoken of religion; we hear even less of God. This perennial explication regarding religion, . . . combined with an insignificant or even suppressed explication regarding God, is a unique manifestation of the intellectual culture of the time" (BDG 46). Equivalently this

---

[16] In a publisher's note to BDG (the latest edition), it is remarked that, although earlier editions published these lectures as an appendix to the *Lectures on the Philosophy of Religion*, more recent scholarship has shown that they not only constituted an independent series of lectures (delivered in 1829) but also treated the topic in a manner quite independent of that of the *Lectures on the Philosophy of Religion*. Fackenheim (*Religious Dimension*, note 31 to page 175) refers to these lectures as "vitally important and much-neglected."

[17] For a reason which the editor can throw no light on, this lecture, which is clearly independent, was in the earlier editions an "insert" between lectures ten and eleven. It is no longer possible to date it.

is saying, Hegel remarks, that divine revelation does not reveal God, since God is not a content with which the mind can cope (BDG 48). In this context it is interesting to note that throughout these *Lectures* Hegel speaks of "the ascent of thinking spirit to God," i.e., when philosophy thinks what religion represents. Since it is known that Hegel was familiar with St. Anselm, one is tempted to ask whether he is applying to *philosophy* Anselm's famed definition of *prayer*: *ascensio mentis in Deum*.

In any event, we are back with the problem with which we are already familiar, the finitude of human spirit over against the infinity of God. If we are not to say that the human spirit cannot grasp God at all, and this Hegel will not permit, are we to make this grasp possible by finitizing the infinite or by infinitizing the finite (see BDG 110)? If nothing else, putting the question this way makes "Religion" as a dialectical moment in the movement of the *Phenomenology of Spirit* more intelligible. Because the infinite object has been presented to man in religion, the human spirit must rise to infinity if it is to be adequate to its object—it cannot simply leave that object unthought. What stands in the way of admitting that human thinking can know God is, first of all, the assumption that the passage from finite thinking to an infinite object is a "leap" (BDG 111–12); secondly, the presupposition that the finitude of human spirit is "absolute," i.e., contained within itself (BDG 112–13), sufficient to itself as finite; and thirdly, a refusal to see that the activity of the infinite in the finite does not cease to be an activity of the finite (BDG 113). What needs to be grasped is that the relation of God to man, unlike the relation of objects in the world to subjects in the world, is the relation of spirit to spirit.

> That man knows of God is, on the basis of the essential community [of God and man in spirit], a communal knowing—i.e., man knows of God only to the extent that in man God knows of himself; this knowing is God's consciousness of himself, and at the same time it is God's knowledge of man, and this knowledge of man by God is man's knowledge of God [BDG 117].

Strong words, to be sure, and they have led some to conclude that in knowing God either man is no longer man or he no longer really knows, since it is God who is doing the knowing.[18] It would seem preferable to see in what Hegel is saying an echo of what Meister Eckart and other mystics said when they spoke of a union with God which "divinizes" man. Hegel's philosophical knowing, certainly, is more analogous to the *ascensio mentis in Deum* of the mystics than

18 See Joseph Donceel, s.j., "Can We Still Make a Case in Reason for the Existence of God?" in *God Knowable and Unknowable*, ed. Robert J. Roth, s.j. (New York: Fordham University Press, 1973), pp. 159–86.

it is to the critical thinking of Kant. Is it too much to say that philosophical thinking itself can see more than its finite self in its thinking
of God? Kant, it is true, will see a contradiction in this unity of the
finite and infinite, and, as he does always when the mind gets into
contradiction, he will see the contradiction in reason, not in reality.
Hegel, too, sees contradiction, as he does wherever he sees life, but
he feels that both reality and reason are equal to the contradiction,
especially if that is the only way in which life (here life of the spirit)
avoids stagnation. In his lecture "On Kant's Critique of the Cosmological Proof" he tells us:

> In fact, however, reason can decidedly put up with contradiction—and, of
> course, also resolve it—and things at least know also how to put up with it,
> or rather they are simply existing contradiction, whether it be that Kantian
> schema of the thing-in-itself or empirical things—and only to the extent that
> they are rational do they also at the same time resolve the contradiction in
> themselves [BDG 148].

The unity of finite and infinite does not present an irresolvable contradiction; it is a condition for the very being of being. If we look
back at the overall movement of the *Logic*, we find that it begins with
a being which is infinitely empty—and therefore in no way different
from nothing—and ends with a being which is infinitely full, and that
the path from the one to the other has been marked by a progressive
negation of the limitations of abstraction. In a very important sense
it is the same being which is infinitely empty and infinitely full, the
same being which is finite and infinite. Hegel's point is that if we begin at all, we must continue, and the movement from the finite is a
continuous movement. The finite makes sense not in itself but in
being integral to the movement toward the infinite. The question,
then, is not so much whether reason can know that the infinite really
is; rather it is whether reason must know that being is infinite (BDG
149–51). Being must be known as both finite and infinite, or not
known at all. "Being is to be characterized not only as finite but also
as infinite" (BDG 152). It is for this reason that Heidegger characterizes Hegel's metaphysics as essentially "onto-theological"; the being
without which no being makes sense is the highest being, or God.[19]
To return to Hegel's own words: he is convinced that the mistake
which has been made is to look upon the finite as the originally affirmative which is negated in the infinite. Rather the infinite is affirmative;
it is negated in the finite, and reaffirmed in the negation of limitation.
"The essential point in this mediation, however, is that the being of
the finite is not the affirmative, but rather that it is the self-superseding

---

[19] See Martin Heidegger, *Identity and Difference*, trans. Joan Stambaugh (New York:
Harper & Row, 1969), pp. 59, 70–71.

of the finite whereby the infinite is posited and mediated" (BDG 152). There has been no leap from the finite to the infinite; the very positing of the finite as real entails the positing of the infinite as real. Moreover, the spirit which posits both finite and infinite is itself both finite and infinite; its movement and the movement of being are not to be separated (see BDG 153–54). Kant was certainly not wrong in criticizing the form in which proofs for the existence of God had been presented; what he failed to do, however, was to see the profounder foundation upon which they rested (BDG 154). The exposition of this profounder foundation, Hegel is convinced, is his own *Logic*. There we are told there is no being which does not imply the infinity of being, no thought which does not imply the infinity of thought; and the infinite, God, is the perfect identity of thought and being (JL 159).[20]

20 It may seem strange that throughout this article no reference has been made to the *Enzyklopädie der philosophischen Wissenschaften*. Although it is true that the *Enzyklopädie* is a rich source for the kind of thinking we have been describing here, containing abundant passages which would be very much to the point, we have omitted references to it since it is primarily a summary of Hegel's abiding conviction of the truth of what he has said elsewhere.

9

Hegel on the Identity of Content
in Religion and Philosophy

FEUERBACH'S JUDGMENT OF HEGEL'S PHILOSOPHY was that it was not philosophy at all but only religion in disguise. Since that time more than one effort has been made, by friends and enemies of Hegel alike, to show that Hegel's thought was not religious at all but rather the culmination of a process of secularizing philosophy which began with Bacon and Descartes. When dealing with a thought so complex—and even tortuous—as Hegel's, it would, of course, be difficult *to prove* that either side is in error, but no conscientious interpreter can gloss over the fact not only that Hegel constantly speaks of God and of religion—more, perhaps, than any modern philosopher—but also that the consciousness of the absolute which he calls religious consciousness is for him integral to the process of thought which he calls *Wissenschaft*.[1]

What can seem—and has seemed—paradoxical in this is that Hegel need yield to none in his emphasis on the secular character of thought, in the sense that he sees thought as thoroughly rooted in the autonomy of human spirit. He will accept no authority outside human thought as arbiter of that thought's validity. The rationality of thought and its autonomy are identified. Nevertheless Hegel is unequivocal in his insistence that the content of philosophical thought is religious. Philosophical thought does not merely concern itself with religion as with any other phenomenon of human consciousness; thought, for Hegel, is not philosophical if it is not religious. We can to a certain extent understand this if we grasp the dialectical movement of Hegel's *Phenomenology of Spirit*, in which each form of consciousness finds its "truth" not in itself but in the succeeding form which supersedes it. If each successive stage in the dialectical process is the truth of the

An earlier version of this chapter appears in *Hegel and the Philosophy of Religion*, ed. Darrell Christensen (The Hague: Nijhoff, 1972), pp. 261–78.

[1] *Wissenschaft*, which for Hegel is not a characteristic of philosophy but rather identical with it, is the totality of the process whereby man comes to *Wissen*. That process is described in detail in the *Phänomenologie des Geistes*, the original title of which was "Wissenschaft der Erfahrung des Bewusstseins." Therein the stage of consciousness immediately preceding knowledge in the fullest sense is the stage of revealed (Christian) religion, and nowhere in his writings does Hegel alter this.

preceding stage, then religion will be the truth of moral consciousness (and revealed—Christian—religion the truth of religious consciousness as such). At the same time, however, religion will be the
truth of all that precedes it. Thus, with religion the absolute as absolute is first recognized as the object of consciousness, self-consciousness, and reason. It is noteworthy that, at each stage of the dialectic,
immediate certainty is overcome by a progressively more concretely
universal content. Obviously this process cannot stop until the content becomes the totality of all content, wherein reason's certainty
"that it is all reality" is concretized. Thus, the "truth" of reason is in
spirit, i.e., beyond mere reason, and spirit in its completeness is the
content of religion—a content which, it is true, philosophy must make
its own. The point is, however, that philosophy cannot make this
content its own until in religious consciousness the content is grasped
as the fullness of Spirit, absolute Spirit, God. To present Hegel's
thought in this schematic way, however, is to ignore the process
whereby it became the "system" it was.

We know that Hegel—like his friends Schelling and Hölderlin at
Tübingen—was in his youth destined for the ministry. We know too
that he—like the others—could not accept ordination in a Church
whose official religion did not make sense to him; nor could he accept
a far-away, authoritarian God, who did not make sense to modern man
with his conviction of autonomous reason. We also know, however,
from his letters during the period following his departure from Tübingen—and from the cryptic password, *Reich Gottes*, which he and
Hölderlin exchanged as they took leave of each other—that he left with
the intention of finding a religion—and a God and a theology—which
would make sense. A glance at his *Early Theological Writings* will
indicate to us that his quest took him first to Kant's moral religion
and Fichte's God, who was the principle of moral order (cf. TJ 3–71).[2]

In 1792 Fichte published anonymously his *Kritik aller Offenbarung*,
which was first attributed to Kant, and in 1793 Kant published his
Religion innerhalb der Grenzen der blossen Vernunft. Both these
works Hegel read and annotated avidly. For us to whom the concept
"philosophy of religion" has become something of a commonplace it
is difficult to appreciate the effect these works had on the mind of
young Hegel. Here was a chance to make rational sense out of what
had previously been presented simply as unquestioned divine revela-

---

2 Here Hegel agrees pretty much with Kant that religion stands in the service of
morality. Still, Theodor Häring, in his *Hegel, sein Wollen und sein Werk*, 2 vols. (Leip-
zig and Berlin: Teubner, 1929, 1938), makes it abundantly clear that even at this early
stage Hegel did not accept fully the Kantian subordination of religion to morality (cf. 1
66, 188–89).

tion.[3] Kant in particular emphasized a principle which he had already enunciated in 1766: that religion is based on morality rather than vice versa. If religion is to be justified, it must appeal to reason, and the only reason to which it can appeal is moral reason, which needs neither a superior being in order to know duty nor a superior motive in order to accomplish it.[4] Still, although an ultimate appeal to reason cannot be an appeal to God (unless they are identified), moral reason does inevitably lead to religion.

> If morality recognizes in the sacredness of its law an object of greatest reverence, by the same token, on the level of religion morality represents in the form of a supreme cause completing those laws an object of adoration and thus becomes manifest in the majesty of this cause.[5]

Kant does not say explicitly that God is simply absolute moral will, but he does say that the only religious teaching which counts is moral teaching, which is set forth as the will of God.[6] God, then, becomes the personified idea of the good principle who can be recognized only by the good man,[7] and religion consists in recognizing the demands of moral reason as divine commands.[8]

> *Religion* (considered subjectively) is the recognition of all our duties as divine commands. The religion in which I must know ahead of time that something is a divine command in order to recognize it as my duty is *revealed* religion . . . ; on the other hand, the religion in which I must first know that something is duty before I can recognize it as a divine command is *natural religion*.[9]

God is, so to speak, the universal lawgiver corresponding to universal law,[10] but he is not the one who enforces the law.[11] There is, then, a divine command, but its authority resides not in its being divine but in the intrinsic moral value which reason finds in it. We do, however, sanctify moral duty by interpreting it as God's com-

---

[3] Hegel did, of course, know Spinoza's *Tractatus theologico-politicus* and Lessing's efforts at biblical interpretation, but Kant and Fichte opened up to him a new world of rational religion.

[4] Kant, *Die Religion innerhalb der Grenzen der blossen Vernunft*, ed. Karl Vorländer (Hamburg: Meiner, 1956), p. 3.

[5] Ibid., p. 8. Cf. Kant, *Der Streit der Fakultäten*, ed. Klaus Reich (Hamburg: Meiner, 1959), p. 74: "He feels that he is created for a realm other than that of the senses and of understanding—that is, for a moral realm, a kingdom of God. He recognizes his duties as none other than divine commands, and there arises in him a new knowledge, a new feeling: namely, religion."

[6] Cf. *Religion innerhalb*, p. 10; *Streit der Fakultäten*, p. 31.

[7] Cf. *Religion innerhalb*, p. 63.

[8] Ibid., p. 92.

[9] Ibid., p. 170.

[10] Cf. ibid., p. 105.

[11] Ibid., pp. 106–107.

mand,[12] and we honor God by observing the duties dictated by reason, since it is his command that we do so.[13] It is important to note that the reason here in question—as in the three *Critiques*—is individual reason universalized, i.e., recognized as authentically reason.[14]

In all this it would be going too far to say that Kant identifies morality and religion; he does, however, say that they are identical in content, even though their form is different.[15]

> The only true religion contains nothing but laws, i.e., the sort of practical principles of whose unconditional necessity we can be conscious and which we can, therefore, recognize as revealed through pure reason (not empirically).[16]

We find much that is similar to this in Hegel's *Early Theological Writings*, especially in his critique of the "positivity" of religion and religious institutions, and yet precisely in these early essays Hegel is already beginning to break with Kant in his religious thinking. It is important to note, however, right here at the outset that, although we cannot ignore these youthful efforts of Hegel's—for they give testimony to his development and to Kant's influence on it—we must beware of seeing in them a definitive position.

The first important document to indicate the direction of Hegel's mature religious—and philosophical—thought is the *Phenomenology of Spirit*. Not only does the *Phenomenology* at various stages in its description of the process of consciousness turn to forms of religious consciousness as integral to that process, but it also introduces religion in its developed form as the link between moral reason (in which spirit is present in an immediate and almost unconscious way) and the ultimate in philosophical thought, which is "absolute knowing." Gone is the emphasis on moral reason as the only possible basis of religion, and in its place stands the insistence that moral reason will find its own truth only if it moves on to the further (higher) stage of religion, where for the first time absolute spirit reveals itself as the content short of which consciousness can never become knowledge. For the first time we see emerge clearly the paradox which Fackenheim claims characterizes the whole of Hegel's mature thought, the gigantic endeavor to synthesize a faith which is essentially receptive of the divine with a rational thought which is autonomous and

---

12 Cf. ibid., p. 111.
13 Ibid., p. 114.
14 Ibid., p. 143.
15 *Streit der Fakultäten*, p. 31.
16 *Religion innerhalb*, p. 187.

self-creative. Herein is presented the mystery of a human thought whose origin is both human and divine, which is no less human for being divine.[17]

What Hegel has done effectively is to dissociate himself from the rationalism of the Enlightenment and from the critical philosophy of Kant and Fichte, to insert his own thinking in the tradition of Plato and Aristotle, Plotinus and Augustine, Anselm and Spinoza, all of whom saw human thinking as somehow divine. Thought reveals itself as infinite activity (which it will do more definitely in the *Science of Logic*), and infinite activity is seen as activity of the infinite. It could be argued, of course, that what Hegel has done is to reduce the divine to the totality of the human—and if all we had to go on were the *Phenomenology*, a case might be made for that interpretation—but there are simply too many texts (even in the *Phenomenology*) which are not susceptible to that kind of reading. The result of the *Phenomenology* is to show that the ultimate *subject* of philosophical thinking, the thinking itself or thinking spirit, is at the same time the ultimate *content* of philosophical thinking. It is conceivable, of course, that one could arrive at such a conclusion without including religious consciousness in the process at all—Fichte tried it, and so did Schelling—but the fact is that Hegel considered it impossible. For him it is sheer nonsense to consider consciousness apart from its content, and the form of consciousness wherein absolute Spirit first reveals itself as content—prior to that form which is thinking in the full sense—is religious consciousness. "The content of religion, therefore, expresses sooner in time than does science what spirit is; the latter alone, however, is spirit's true knowing of itself" (*Phän.* 559). We might note here that what motivates Hegel in his insistence that the content of religion and of science (philosophy) is identical is not his desire to rescue religion. It is, rather, his desire to rescue philosophy, which would be less than universal science if the object of religion were out of its domain.

This has been long in coming. As we noted before, religious consciousness has already made its appearance in the *Phenomenology* before this, i.e., as consciousness of absolute being. What had not yet appeared was absolute being itself, i.e., spirit conscious that it is itself of which it is conscious (*Phän.* 473). When we get to the end of the *Phenomenology* we see that what has been happening all along is that human spirit has been progressively coming closer to a grasp of what it truly is, which is to say that spirit has been progressively manifesting itself as the truth of human spirit. Each manifestation, however, had

17 Cf. Emil L. Fackenheim, *The Religious Dimension in Hegel's Thought* (Bloomington: Indiana University Press, 1967), p. 206.

revealed itself as inadequate, because spirit is more. In religion spirit reveals itself for what it truly is, infinite subject, self, but the manner of self-revelation is still inadequate since the truly spiritual element in which it can reveal itself fully is thought, not emotion or representation (cf. *Phän.* 480).[18]

What has happened, then, is that the story of the absolute's appearing has slowly been unfolded before us. It takes a long time, however, before we become aware that the absolute is the ultimate content of consciousness (if it were not, knowledge would not be knowledge, because only partial). Even when we do see this we do not at first see it as the content of *knowing* consciousness. First it is imaginatively or emotionally present in consciousness, as *represented*. Only at the end is it the content of *thought*. In the overall process it is with religion that it becomes manifest that the true content of consciousness is precisely the absolute (unconditioned, infinite). It could not ultimately be the content of thought if it were not first manifested as the content of religious consciousness. This is a position which Hegel never thereafter repudiated. It is not accidental to the process of consciousness that it passes through the stages through which it does, but the relationship of religion to philosophy is closer than simply that of one of the stages (or "moments") of the process to the whole of the process. The goal of the process is the grasp of what is true in all its truth, and it is only with religion's grasp of the absolute that the goal is finally in sight.

We can see, then, that although Hegel did treat explicitly of the philosophy of religion, there is a very real sense in which, for him, religion is not something *about which* one philosophizes; it is part and parcel of the process whereby philosophy becomes philosophy. Our task here will be to discover what it can mean to say that religion and philosophy are two forms of consciousness having the same content. We have already seen that for Kant religion and moral reason are two forms with one content, i.e., duty, but that is a far cry from what Hegel is saying, although it should be remarked that Hegel—even in his later

---

18 The term which we here translate by "representation" is *Vorstellung*. It is impossible to find one English term which will adequately translate the German term in each of its occurrences. The notion which Hegel seeks to get across in using it is that in a *Vorstellung* the object of thought is not itself present to thought but is represented by a subjective medium which stands in its place (its "representative," i.e., *Stellvertreter*). "As interiorized intuition, representation is the mean between immediate being, determined of intelligence, and intelligence as free, as thinking. Representation is *proper* to intelligence in its still one-sided subjectivity, insofar as what is proper to intelligence as still conditioned by immediacy is not in itself *being*. The path of intelligence in its representations consists just as much in making immediacy interior by positing *itself as intuiting* as it is to supersede the subjectivity of interiority, to exteriorize itself within itself and to be itself in its own exteriority" (EPW 363).

years—is one with Kant in affirming the moral roots of religious consciousness.

> True religion, or religiousness, arises only for morality; it is thinking
> morality, i.e., a morality becoming conscious of the free universality of its
> concrete essence. Only from the standpoint of morality are we conscious of
> God as free spirit; it is vain, then, to look for true religion, or religiousness,
> apart from the moral spirit [EPW 431–32].

The question, however, does not concern the derivation of the subjective response called religious; it concerns, rather, the object which religion and philosophy have in common. "Both [religion and philosophy] have the *truth* as their object, and that in the highest sense—in the sense that God, and God alone, is the truth" (EPW 1). It must, of course, be remembered that truth is truth in the full sense of the word only when it is thought, i.e., grasped in concept, since thought is the proper locus of truth. Philosophy, then, is the transforming of other forms of consciousness into thought (EPW 37), while in the case of the religious consciousness, the content, i.e., *Wirklichkeit*, remains the same (EPW 37–38).

The significance of this is highlighted most strikingly, perhaps, in Hegel's *Introduction* to the *Lectures on the History of Philosophy* in which he tries to say just what this philosophy is, of which there is a history. There we are told that philosophy is the highest form in which spirit manifests itself at any time or place—among a people (EGP 38–39). To say that it is the highest form, however, is not to say that it is the only form; there are also non-philosophical ways in which the supreme idea (spirit) can be present, and these are art and religion: "The way in which the supreme idea is present for non-philosophical consciousness, for sensitive, intuitive, representative consciousness" (EGP 42). It would be a mistake, however, to look upon this non-philosophical presence as non-rational; it is not totally spiritual—since only thought is that—but it is supremely rational:

> (It has been remarked above that like philosophy so too religion must first
> of all be comprehended, i.e., it must be recognized and acknowledged as
> rational. For it is the work of self-revealing reason, its supreme, most rational
> work.) Those are but absurd notions according to which priests out of self-
> serving deceit have simply manufactured a religion. . . . Rather, this *region of
> the spirit is the sanctuary in which the remaining deception of the sense-
> world, of finite representations and goals, the area of opinion and arbitrari-
> ness, has been dissolved* [EGP 43].

From the point of view of the subject, perhaps, the grasp of this supremely universal object is not purely rational activity; its presence, nevertheless, is the work of reason; only that which has the mark of reason on it is, properly speaking, human. "We are men, and we have reason. Whatever is human, rational, finds an echo in us, in our feeling, emotion, heart, in our subjectivity in general" (EGP 46). It is, in fact, the object of thought, even though the manner of grasping it is not, properly speaking, thinking (EGP 48). Universal reason—which, for Hegel, is not individual reason universalized—reveals itself best in human reason, but it is not limited to that form of manifestation (EGP 52).

It is a traditional commonplace that God reveals himself in nature.[19] But, says Hegel, God does not manifest himself primarily in nature but in the activity of man's spirit; it is man who *makes* nature the mirror of God (EGP 201). What is more, God reveals himself preeminently in the symbols of religion (EGP 57); they do not hide God, they are means of permitting him to come into human consciousness (EGP 55–56). What must be recognized is that, historically speaking, religion everywhere precedes philosophy. More significantly it does in two steps what philosophy does in one: in religion man first sets God over against himself, and then through the activity of cult he unites himself with God (EGP 167). The point is that in religion men have set forth the consciousness they have of the supreme being, and this, no matter what the subjective form of setting forth, is a function of reason (EGP 168). The difference would seem to be that, although truth is present in religion, it is present as a *given* which cannot be verified in religion itself, whereas the truth in thought is verified in the very process of thought (cf. EGP 173–74). Nevertheless, it is precisely the same *truth* which is common to both (EGP 175). Ultimately, then, the God of philosophy (Spirit) is simply identical with the God of religion—although only philosophy can see this, and only philosophy knows God for what he is (EGP 175).

> From this, then, we gather the relationship between Spirit and human spirit. We must, of course, abstract from the atomic manner of representing individuality as fragmented and isolated. Spirit truly represented is simply what is aware of itself. The difference between individual and universal spirit, then, should be expressed thus: The subjective, individual spirit is the universal, divine Spirit, to the extent that the former is aware of the latter, to the extent that the latter manifests itself in each subject, each man. Thus, the spirit which is aware of absolute spirit is subjective Spirit [EGP 176].

When the individual subject knows God, it is God who is doing the knowing, and where the grasp of God is in religious belief, the same is true; it, too, is spirit's testimony to itself (EGP 178): to be truly religious is to be aware of God (EGP 179). At this point Hegel quotes John 16:13, "He [the Spirit of truth] will teach you all truth," inter-

---

19 **Cf.** the section in the *Phenomenology* on "Reason Observing."

preting it to mean that all knowledge of truth is the presence of Spirit in us (EGP 180).

Because the individual as individual is necessarily limited, the manner in which Spirit is present in the individual is necessarily limited. In thinking, this limitation is *aufgehoben*, because thinking is Spirit's consciousness of itself and is more than what any individual subject *does*. In religious awareness the limitation persists, because what is present is not Spirit itself but teaching *about* Spirit, a representation (a *Vorstellung* which is *stellvertretend*) calculated to arouse religious emotion (EGP 182–83). In religion man is truly aware of Spirit, and it is truly Spirit of whom man is aware, but the awareness is not truly spiritual. "In religion Spirit has a peculiar form, which can be sensible . . . a representation" (EGP 184). *Thought* is involved, but in a *mixed* form (EGP 184), "a form which contains more or less of the sensible" (EGP 186). This brings us back to the two-step process in religion, which in philosophy becomes one step: in religion Spirit is external and is rendered *present* in representation, which is followed by identification in *worship*: in philosophy content (spirit) and form (thought) are one: "because what I think, i.e., the content of thinking, is in the form of thought, it is no longer over against me" (EGP 185).[20]

It is unquestionably difficult to see how the content of philosophy and religion can be identical. Religion as such has never been able to see the identity. The philosophical tradition from Plato to the Middle Ages took the identity for granted. Modern rationalism (particularly of the Enlightenment) has been incapable of grasping the identity and has, therefore, been inimical to religion (cf. *Phän.* 187–91). The point is, says Hegel, that rationalism has to be opposed to religion, but *reason* is not.[21] Reason is proper to man as man, and in order that what he do be strictly human—as opposed to what other than man can do—it must be the work of reason. Since, however, the truth of reason is not in mere reason but in spirit—where the transition from individual to universal reason has already taken place—it is only in and through spirit that what man does is truly and adequately the work of reason. If, then, it is true that in religion man relates himself to the absolute, who as absolute must be absolute truth, then religion must be the work of reason. If, moreover, true thinking is ultimately think-

20 Cf. WL I 30: "Absolute knowing is the truth of all modes of consciousness because, as that march of consciousness manifested, only in absolute knowing has the separation of the *object* from *self-certainty* been completely eliminated and truth has been identified with this certainty, just as this certainty has been identified with truth."

21 It should be mentioned that, in Hegel's view, rationalism is also the enemy of philosophy: "This rationalism is opposed to philosophy in both form and content" (EGP 191; cf. EGP 292).

ing of the absolute, then the absolute which thinking thinks cannot be other than the absolute to whom man is related in religion. Hegel is well on his way in his quest for a religion and a God who makes sense in a modern rational world.

What is not quite clear up to this point, however, is just what reason, or spirit, meant for Hegel. That reason is not to be separated from human reason is clear enough, but it is also clear that individual reason does not even merit the name unless it is in tune with universal reason. The problem, then, concerns the meaning which can be given to universal reason. It is simple enough to say that *Vernunft* designates human thinking functioning at its highest and its best (incidentally German translates the Greek νοῦς by *Vernunft*). The term is still empty if it does not say what human thinking does when it functions at the highest and best. By the same token, it is all very well to say, as does the Western tradition, that what reason thinks to be true is true, but by itself that is no more than a tautology, since a thinking which is not true simply is not reason. Thus, if it is possible to institute, as Kant seeks to do, a Critique of Reason, whereby we can determine that it is reason which is functioning, it is also possible to determine that what it asserts to be true is universally true—if not, the assertion would simply not be an assertion of reason. What reason says cannot be other than true, and to know what individual reason, as reason, says is to know what universal reason says, because reason cannot contradict reason; reason is one. So, to speak with Kant, the object of reason is universal because it is the object of reason.

For Hegel, however, the process is reversed. We do not know that a proposition is true *because* reason affirms it; we know that it is reason functioning because what it affirms is true. The same can be said with regard to universal validity. If I *know* what is true, I also know that it must be true for all. But, says Hegel, knowing that it is true for all is the condition of knowing that it is true, not vice versa. There is no question, then, of universalizing individual reason; rather it is one of individualizing universal reason. The whole movement of the *Phenomenology* indicates just this. Consciousness, whose apex is reached in understanding (*Verstand*), is *aufgehoben* in self-consciousness, where the self can be recognized as a self only in a community of selves. Self-consciousness in turn is *aufgehoben* in reason (ultimately moral reason), whose dictates are not those of the individual but of the *Geist der Gemeinde* (*Phän.* 391). Finally, reason is *aufgehoben* in spirit, because only in spirit is there consciousness of identification with the totality of spirit, which is concretely universal spirit. This is where religion comes in. There, for the first time, individual consciousness becomes aware that the object with which it seeks to be identified is universal spirit. Religion too, however, must be *aufgehoben* in absolute knowing (which is philosophy or *Wissenschaft*), because only there is there an awareness that the absolute can be object only if the absolute is subject. The individual subject has not been lost in the process; it has been found, because it realizes that only in the universality of subjectivity can it find the guarantee for the universality of what is objective for it.

Now, in all this one can, I suppose, argue that the absolute, or spirit, is not God in any intelligible sense of the term. One might even argue that when Hegel says of God the same things he says of absolute Spirit he is speaking metaphorically. It is difficult to see, however, how one can argue in this way and still make sense of the mountain of texts in which the God who is the object of religion is identified with the object of philosophy.

What Hegel set out to find, as we saw before, was a religion and a God which would be compatible with modern philosophical thinking. In the beginning he may have thought that what he would find would be substitutes for the Christian religion and the Christian God—perhaps the unified reason of the Enlightenment or the supreme moral principle of Kant and Fichte. What he came up with, however, was a transformed Christian religion and a transformed concept of God. As Fackenheim puts it so well, "For the early Hegel, philosophy will produce a new religion on the ruins of the old. For the mature Hegel, philosophy comprehends the old religion, and this latter is not and cannot be ruined." [22] In another place he goes even farther: "Hegel asserts, with unwavering insistence, that Christianity is the absolutely true content, and that his philosophy both can and must give that content its absolutely true form." [23]

It is scarcely conceivable that Hegel would have devoted so much time in his *Lectures on the Philosophy of Religion* to a justification of the "ontological proof" and then append sixteen additional lectures on the same subject if he did not take seriously the God who is there identified with *the* concept. As early as *Glauben und Wissen* Hegel finds fault with Kant, Fichte, and Jacobi for giving up on absolute knowledge and assigning to belief the content which is absolute, i.e., God.[24] In the *Phenomenology*, as we have seen, the language may be

---

[22] Fackenheim, *Religious Dimension*, p. 209.

[23] Ibid., p. 112.

[24] Cf. EPW 431, where he comes back to the same complaint. By putting the infinite out of reach of reason and handing it over to faith, Kant, Fichte, and Jacobi are simply settling for a reason which is not *reason* but *understanding*. When Hegel makes reason capable of the infinite (in fact, that is what distinguishes it as reason), he is making it an infinite capacity. This it cannot be if it is merely the function of the individual (even the universalized individual).

ambiguous, but the affirmation is unequivocal: what *Wissenschaft* knows in the form of thought is the same object which religion represents symbolically.

> Thus, what in religion was *content* or form of representation by *another* is here the proper *doing* of the *self*. The concept guarantees that the *content* is the proper *doing* of the self—for, as we see, this concept is knowledge of the self's doing in itself constituting the very essence of all reality, a knowledge of this *subject* as *substance* and of the substance as this knowledge of its own doing [*Phän.* 556].

The thinking knowledge with which the *Phenomenology* ends is that whose content is "God, as he is in his eternal essence before the creation of nature or of a single finite spirit" (WL 1 31) with which the *Logic* begins. To know God is to know all reality, and to know all reality is to know; short of God knowledge is not fully knowledge. The thinking with which the *Logic* is concerned from beginning to end is infinite activity. But infinite activity is the activity of an infinite subject, whose object too is infinite. Thought is truly thought only if it is of infinite being. Thus, the *Logic* is the detailed working out of the "ontological argument," the proof of God from the infinity of thought. In this Hegel is not saying that there is no finite thought or that finite thought is not valid. What he is saying is that the finite bespeaks the infinite and is nothing without it.

> It is the nature of the finite itself to go beyond itself, to negate its negation and become infinite. Thus the infinite does not stand *over* the finite as something complete for itself, in such a way that the finite would continue to be *under* or *outside* the infinite [WL 1 126].

It is too obvious to need mentioning that there are finite subjects as well as finite objects (the very use of the plural indicates that). By the same token, there are finite thoughts and finite concepts. The point is that only in the process of passing beyond its own limitations is the finite significant at all. For it to be true it must determine itself to its truth in the totality of being: "The infinite is the finite's affirmative determination, that which it truly is" (WL 1 126). There is, of course, distinction between the finite and the infinite—to deny it would be to affirm "the dark night in which all the cows are black"—but it is the dialectical distinction of dynamic relationship, where finite and infinite are only in the passage from one to the other (WL 1 125).

It is for this reason that it is necessary to identify the whole movement of the *Logic* with the "ontological argument"; not, however, in the sense that the *Logic* justifies the argument, but in the sense that the *Logic* depends for its justification on the validity of the argument. The "ontological argument" is not an inference from the being of the finite world to the being of its creator; it is a passage from the essential non-being of that which is *merely* finite to the essential infinity of being. The thought which thinks infinity is infinite thought, and infinite thought is the thought of God himself. To think truly (in reason) is to discover infinite thought, and to discover infinite thought is to discover God, i.e., to discover God thinking.

It is certainly not without significance for our present purpose that Hegel has much the same to say about the relation of finite and infinite, thought and reality, man and God, in the *Lectures on the Philosophy of Religion.*

> That man knows of God is, on the basis of the essential community [of God and man in spirit], a communal knowing—i.e., man knows of God only to the extent that in man God knows of himself; this knowing is God's consciousness of himself, and at the same time it is God's knowledge of man, and this knowledge of man by God is man's knowledge of God [BDG 117].[25]

Once more, then, we are back with the identity of content in religion and philosophy; the God of philosophy is the God of religion.

> Insofar as it has achieved the universal, thought is unlimited; its end is infinitely pure thought, such that any cloud of finitude has disappeared, because it thinks God, and thus religion, the thinking of God, begins [PR II 225].

Religion, then, *thinks* God, and the God whom religion thinks in one form is the God whom philosophy thinks in another—more adequate—form. God is ultimate truth, but there are not two ultimate truths, one for philosophy and another for religion, since ultimate truth is the truth of all truth.

> Truth is, of course, contained in every other sphere, but not the highest absolute truth, for this is to be found only in perfect universality of determination, and in the fact of being determined in and for itself, which is not simple determinateness having reference to another, but contains the other, the difference, in its very self [PR I 40].

Thus, whether the thought which thinks God is religious or philosophical, the God it thinks is the same God, and the thinking is God's revelation of himself to and in the spirit of man.

> Let it suffice here merely to observe regarding the supposed opposition of the philosophy of religion and positive religion that there cannot be *two kinds of reason* and *two kinds of spirit*: there cannot be a divine reason and a human, there cannot be a divine Spirit and a human, which would be *absolutely different*. Human reason—the consciousness of one's being—is indeed reason; it is the divine in man; and spirit, insofar as it is the Spirit of God, is not a spirit beyond the stars, beyond the world. On the contrary, God is present, omnipresent, present as Spirit in all spirits [PR I 50].

25 For the relationship between the *Lectures on the Proofs for the Existence of God* and the *Lectures on the Philosophy of Religion*, see chap. 8, note 16.

It should be noted in the text just quoted that the "philosophy of religion" of which Hegel speaks is not a philosophizing about religion; it is the thinking philosophically what religion thinks religiously. It is, then, philosophy itself, the source and object of whose thinking is the divine Spirit himself. Thus, Hegel's God is not one who is out there, beyond the world, but one who is present in his works, chief of which is thought as it occurs in human spirit, whether that thought be religious or philosophical.

> Religion is a product of the divine Spirit; it is not a discovery of man's, but a work of divine operation and creation in him. The expression that God as *reason* rules the world would be *irrational* if we did not assume that it has reference also to religion, and that the divine Spirit works in the character and form proper to religion. But the development of reason as perfected in thought does not stand in opposition to this spirit, and consequently it cannot be absolutely different from the work which the divine Spirit has produced in religion [PR 1 50].

With the *Lectures on the Philosophy of Religion* Hegel has reached a stage of development in his thought on religion which was not clearly elaborated in the *Phenomenology*. No longer is there question merely of an identical content in both religion and philosophy; religion itself is perfected in philosophy in such a way that the two are no longer distinct; religion is now philosophical religion, because it is complete as religion in the form which is proper to philosophy. In religion at its former stage the infinite (God) is present in a thought which is itself finite; the being which was present is infinite, but the manner of its presence was finite. In philosophy—or philosophical religion—the same infinite being is present, but the manner of its presence is its own infinite self-consciousness.

> We have now reached the realized concept of religion, the perfect religion, in which it is the concept itself which is its own object. We defined religion as being in the more precise sense the self-consciousness of God. Self-consciousness in its character as consciousness has an object, and it is conscious of itself in this object; this object is also consciousness, but it is consciousness as object, and is consequently finite consciousness, a consciousness which is distinct from God, from the absolute. The element of determinateness is present in this form of consciousness, and consequently finitude is present in it. God is self-consciousness. He knows himself in a consciousness which is distinct from him, which is in itself God's consciousness; but it is also this for itself, since it knows its identity with God, an identity which is, however, mediated by the negation of finitude. This concept constitutes the content of religion. . . . This concept is now realized, consciousness knows this content and knows that it is itself simply interwoven with this content; in the concept which is the process of God it is itself a moment. . . . This is perfect religion, the concept become objective to itself. Here it is revealed what

God is: he is no longer a being above and beyond this world, an unknown, for he has let men know what he is, and this not only in external history,[26] but in consciousness [PR II 191–92].

By the time we reach this over-long quotation we have no difficulty in seeing that Hegel has instituted a speculative transformation of revealed religion. What is perhaps more significant here, however, is that he has also instituted a transformation of modern philosophy. Not only may philosophy, in Hegel's eyes, not ignore God; it is, precisely as philosophy, the thought of God. Philosophical thinking is infinite activity; it is the presence of infinite Spirit in the spirit of man, wherein the latter is *aufgehoben* in a thinking which must be infinite if its object is the truth.

With this the pieces of a complex puzzle begin to fall into place. It can be doubted—and has been—that the religion Hegel speaks of is really the Christian religion, or whether the God he speaks of is truly the Christian God. Be that as it may, there can be no doubt that the God-question concerned him very deeply and that he sought to understand God in such a way that God not only would not conflict with the autonomy of philosophical thinking but also would not be an object which simply exceeded the capacity of human reason. The Christian God has always been looked on as the supreme being, infinite spirit, and absolute reality. Of Hegel's God the same can be said. Hegel's, however, is a philosophical endeavor to understand what such attributes can mean to modern man.

The other side of the same picture, the philosophical, has also become clearer. For Hegel, philosophy is a science which has absolute truth for its object and absolute knowledge as its manner of grasping this object. That knowledge is knowledge he never doubted; his problem was to describe knowledge in such a way that it would manifest itself as precisely that. When all is said and done Hegel is still working in the tradition of "transcendental" philosophy, whose task is not to *discover*—either empirically or deductively—what is the case, but to uncover the necessary conditions for what he knows to be the case and to affirm the absolute reality of those conditions. For Hegel, then, if what he has described is not true, then knowledge is not knowledge, philosophy is not philosophy.

With regard to the *reality* of this concept, *science* does not appear in time and in *actuality* until spirit has achieved this consciousness regarding itself. As the spirit which knows what it itself is it does not exist sooner, never

26 This notion of "external history" (*äusserliche Geschichte*) is familiar to us from the *Phenomenology*. It designates an *account* of the events of history, which, as the work of the historian, is external to the events themselves, which have in themselves an internal relationship constituting the historical process.

before the completion of the work of overcoming its imperfect form, of shaping its own consciousness, its essential form, and in this way identifying its *self-consciousness* with its *consciousness*. The spirit which is in and for itself and distinguished into its moments is knowing *for itself*, conceiving in general, which as such has not attained *substance*, i.e., in itself is not absolute knowing [*Phän.* 557].

The paradigm of all knowing is divine knowing [27] where the knowing itself is infinite and what is known is the finite totality of the knowable (cf. WL II 502).[28] If human knowing is to be truly knowing, it must in some sense be divine. This it is in religion, but religion itself can ultimately know what it is knowing only in and through philosophy, which is to say that in religion man *believes* in God, but only in philosophy can he *know* what God (in whom he believes) is. Until then he knows not what he says when he says "God."

Thus, we might say that Hegel's has been a gigantic effort to rescue both Christian religion and philosophy by ultimately identifying them. It is, for him, inconceivable that philosophical knowledge should merit the designation "knowledge" if it falls short of grasping the ultimate totality of reality which religion presents. On the other hand, religion will be dealing in little more than empty words or symbols if philosophy does not make known to it the meaning of its own content.

[27] This same theme we find as early as the *Early Theological Writings*; see TJ 75.

[28] Cf. also EPW 182–83, where Hegel says in a slightly different vein that only as Idea is the concept fully defined, because only thus is it explicitly identified with the totality of reality.

10

Philosophy and Social Change

IT REQUIRES NO GREAT PERSPICACITY on the part of the philosopher (or, for that matter, the non-philosopher) to recognize that the age in which we live is one of extraordinary changes and that those changes have had and are having an as-yet-uncalculated impact on the way men live their lives. Nonetheless, it does take more than ordinary discernment to evaluate both the changes and the impact they make. It can be said, of course, that in the dynamics of history any age is necessarily a period of change; but it is also true that one age more than another will in the course of history constitute a particularly significant turning point in the ongoing process of human living. There are periods in history when the forces of change are concentrated in such a way that the periods in question stand out as milestones on man's pathway through time. What characterizes our present age is not only that it is one of those milestones, one of those points in which the energies of change are concentrated, but also that at present the tempo of change has been accelerated to a degree unprecedented in past history.

The rapidity of contemporary change is such that, before we can become effectively adjusted to one change, another has supervened to challenge our adjustability even more. It is, in fact, precisely this factor of adjustability which makes today's "generation gap" so poignant; it is far easier to adjust to change when what is faced is not recognized as change but only as the way things are. One generation must adjust; a succeeding one need not. Paradoxically, to have lived longer is to have experienced more acutely our incapacity to come to terms with life in the framework of the categories to which we have become accustomed; and the result is schizophrenic.

On the surface the changes we are witnessing can appear as simply extraordinary and unmitigated progress. Man's capacities, after all, are steadily increasing, and no limit to that increase is clearly in sight. With the elaboration of more and more intricate, more and more refined, instruments, man's capacity for perception has been extended enormously. In a period of twenty years scientific knowledge has

An earlier version of this chapter appears in *Person and Community: A Philosophical Exploration*, ed. Robert J. Roth, s.j. (New York: Fordham University Press, 1975), pp. 1–24.

progressed both quantitatively and qualitatively more than it did in the centuries between Archimedes and Einstein. Keeping pace with this growth in man's knowing is the equally extraordinary increase in his know-how, in his productive capacity to fulfill his needs (this last, of course, accompanied by a vast increase in those needs). Both these advances might simply be included under the heading of an increased capacity to dominate nature—unfortunately most dramatically ex-emplified in the capacity for destruction, but also experienced as a capacity for construction. The forces of nature have been harnessed for good as well as for evil.

THE NEED OF CRITERIA FOR CHANGE

When we witness the unquestionable increase in man's power over his environment, however, we cannot but wonder whether this increase is not inseparable from a diminishment in man's capacity to know himself, to control himself, to be creative of a life suitable for man as man. With the enormous growth in his capacity to know and do, there remains the gnawing question whether man himself has grown. Along with growth in man's capacities goes a multiplication of the problems which he must face in his changing world, and we must at least ask the question whether he has proved himself adequate to the task of facing them. It would certainly be incredibly naïve to think that change, just because it is change, is necessarily healthy change. But has contemporary man increased his capacity for distinguishing between healthy and unhealthy change; has he perhaps relinquished any criterion for making that distinction? In a world which is charac-terized by rapid change, by constantly accelerated change, it might be questioned whether man has retained a capacity to give meaning to the term "should," to say what should or should not be, or whether he has simply surrendered to what is or is in the process of coming to be. In an age far less externally complex than our own, Plato in his *Sophist* asked searching questions about the being of becoming, and the questions are no less in need of answers today than they were then. It may be that we see more clearly today that if philosophy is an at-tempt to grasp ultimate reality, and if ultimate reality is in process, then philosophy must come to terms with process. To know that this is so, however, is not to have solved the problem; it is not even to have attempted to understand the problem. If there is a *being* of process, then, it would seem, there should also be a *logic* of process. But what can this logic be? Can there be a static logic of dynamic process, or must the logic itself be dynamic? What can a dynamic logic be; can it be arrived at by an analysis of concepts, or must it somehow emerge from the process itself? Can an analysis of concepts ever do justice to the process from which they emerge? Whether or not definitive answers can be given to questions such as these, they make it clear that the issues involved are too problematic simply to be passed over in silence.

At one extreme, then, in relation to change is the attitude which either sees change as simply a fact which need not be judged in the light of any criterion whatever or accepts change as good merely because it is change. The problem generated by this extreme attitude is rather obvious: the attitude is not merely uncritical and, therefore, irresponsible; it is a relinquishing of the genuinely human role of determining what one is to be. It is the sort of attitude which, in recent years, has permitted B. F. Skinner to get such mileage out of his theories of human manipulation. At the opposite extreme is the attitude of a resistance to change because it violates an established order which itself has become the criterion for what is as it should be. The problem here is a subjective one (although the response to it may have objective overtones): the problem of identifying with one period in a world which is in fact changing. One who thus identifies what ought to be with what was or has been can quite readily assign to himself the vocation of reversing change—to bring it into conformity with the arbitrarily accepted criterion—thus romanticizing the past, without reflecting that the past in question represents a change over a more remote past (the accelerated pace of change of which we have spoken can render this problem more acute without making the simplistic solution to it more valid). At no stage in history can it make sense to insist that only methods from the past are adequate to solve questions of the present or, worse still, that problems of the present must be adapted to solutions of the past. Here, too, the problem can be made more complex by a failure to see just what is changing, the sign or the thing signified. Where sign and signified are identified, a commitment to what is signified can result in resistance to any change in the manner of signifying it. A solution can be found, perhaps, in a knowledge of the past which permits one to understand and cope with ongoing change in the light of past change—if this is not, in turn, complicated by the difficulty of understanding a past which exists only in the record of it or of knowing just what happens when a change takes place.

CHANGES IN PAST CIVILIZATIONS

To illustrate this on the grand scale and with broad strokes, we might look at a series of stages in civilization as we know it, each ushered in by a cataclysmic change, even though not with the rapidity to which we are now forced to become accustomed. The story of the ancient

East (i.e., that part of the East whose history has directly influenced the West—Egypt, Mesopotamia, Babylonia, Persia) is necessarily somewhat foggy, but it represents a civilization which had little in common with the Greco-Roman civilization which succeeded it in our history. The disintegration of the Roman Empire was, in turn, a change which gradually resulted in another diametrically opposed civilization, that of the Holy Roman Empire and of the feudal structures within it. As a sort of extension of feudalism we can see the great monarchies of the West, whose gradual demise was ushered in (symbolically perhaps) by the French Revolution, and which were superseded by the constitutional nation-states of nineteenth-century Europe. When we reach this stage we are faced with another revolution which was chronologically concomitant with the rise of nation-states but the repercussions of which wrought a tremendous change in civilization— we call it the Industrial Revolution. This stage in Western civilization was succeeded by a sort of vacuum wherein industrialization continued, but a style of life was coming to an end. The cataclysmic dividing-line was World War I (World War II simply continued the process of disintegration). A new age has been ushered in, and its multiple changes are ours to cope with—we can call it the atomic age, the space age, or what-have-you. The point is that the mentality of a former age cannot cope with it, any more than the mentality of feudal Europe could cope with the Industrial Revolution.

To speak of changes such as these, of course, is to say nothing of the myriad other changes which have taken place in the course of history; it is not even to spell out the implications of these major revolutionary changes. It does, however, show to some extent what change can be: not merely differences in living resulting from advances in technical knowledge, skill, development of transportation and communication, growth of population, etc., but changes in mentality, in ways of seeing reality, in taste, in values—in short, in most of the things which make up the spiritual life of man. Quite obviously, too, the changes which take place are not immediately worldwide—until most recent times changes have never been worldwide—but they do belong to a steady process which ultimately makes the life of every man vastly different from one age to another.

The kind of change envisioned here can be illustrated by one vastly significant example: even granted that in the course of human history God does not change, there can be no question that man's view of God changes again and again. Even apart from revelation, there is a passage from a plurality of gods to the one God, from the God of nature to the anthropomorphic God, from the purely transcendent to the more immanent God, from the God who is power and might to the God who is spirit and love. The change is one in man's awareness, it is true, but precisely that is significant. The fact is that we simply do not continue to say exactly the same when we say "God"—whether in successive periods in our own individual lives or in the course of history—and the change is a fundamental change in us, a change not only in our way of seeing God but in our way of seeing ourselves and the world. And this is as it should be. It is one of the reasons why we can—and perhaps should—have an unchanging commitment to God accompanied by a changing response, without inconsistency. More than that, changes such as these can be—and perhaps should be—paradigmatic for the changes which come about wherever there is vitality. It is not merely that with the passage of time man sees himself *differently*; what he sees in seeing himself is *different*; a changing image of man means a changing man, and our problem is to discover how the philosopher comes to terms with that.

There are, however, two questions here, one regarding the fact of change, and the other the desirability of change; and the questions can be kept separate. When philosophy enters upon the scene it can concern itself with either or both; it can seek to evaluate changes which take place or perhaps the desirability of effecting change. When Aristotle, for example, recognized the experience of change as incontrovertible evidence for the fact of change, he sought to describe the structure of reality in such a way as to account for the fact (Parmenides and Zeno, on the other hand, opted for a structure of reality which reason seemed to demand, thus preferring to ignore the evidence of experience). Philosophy, then, neither initiates nor guides change; like the Owl of Minerva it takes flight at dusk to gaze on what has already taken place and to give an account of it. Its task, however, is not simply to watch; it must also seek to understand, to evaluate, perhaps even to predict and warn. If, with Marxism, it seeks not merely to understand but also to bring about change, it may well be doing something admirable, but in becoming thus admirable it has become something other than philosophy.

EFFECT OF CHANGE ON MAN

Now, the change with which we are here concerned is not simply physical change, which might conceivably be explained by a theory of potentiality and actuality and not evaluated at all. Our concern is the more profound and ultimate concern of all philosophical investigation, which is man—man in the process of becoming what he is not yet. We seek to understand man, and we recognize that throughout the process man is always identifiable as man. This requires that we be able to distinguish between what belongs to man substantially and what belongs only to his changing styles of life; but it also requires that we do not allow a seemingly once-and-for-all answer regarding the meaning of man to blind us to the progressive realization of what it is to be man. There is a delicate balance to be maintained here. We can, after all, still read Homer and Sophocles, Plato and Aristotle, or the Bible, and recognize that the man we meet there is the man we meet when we know ourselves or when we reflect on our contemporary civilization. At the same time we must recognize that there is a difference, a vast difference, and one which cannot be accounted for by the mere passage of time. We must recognize, too, that the process of man's becoming will not be understandable by reference to some "plan" in the mind of God, which, even if it were the case, would not be available to the mind of man. We must seek to understand what man is by examining what man does, without at the same time surrendering to the sort of humanism which claims that man is intelligible as man only if God is eliminated from the picture.

The ultimate point of reference for all philosophy, then, is man, and all that man knows is ultimately a contribution to his knowledge of himself. This does not mean that all philosophy is reducible to psychology (or anthropology)—that would be inadequate, even as a "philosophy of man"—but it does mean that all that philosophy knows is significant only in reference to man. It is man who knows, who does the questioning, and every answer he attains tells him more about himself. One might conceivably be interested, with Husserl, in the "essence" of consciousness, or of life, or of reality, independently of whether it is man's consciousness, or man's life, or reality in relation to man; but it is doubtful that the results of such an interest could mean a great deal, or that one could really escape the ultimate reference to him who is interested. We may be interested in logic or epistemology, but only because they tell us of human thinking. Our concern may be metaphysics, but it tells us of being-for-man. Ethics, too, is a guide, not to action in general, but to human action. A philosophy of nature (as opposed to science) seeks to penetrate the "meaning" of nature—for man. Even a philosophy of God seeks a knowledge which is significant as determining man's relationship to God.

We can go further and say that any particular philosophy—distinguished from philosophy as the total process of philosophizing—is significant not so much for its "truth value" (although that need not be negligible) as for the light it throws on ongoing human experience. Philosophy asks the kind of questions which are ultimately unanswerable—at least in the sense that what answers there are are not ultimate; that is why it is *perennis*—and the questions are those which no other discipline is even competent to ask, much less answer. To take but the most obvious example: the question of life. We cannot simply take life for granted, not our own view of it nor the most commonly accepted view of it. We must ask questions about it, and the questions are significant, even where no definitive answer is forthcoming—the questioning itself reveals man to himself. Is life better than non-life? Is biological life a supreme value, such that it may not be sacrificed for any other value? Is life a value only for the one who lives it? Is human life superior to other forms of life? What does "superior" mean in the context? As scientist, artist, jurist, politician, businessman, athlete, a man can get his work done without asking these and a host of other questions which his science, art, law, politics, business, or sport can neither ask nor answer. As man he cannot be satisfied not to ask the questions, even though the lack of definitive answers forces him to ask them over and over again. Here, perhaps, we can detect a purpose which the philosopher serves, precisely as philosopher; he does in a disciplined way what all men have a tendency to do but most men do not have the time to do.

MAN IN SOCIETY

All these questions are questions about man, even where the direct object of the question is not man himself. The meaning of what is, what happens, what is done, is to be found in man, because only man is a bearer of meaning. Man, however, is concretely intelligible, concretely meaningful, only as he concretely is—and that is in society. We have said that to be conscious of man as man is to be conscious of man in process, but consciousness of man in process is inseparable from consciousness of society in process—and that is history. History bears witness to repeated changes in man's mentality, his way of seeing reality, his taste, the values he lives by; but these changes are inseparable from the changes of social structure wherein man lives.

Much of what has been said up to this point can, it is true, sound strange to Aristotelian ears. In the Aristotelian tradition, although man is "essentially" social and political (and perhaps, therefore, historical), he is still only derivatively so. His social and political character flows from his "nature"—his life follows from and, therefore, is not constitutive of his nature (the priority of *esse* over *agere* is looked upon as not simply logical but in some sense ontological). In this view, which in reality is basically a metaphysical view antecedent to any concrete consideration of man, relation is simply subsequent to and, therefore, not constitutive of substance. Now, where man as "nature" is significant (i.e., considered abstractly), it may make sense to speak in this way; where, however, there is question of man in the concrete, as "person," it makes little sense. It is, in fact, a moot question whether it makes sense at all to speak of man as a being of nature; man is truly man only as a person, and man is a person only as related to other persons (the Trinitarian analogy is not accidental). This means, then, that man is authentically human only in the framework of society, with its multiple relations. By the same token the process whereby man becomes what he is (better, perhaps, *who* he is) is inseparable from the process whereby society becomes what it is, and both are inseparable from what man does.

To say this is not to say that the Aristotelian view of man is erroneous—except in the sense that any partial view is erroneous if it is taken as total. It is a commonplace that many men can look at the same thing and yet *see* something different. The biologist, the psychologist, the social scientist, the rhetorician, the advertising man, the philosopher, and the theologian—all look at man. What each one sees is different, and what each one sees can in some sense be true. Similarly, different philosophers can see man differently, and their views can be partially true.

We are not saying, then, that to speak of man in society, of man as effectively human, acting precisely as concrete man and not as an abstraction, of man as intelligible only in a social framework, is to say all that can be said of man. The abstract foundation of human "nature" may well be necessary if all else we say is to be intelligible. We are saying, however, that not to speak of man in society is not to speak of man as he is; it is to look at the evidence available and not to read all of it. When the individual enters the world, he enters a world which is not only already there but which already has a sense (the term signifies both "meaning" and "direction") which he does not give it and which he is not free to take away from it. He chooses neither to be born nor to be born in these circumstances. The society in which he lives has been structured by a sum of human activity and environmental forces in the past in which neither he nor those around him have had any part. It is a society which can, it is true, also be restructured, but even the restructuring will be socially conditioned. He will speak a language which he as an individual does not choose, a language which is a given in the community and which will condition the way he experiences the world and life in it. He will neither create nor discover values independently of others; his very thinking will be conditioned by the structured community of which he is part. The world of values in which he shares does not flow from nature—not even from "human nature"—although it may be "natural" for him to accept a certain set of values. As time goes on he will, undoubtedly, change in many ways, but the changes will not be independent of changes taking place in the social framework. In short, he will inevitably be part of a vital social organism which follows the two basic laws of all organisms: that the whole is greater than the sum of its parts and that the whole is somehow present in each of its parts.

In the course of his life the individual will learn many abstract truths, but because the whole of that life will be conditioned by a social context, he will also learn that those abstract truths are rarely adequate to the concrete situation where the action is. If he is not to perish in the vacuum of those abstractions, he must discover that a certain healthy relativism is in order—not that the abstract truths will ever become abstractly untrue, but that in being concretized they will not be quite the same truths. What is abstractly true can continue to be true and yet be found concretely (practically) to be untrue, because things do not happen in the abstract, and what does happen deviates, be it ever so slightly, from the abstract prescription of how it should happen. Plato was not wrong in looking for the definition of abstract justice, any more than Galileo was wrong in calculating the formula for the rate of acceleration of freely falling bodies, or Kant in formulating the categorical imperative, because Plato, Galileo, and Kant knew that rules valid for an ideal order are only approximately valid for the real order. Moreover, circumstances can change so much that what could have been concretely meaningful in one set of circumstances becomes meaningless in another.

What immediately comes to mind by way of dramatic illustration is the defense of war drawn from the enumeration of the conditions for a just war. One need not deny the validity of the conditions nor the justice of the war they describe in order to be convinced that we have reached a point in history where the conditions cannot be concretely realized and where, as a consequence, "just war" has become a meaningless abstraction. We can, of course, speak in the abstract of intelligence, of beauty, of right, and we can know what we mean when we do. But we can also make the mistake of thinking of intelligence as the capacity for abstract conceptualization which is verified in IQ tests, or of beauty as the form which has been concretized in the art of a particular era, or of a right as the sort of claim a person has to a thing (e.g., to private property) within the framework of social relationships which are no longer existent. If we do this we run the risk of not recognizing intelligence, or beauty, or right, when they appear in forms or contexts to which we are not accustomed.

There is a tendency among philosophers to want what is true to be eternally true; it is more comfortable that way. If, of course, philosophers are content with abstractions, they may very well get what they want, but they may thus prove rather unreliable guides through life. We can, for example, speak of "inalienable rights," which, presumably, flow from nature and are not dependent on the relationships of society. The fact that at some time in history every one of those "rights" has been contravened by one society or another, or that only relatively recently have any rights been recognized as belonging to man as man and not merely to some particular kind of man (e.g., a free man), does not contradict the fundamental inalienability of the rights in question. That the list is so short, however, might lead one to suspect that a more fruitful approach to the question of rights might be through the social and political structures in which rights become effective. Kant set down as an eternal, necessary, and universal truth that a human being is never to be treated as a means but only as an end. By this Kant certainly meant that human beings do not evolve in society to a point where such a categorical imperative becomes true (if, indeed, Kant was even capable of thinking of man as evolving). It may be that Kant was correct; but we should remember that the Kant who thought so was the same Kant who thought that physical laws were not merely descriptive of what does happen but prescriptive of what must happen, and who saw both physical and moral laws as prescribed by reason alone. It may very well be that inalienable rights are truly inalienable, but need the source of this inalienability be "nature" and not a set of relationships which have developed with the evolution of man's social consciousness?

THE DYNAMICS OF SOCIETY

Nothing which has been said so far should be taken as a claim that all other forms of explanation—in the physical, psychological, epistemological, metaphysical, or moral orders—should be dropped and replaced by sociopolitical or historical explanations (although it may well be that man's awareness of any and all explanations is conditioned by the social context within which he seeks explanations). It claims no more than that the philosopher should take the social into account in all his investigations. This is particularly true where what the philosopher is investigating are changes in human consciousness, changes in man's image of himself, of the world, and of God. Here it is important to stress that the social context, the social structures, of which we have been speaking are not static but dynamic. To investigate social or political changes themselves is, of course, the work of the sociologist or the political scientist, but to investigate the impact of these changes on man, on the way man changes, or on the way his image of himself changes, is the work of the philosopher. Nor need this mean that the philosopher has made unnecessary concessions to the Marxist by interpreting all change exclusively in terms of the relationships which develop in the productive process (although these, too, should not be ignored—a theory need not be totally true in order to make important contributions to social understanding).

It does mean, however, a considerable reduction in the importance of studying man's "nature"—except to the extent that both his social being and the development of his consciousness through action and interaction reveal the need of a constant core of intelligibility which is indispensable—if process itself is to be intelligible. Only if that which evolves in the process is always identifiable as man and not as something else can talk of change in man's consciousness make sense. In fact, history can make sense only if it is constantly of man that it is the history. We can speak of a process of evolution whereby man comes to be man, but we cannot meaningfully speak of a history prior to the advent of man. By the same token, however, once man has evolved to the point of having become a social being, his development thereafter is inseparable from the development of the social structures within which he lives, acts, and interacts. So true is this that effectively the history of man and the history of society simply coincide. To speak with Teilhard de Chardin, we might say that social evolution is the form which evolution takes once biological evolution has made of man a social being. Thus, his oft-quoted dictum that "the history of cosmogenesis is the history of anthropogenesis" can be expanded by saying that the history of anthropogenesis has become the history of sociogenesis—that is what the process of "complexity-consciousness" has become.

It is not without significance that philosophy as we know it, or history as we know it, or, for that matter, human awareness as we know it, began when man began to be aware of his social dimensions. A simple answer to this could be that man experienced no need to reflect on the meaning of reality, or of process, or of human awareness as such, until he experienced what it was to be with others with whom he felt a need to communicate. This is, after all, in its own way correct; the need of reflection on the meaning of existence is inseparable from the need of communicating one's reflections, no matter how solipsistic the "existentialist" may appear to want to be. Human thought thrives almost exclusively on the need and the desire to communicate itself. Communication, however, is meaningless unless there is a community within which communication can be accomplished. Man asks himself many questions, but the very asking of them would be devoid of meaning were there no community within which the questions could be asked. The individual cannot simply ask himself questions: unless the questions are asked against the background of a society which gives meaning to the individual, the individual cannot ask questions which make sense—to say nothing of the impossibility of supplying answers. What it comes down to is that, although man can conceivably ask questions about man as man without reference to the social context in which man is found, he himself cannot be independent of the social context in asking such questions. Actually it is inconceivable that man in isolation (if there can be such) could even ask himself what it means to be man; the question could not occur to him outside a framework in which it is significant that others, too, should be men. So far as we know, dogs and cows, and cats and snails, do not ask themselves what it is to be what they are—not simply because they lack the intelligence to ask such profound questions, but because they lack the social framework within which alone such questions could possibly make sense. The result, then, is that the question regarding the meaning of man can be asked only in a framework within which the relationship of man to man is constitutive of the answer which can be given to the question. If this is so, however, then the answer to the question regarding the meaning of man is not to be found in abstract speculations concerning his "essence" or "nature," but in a concrete inquiry into the social structures which condition his life as he lives it. We can know neither what man is nor what he should be independently of the concrete relationships within which "is" is significant. We do not know man adequately, we might say, by simply knowing what he is or even what he does; we must also know how he relates.

This, however, brings us back once more to the problem (or the dilemma) of constancy. Change can be meaningful only if it is change in that which remains constant; constancy can be meaningful only if it is constancy enduring through change. The dilemma, of course, is not a new one for human thought; nor is it limited to the constancy and changeableness of man himself. The dilemma is as old as philosophy itself; it might even be considered the greatest single impetus to philosophizing. To deny change (as, presumably, did Parmenides and Zeno) is to fly in the face of experience which is not to be rationalized out of existence. To deny constancy would be to condemn experience to meaninglessness. It may be that with Hume we will want to say that there is no way of "knowing" that what we experience retains a continuing identity with itself, that there is no "logical" contradiction in its being repeatedly annihilated and re-created. We do know, however, that we cannot *live* without supposing its continuing identity. If experience is to be experience *of* anything, there must be constancy.

Thus, to say, as we have said, that man (or perhaps simply the image of man) changes, as social structures come to be and pass away, is to say that what is constantly identifiable as man has undergone significant development in a process we call history. The man of the

Bible, of Sophocles and Plato, of Dante and Thomas Aquinas, of Hobbes and Rousseau, Hegel and Marx, Whitehead and Dewey, is the man we meet today when we experience ourselves or those who with us make up contemporary society. Nor is this necessarily to speak in any but an abstract sense of an enduring "nature" of man. There is, in fact, a danger that we shall look upon man as an eternally given, who may have his ups and downs but who can always be judged by the same standards because he is an unchanging instantiation of an idea in the mind of God. To be changeless in this sense is to be a thing, not a person, and the most significant thing which can be said of any man is that he is a person, unique in the class to which he belongs. It may, of course, be that the requisite constancy of man also demands that certain characteristics, such as rationality or immortality, must always be true of him (although what we *mean* by these may also change), but this in no way requires that many of the things we say of him with utmost confidence need be true of him at every period in his history. To distinguish what we must always say of him (and the manner in which we say it) from what we must say of him in certain temporal and social circumstances is one of the tasks which confront the philosopher. There are questions which must always be asked with a realization that the same answers are not always valid, or at least that the answers do not retain exactly the same meaning.

CHANGES IN MAN'S VIEWPOINT

With Plato we can, for example, ask such questions as "What is justice?" The likelihood is that, along with Plato, we shall never find a completely satisfactory answer to the question, even though, if in formulating the question we come up with something like the *Republic*, we shall have done a very worthwhile thing. We are more likely, however, to ask what the just thing to do in a given set of circumstances is, or when a situation is just or unjust (with an effort, of course, to ensure that the *terms* "just" and "unjust" retain a constant *meaning*). It is when we ask this second sort of question that we must take into account all the circumstances which can vary the situation and, thus, the answer to the question. No one doubts that a knowledge of the circumstances is tremendously significant in arriving at this sort of judgment—that is one reason why a "categorical imperative" has such reduced practical value. It is important to note, however, that the structure of society in which events take place and choices are made is one of the most important circumstances to be taken into account, and that the structure of society can and does change with the advance of history. Perhaps what could correctly be called just or unjust in one form of society (e.g., a monistic one) cannot be so readily judged in another (e.g., pluralistic) form of society. We have already considered how questions regarding war or private property have to be asked differently within the framework of contemporary world society. There are other questions which have to be asked (and perhaps answered) differently against the background of changing relationships.

In any event, we should not take it for granted that an answer which could legitimately be considered adequate for a given social framework continues to be adequate when the framework has changed. It may be—to take a somewhat specialized example—that within the society for which the law was promulgated the indissolubility of marriage was unquestionable. It may be, too, that where the marriage union exactly reproduces the union there spoken of, its indissolubility is today equally unquestionable. But is the union exactly the same? Does the view which society takes of the union have some influence on the very "nature" of the union? Where the view that the "dynamics" of the union require a second look at its alleged permanency is socially so widespread, are we justified in ignoring it in favor of a view based on an abstract analysis of the "nature" of marriage? We might illustrate the nature of the question being asked by referring to what is today a dead issue (in the West at least), that of polygamy. There was a time when polygamy was quite normal, even among the chosen people of God. We may find it convenient to see this as a case of God's "permitting" what in itself was really evil; but, to say the least, that is a singularly unphilosophical (perhaps even blasphemous) convenience. We might also prefer to say that where society looked upon women (and women looked upon themselves) as possessions and, therefore—at least in this relationship—not as persons, it was perfectly logical not to consider the marriage union (or, perhaps, the procreative society) as an exclusive union of two equal partners. Or we might even prefer to say that the structure of early society did not make it imperative that there be one wife to a husband, whereas in contemporary society it is imperative. (What the situation may be in future society is a question we can mercifully leave unasked.)

Considerations such as these can permit us to approach other questions too. The arguments against birth control, for example, do not necessarily become bad arguments because the vast majority of people ignore them (although the *maior et sanior pars* argument might make moralists more humble). They might, however, become inapplicable arguments where it is recognized that the marriage union is not primarily a procreative union and that intercourse is not merely a procreative act, or where overpopulation of the world is seen as a concrete problem, for which abstinence is too drastic a solution. We all recognize, of course, that the question of abortion cannot be solved by an appeal to the same considerations as those which apply to birth control. Nevertheless, without even going into the morality of abortion, we can ask ourselves whether it is always a good thing for morality to be legislated—particularly in a pluralistic society where the consciences of vast numbers of people differ so sharply. We are not likely to think that all the things which Plato legislated for in his *Laws* should be legislated for today. Perhaps we are ready to recognize that the legislation of morality in general should decrease—without, of course, denying that the "common good" is still a valid goal of legislation *if* there are those who are truly wise enough to know what the common good is.

Perhaps we have even reached a point in history where we do not have to condemn out of hand those who argue that a law recognized as just can sometimes be justly disobeyed. I do not wish here to enter into the arguments for "civil disobedience," but I should like to suggest that an examination of them will reveal that they are not idiotic. In any event it would seem not inconceivable that the consideration of man as a member of society structured in a certain way can demand or permit what a consideration of man's abstract nature (or of society's "nature" in the abstract) does not.

It may be that there is an absolute morality which does not change with a change in social relationships, but it may be, too, that we have been wrong about the extent of such an absolute morality. It scarcely seems necessary to stress that there are existential moral demands which are no less binding because they did not aways bind; moral necessity is not a function of either eternal or universal validity. It might, of course, be said that fundamental moral principles remain always the same, and that change is only in that to which they are applied; but that is only another way of saying that the abstract remains always the same, while the concrete is process. This leaves intact the need of distinguishing between the abstract and the concrete. One can say, for example, that incest is always morally reprehensible, and that the application of this prohibition differs in different societies. Since, however, there is scarcely any form of what one society considers to be incest which is not permitted in some other society, the suspicion is that the relevant abstraction is not incest at all but something even more vague called "social desirability," which is meaningless except in the concrete context of the society where it is interpreted.

One of the reasons why laws change is that the social desirability of their implementation changes. There are a number of reasons why it is socially undesirable that fathers and daughters, mothers and sons, or even sisters and brothers, should marry. There was a time, in the era of the "extended family," when it was socially undesirable that third cousins should marry. We know, however, that Thomas Aquinas and the Scholastics sought reasons rooted in the abstract nature of love or in the rather tenuous ties of "blood" to explain *a priori* what was in fact a purely practical prohibition. Presumably there was a period in history (or there are social structures in existence) in which the marriage of brothers with sisters was (is) a practical social necessity. Whether there are biological reasons for frowning on such a practice is another question and one whose moral repercussions are quite different (here the biologist must speak before the philosopher can).

The point is that there are a great many givens in any society (and in history) which have long been considered to belong to the nature of things but which turn out to be social conventions and quite justifiable as such. The family, we are told, is a "natural" society, and so, for the sake of argument, let it be (although certain experiments in Israel might cast doubt even on that). Where there is a society, there should be some form of authority, and so, tradition tells us, the father is the "natural" head of the family, just as the husband is the "natural" head of the wife. The difficulty with this is that there are societies in which the mother is the head of the family, and it would be rather arbitrary on the part of Western moralists to say that this is "unnatural" or wrong. Even in our own society it is becoming increasingly evident that to speak of the husband as "head" of the wife is nonsense, and to call either father or mother, rather than both, "head" of the family is unrealistic. Involved in all this, of course, is the even larger issue of the dialectical character of authority, which makes it doubtful whether authority "resides" in anyone rather than simply being exercised by one rather than many.

It has always been recognized by moralists that certain rights and obligations are necessarily vague and unspecified, and that they are made specific by legislation in society. Thus, in human life there is a time when one passes from the relative irresponsibility of childhood to the beginnings of responsibility in adulthood, and this seems to be tied up with the capacity to reason adequately. Different societies (even different segments of one and the same society), however, determine that age differently; they even determine (rather arbitrarily) a different age for different responsibilities. Thus, there is a voting age, a draft age, a driving age, a drinking age, an age when people can marry without parental consent, etc. Sometimes there are objections to the arbitrariness of such specifications, particularly when they seem to contradict each other, but it is generally acknowledged that they are specifications which society is competent to make. The question arises whether society does not specify a great deal more in the area of rights and obligations, without resorting to legislation but simply by the way it is structured. It is as though, with the passage of time and the change in relationships brought about by myriad factors not consciously brought to bear on its development, society gradually recognizes the anomaly of certain things which it formerly took for granted. Perhaps, too, they become anomalies as circumstances change.

In any event, the impression can be created that new rights are being developed when what is happening is that former ways of doing things are becoming incongruous in the light of the image of man which develops with society itself. Thus, for example, new aspects of the right of personal privacy develop, and such things as reading the letters of others—whether it be parents who read letters written by or to their children, or government officials who censor the letters of citizens—become unacceptable. What is happening, of course, is that the very thinking in regard to the relationship between authority and subjection to authority is being revamped and privacy takes on a new meaning. By the same token we are witnessing a change in attitude which no longer takes it for granted that the police may at their own discretion employ wiretapping or lie detectors in their efforts to combat crime. Perhaps, of course, authority—parents, government, the police—never had these rights, and we are just finding it out. But perhaps, too, the image of man which develops in a modern social context is what makes the formerly acceptable now incongruous. There was a time, after all, not only when authorities could act rather arbitrarily toward their subjects, but when it would not occur even to the subjects to question their right to do so.

Something similar has happened with respect to the ideas we now hold regarding the bodily integrity of the person. Although philosophers, it is true, have had many eloquent things to say (not all of them terribly convincing today) about the inadmissibility of bodily mutilation, that in itself came at a relatively late date in human history. Nor were the same philosophers quite so sensitive as we are today regarding torture or corporal punishment short of mutilation. There still are, of course, such things as "police brutality" and "revolutionary terrorism," but by and large such tactics are repudiated by society (with significant abstentions on the part of those who advocate violence as a means to the righting of wrongs). More significantly, the whole question of punishment (particularly capital punishment) has come in for serious rethinking.

What all this comes down to is not only that we apply principles to fundamentally different situations and thus come up with answers which could well have been unintelligible in another age or another situation, but that we give different meanings to the terms we use in describing man's condition. The most obvious example of such a term which takes on different meanings in different forms of society—whether the differences be historical or ideological—is the term "freedom." I do not know whether the term, or even the concept, existed in the ancient kingdoms of the East, but it certainly existed with limited applicability in Greece and Rome. With the advent of Christianity, however, the term took on new meaning, because it was used to characterize the child of God as such. Strangely enough, even in Christianity, the term "free" became bogged down as a qualifier of *arbitrium*, and effective freedom was still long in being realized. Ever since then the term has had its ups and downs. In feudal times it did not say a great deal, and with the advent of capitalism it became something to characterize business enterprise or trade (i.e., the freedom of some to exploit others for the advantage of the former). All in all, however, despite advances and regressions, the term "freedom" seems to have taken on more concrete meaning, even though there may still be some doubt whether people know what they want when they want freedom. This is made all the more manifest when, in the same historical period, the notion of freedom can be ideologically so different. It is difficult to know whether the term means the same when used by an American capitalist, a Russian Communist, or a member of the "Third World." Nor is the difference merely one of different philosophies; the meaning of the term is conditioned by the social framework within which it is used and within which the freedom in question is to be exercised.

To confine ourselves to the social context with which we are familiar, we can say that significant changes have taken place, if not in the meaning of the term "freedom," at least in our conception of what we are free to do or not to do. It is recognized, for example, that the freedom associated with private enterprise can and should be severely limited by public responsibility. The industrialist is simply not free to dispose of what he owns if in doing so he will affect adversely the lives of thousands of workers. Little by little we have come to recognize that it is a function of government to regulate free competition, to limit the freedom of producers, to control those industries whose public impact is greatest. Although our society still recognizes in principle the private ownership of the means of production, it no longer accords absolute dominion over that private property. We see more and more clearly that what one does with one's private property can have an effect on the public domain (e.g., through pollution), and so we stress the necessity of control.

For a long time it was assumed that a wage contract was one entered into by two parties, an employer and an employee. Strangely enough, with the introduction of multiple (private) ownership of the means of production, the assumption remained that management still constituted one party to the contract, while the individual employee (worker) was the other. With the growth in size and wealth of the industrial enterprise, however, it becomes quite obvious that equality of rights between employer and employee is actually the grossest inequality; there is an extraordinary disproportion in bargaining power. The development of labor unions evened the balance somewhat; but even with the increased bargaining power for the employee thus brought about, the need for some sort of government supervision and control becomes rather obvious. The result is that social changes have brought about a change in our thinking so that we now simply take for granted both collective bargaining and a measure of government control, not as obstacles to freedom but as guarantees of equal freedom.

In a somewhat more subtle way the notion of "social justice"—a relatively new concept for the philosopher—provides an additional set of checks and balances for freedom. To a great extent it has become illegal to discriminate against human beings on grounds of race, creed, color, national origin, and even sex. Gradually it is becoming clear that it can even be immoral to discriminate in cases where it is not yet illegal. It can be immoral to exercise one's "freedom of choice" in choosing one's companions on such a basis (e.g., in private schools or clubs). One could, of course, argue that it always was immoral, and that we are just beginning to realize it. The fact is, nevertheless, that a relatively extensive change in thinking has taken place, and that the social change has preceded and influenced the change in thinking. It seems, therefore, necessary to say that what is justifiable exercise of freedom in one age or social context can become unjustifiable in another. If we add to this that world society has become a reality in a way it never was before, it may become necessary to redefine the relationship of man to man as such.

Although it would be out of place here to introduce even the terminological opposition of "conservatism" and "liberalism" since the very meaning of the terms varies so greatly, it does seem necessary to ask whether there is not a certain self-defeating factor in the kind of conservatism which resists change on principle. When, as we noted before, the attempt is made to adapt methods of the past to problems of the present, one wonders whether in reality the attempt is to adapt the problems of the present to the methods of the past. This brings up the question of the need for rethinking many of our categories, not in order to get rid of them, but in order to test their validity in circumstances out of which they did not emerge. This, of course, can work in two directions: it should prevent us from seeking to understand present situations in the light of inapplicable past categories; but it should also keep us from judging past situations in the light of categories which have emerged more recently in the process of history. It is too obvious to need mentioning that there have been many changes of thinking in the course of time, but it still needs to be asked whether to these changes in thinking there correspond real changes in man; changes in social attitudes, it would seem, are attended by concrete changes in personality. If the image of man changes from age to age or from social context to social context, is there not some real sense in which man changes?

It is all very well to say categorically that no man can own another man. Effectively there was a time in history when men did own other men precisely because the image of man which was then current did not make such ownership abhorrent. Was, for example, the fact of slavery in the early United States an evil simply because it was slavery, or because the Western image of man had advanced to the point where slavery had become an anachronism? We have little doubt today that the kind of serfdom which was common in the Middle Ages is simply intolerable. Can we honestly say that we know now that it was intolerable then? Most of us have little difficulty in accepting today's wage contract as justifiable at least in principle. May the situation not change to the point where the wage contract will be as unacceptable as serfdom? It may, of course, be argued that what is or is not acceptable along these lines will depend on legislation. Strictly speaking, however, the legislation becomes an effective possibility only when a way of thinking changes, and a way of thinking changes only when a set of relationships has already changed. There are other changes which we may be slow to accept, but they are with us to stay—at least for a while—and we shall have to adapt our thinking to them. We can, of course, delay the process by, for example, concocting funny stories about "the organization man"; but one day we are going to have to admit that man has become just that, and we are going to have to adjust our thinking to it. What will our thinking be if in the foreseeable future two per cent of the world's population becomes capable of supplying the material needs of the whole population? It seems clear that the categories for handling such a situation are not yet available.

Perhaps here is where the contemporary difficulty lies. The past has seen changes as cataclysmic as any we witness today. They did not occur, however, with the same rapidity, and men had more time to adapt their thinking—imperceptibly—to the changes. Today changes outrun thought, at least the thought whereby man thinks what it is to be man—and so, the crisis. Perhaps we can weather the crisis only if we adopt an attitude which is illustrated in Nietzsche's image of life. Life, he tells us, is like a pathway which exists only as we walk it. Behind us it is constantly being rolled up, so that we can really not look back and find our direction there. In front of us it unfolds only with each forward step we take. Where the path leads, then, is not antecedently given, and yet the direction it takes is not arbitrary or fortuitous. Only with great courage can we take the risk of walking down that path; but if we do not take the risk, we go nowhere.

11

Authority in the Contemporary World

WHEN PHILOSOPHY TURNS its reflective gaze on the institution of authority—in whatever form it may appear—it is clearly taking flight, like Hegel's Owl of Minerva, at dusk, when the events of the day have already taken place, whether they be the events which have shaped the Western world or the events which shape contemporary attitudes. Wherever human beings, with their multiple individual purposes and aims, engage in a common enterprise, which is the unified purpose and aim of all, there is need among them of a cohesive force which will ensure unity in their multiplicity. The unity in question is obviously not one of mere logical classification which has to do with the static abstractions of ideas but rather one of the dynamic harmonization of action. The point is that harmonious action does not come about automatically from the mere fact that the actors in question are human beings and that they are interrelated in a common enterprise. Action is harmonious only when it is harmonized, and rarely can it be harmonized spontaneously without that principle of harmonization which, since the time of the Romans, has been called authority—although the force designated by that term was in existence long before the Romans had a word for it. Fundamentally, authority is simply the power resident in a community for coordinating that community's functions and thus achieving its purposes.

We can say, then, that authority is as old as community—however diversified the forms community may take—which is but another way of saying that community and authority are correlatives; neither exists without the other, neither is understandable except in terms of the other. It is not, however, as though either authority or community comes into existence only when human beings become explicitly conscious of the need for them; still less do they wait upon philosophical reflection before beginning to function. Philosophical reflection can ask questions regarding the nature of community and authority; it can determine their rationale and specify their relation to each other; it can trace the development or logical implications of both and conceptualize them with a view to understanding them better; but it cannot bring them into existence or even prescribe the conditions for

An earlier version of this chapter appears in *Thought*, 45, No. 178 (Autumn 1970), 325–45.

their coming into existence; still less can it by abstract reasonings argue authority in community out of existence. In the affairs of life fact and action tend to precede and determine ideas.

Although the meaning of a term coined to designate a pre-existing reality cannot determine the nature of the reality thus designated, it is not without significance that the Latin term *auctoritas* has its root in the verb *augere*, which means "to grow." It is never used, of course, except in relation to a human community, and so it would seem to designate the principle whereby a community exercises the kind of life which is proper to it. The life of the community, however—any community, no matter how large or small, significant or trivial—is the common action of the many with a view to a common purpose. Authority, then, guides and determines action. At the same time, however, it itself is an activity and is, therefore, exercised by an acting subject. It is for this reason, perhaps, that traditional interpretation has said little about authority as a function of the whole community and has concentrated on its exercise by those who are in some particular way qualified to exercise it. The result has been that authority itself has been viewed as a quality (or right) which some have to determine the actions of others, rather than as, fundamentally, the community's capacity of self-determination. It should, perhaps, be noted here that the position "philosophical anarchism" has as one of its postulates the conception of authority as a force or power distinct from and imposed upon the autonomy of those considered subject to it.

THE GROUNDS OF AUTHORITY

But the fact is that in the community situation, however narrow or extended this situation may be, some have always manifested, for one reason or another, the capacity to determine the actions of others, that is, to exercise authority. The first and most readily manifested reason why some can determine others is the possession of superior competence or knowledge. The one who knows, the expert, is the authority (exercises authority). It is the sort of authority which is accorded to the scientist because of his superior knowledge or to the business executive because of his superior know-how, his ability to coordinate a multiplicity of efforts. This can range from the authority of divine knowledge accessible in revelation to the authority of the theater critic of *The New York Times*, who presumably knows what he is talking about and in fact does determine what a large number of people are going to do (or not do). Another source of authority which has always been recognized—in the sense that it has always worked, even though, perhaps, it has not always been reflected upon—is the authority of natural leadership. We do not know quite what it is, but we do know that it gets things done. It has been exhibited by military leaders like

Alexander, Cæsar, and Napoleon, but it has also been exercised by industrialists, housewives, and schoolboys. It is indefinable, but it is rarely disputed because it functions in an area in which dispute is not the order of the day or in which it is the very quality of leadership which settles the dispute. From the philosophical point of view the next source of authority is scarcely distinguishable from the preceding; we might call it the quality of charismatic gift. It is the kind of quality which enables one to exercise authority in special circumstances; it is frequently temporary and usually exercised in circumstances in which other forms of authority fail to function effectively. It grounds the authority of prophetic office, from that of Isaiah and Jeremiah to that of Mahatma Gandhi and Martin Luther King. It scarcely ever fails to be disputed; more often than not it is disputed through violence; and frequently its effectiveness considerably postdates its exercise. The last ground which is recognized as justifying the exercise of authority is that of office or of official position in the community. In a variety of ways the community can designate those of its members who are to exercise authority in this way. This sort of official designation in no way precludes the possession of any or all of those other qualities which ground authority—the ideal is a blend of them all—but the other grounds are in no sense a precondition for either the existence or the legitimate exercise of authority in a community. The authority in question is that whereby the community is self-determining through the instrumentality of one or more designated to exercise the authority.

Although only the last form of authority raises any serious problems in our context, since it alone makes demands which can conflict with the freedom of those who are determined thus, it is not without reason that I have listed the other forms along with it, since they highlight at least two elements which the last has in common with them: (a) it is not a quality inhering in the one who exercises it but rather a relationship whose functioning involves a quality somehow resident in a subject who is said to "have" authority; and (b) it is a dynamic relationship of which the response of those over whom and for whom it is exercised is constitutive. Having recognized, however, what the forms of authority have in common we can now confine ourselves to the problematic of the fourth form.

A sort of common sense view of authority, then, would make of it a power which some have to determine the actions of others for the sake of carrying out the purposes of the community. It makes little difference what philosophical reflection says to this; this is the way it works, and arguments against the legitimacy of authority based on the autonomy of human reason simply miss the point. A merely individual reason is not autonomous, precisely because as merely individual it is not reason; it is through authority and its exercise that the community reasons, that its activities are rational.

THE NATURE OF AUTHORITY

Immediately, however, a question arises which makes philosophical reflection indispensable: Is the power being talked about physical or moral? Apart from the Thrasymachuses and Callicleses of this world, whose number, I am afraid, is legion, the answer it would seem would have to be that it is moral power. This, then, immediately raises the further question: What is moral power? It is tempting to assimilate moral power to a right (assuming that it is easy to say what a right is), and thus authority becomes the right to determine the actions of human beings or, simply, the right of some to be obeyed by others. There are, however, difficulties attendant on an explanation such as this, and they are weighty ones.

The first of these stems from a subtle ambiguity in the use of the term "right." We can say, for example, "When one in authority commands, it is right to obey," and this can be correct without its being correct to say that the one who commands has a "right" to be obeyed. The latter expression seeks to describe a relational situation in terms of a "right" possessed by one of the parties in the relationship, whereas the former seeks to describe the situation in terms of the "rightness" of the determination resulting from it. This way of describing the situation seems to me more correct, not only because it does so in relational terms, but also because it makes the response of those who obey more clearly constitutive of the dialectical relationship in question. Where there is an authority relationship, it is "right" that command and response be related, but the "rightness" of the response does not depend solely on either the fact of the command or on the "right" of the one who commands.

Secondly, to speak of authority as a "right" runs the risk of missing the developmental character of the community relationship. If what we mean by authority is a right to determine the actions of the community (and of its individual members), there is danger of conceiving this right as somehow external to the community or, at best, as a right of self-determination which has been transferred by the community to representatives who now speak in the name of the community, rather than as a right which is inseparable from the whole community but which the community exercises through the instrumentality of those who serve as administrators of the authority. As we saw in speaking of what is common to all forms of authority, it is important that the response to the exercise of it always be one of self-determination.

This involves inevitably the relationship of freedom and authority.

It has been recognized at least since the time of Thomas Aquinas that it is meaningful to speak of authority only in the context of freedom: both commanding and obeying must be exercises of freedom, or they are not exercises of commanding and obeying. One is not free to command an action which cannot be performed freely. The driver of a car has no authority over the car; nor, for that matter, does the owner of a dog have authority over the dog. If my car or my dog do what I want them to do, it is not by reason of any authority I exercise, or if they fail to do what I want them to do, they are not resisting my authority; what they do or do not do is indifferent to any moral power I may exercise since the relationship in question is not a moral one at all. The situation, then, in which it makes sense to speak of authority is one of moral relationship, where it can be meaningfully said that something should be done, because—that is, where the rightness of what is done is due at least partially to the relationship involved (we should remember, of course, that morality and legality are not synonymous— even though there can be a moral obligation to be legal).

Now, this sort of relationship is not the one-to-one relationship between one who has a "right" to command and another who has a "duty" to obey. Rather, the relationship is that of community, in which the one common goal of the many requires the functioning of a unifying principle. If all men were perfectly rational, this unifying principle could conceivably be reason, although even perfect rationality would seem to demand on the social level a coordinating principle— a rational one. It simply is not rational to expect that the autonomous exercise of individual reason will produce the harmonious effect which the community needs if it is to survive as community. The point, therefore, is that authority is a need of the community. It is because men need to live in community (if they are to secure what atomized individual effort is incapable of securing) that they also need what will ensure the harmonious functioning of community.

THE EXERCISE OF AUTHORITY

This brings us, I think, to the need of distinguishing explicitly between the authority which resides in the community and the exercise of that authority. Because, as is fairly obvious, authority can at best rarely be exercised by the community as a whole, it has unfortunately become standard practice among theologians (who, in the past at least, were among the only ones to give serious consideration to the problem) to view authority as residing in that member of the community who exercises it. This, of course, was complicated by a tendency to ground authority in the creative will of God (that is, his authorship) rather than in the needs of the community itself. If we see authority as essentially a function arising out of the communal relationship, then we can also see it as dependent on that relationship, with the result that it ceases to be necessary to argue that authority comes from God; indirectly it stems from God's creative will, but to note that solves nothing. It is true, presumably, that God wills what will serve the purposes of community, which is but another way of saying that he wills authority as a service to the community. Whether or not God has also revealed a will regarding the manner of exercising or the persons who are to exercise authority is for theologians to dispute (although I seriously suspect that their disputes will get neither them nor us anywhere).

All of this, it would seem, points to the need of understanding authority as a function within the community and of interpreting its exercise on the basis of different modes of community. Just as there is no single model of community, so there is no single model of authority. There are as many types of community as there are communal purposes, and the types of authority will vary as do the communities. What will be constants, however, are (*a*) the fact that authority has its source in the community relationship, whatever it may be, and (*b*) that the exercise of authority is ultimately responsible to the community it serves. Thus, ideally there should be no conflict between individual autonomy and authority in the community; the community relationship is such that within it the exercise of autonomy is inseparable from a framework wherein authority functions as a determinant —or co-determinant—of action.

Only if it were possible for man to live in complete isolation could autonomy be a completely individual affair; in any other situation it is necessarily limited by the autonomy of others as individuals as well as by the overall purposes of the community, which is but another way of saying that meaningful autonomy is inevitably limited by authority—just as authority has its source in the community, so too freedom. The limitation, however, is not one-sided. Autonomy can be meaningfully limited by authority only if authority is limited by autonomy. Authority and freedom are not merely to be reconciled; they are dialectically related in such a way that each is constitutive of the other.

Lest all that has been said thus far seem unduly abstract and without contemporary relevance it might be well at this point to consider the relationship of authority and autonomy in the four types of community which today might be called problem areas: the family, the school, the state, and the church. Each is a type of community in which spontaneity is incapable of achieving the kind of coordination necessary for a viable structure, and in each it will be necessary to recognize both the dialectical relationship of elements in the structure and the developmental character of the functions called authority and autonomy.

Without entering into the question concerning the "natural" as opposed to the "conventional" character of the family community—that is, the union of father, mother, and children—it can, it would seem, be said that the family provides the first and most obvious model of community, an identifiable unity of a number of persons whose actions and purposes are coordinated with a view to attaining a common goal. The point is that the family admirably illustrates both a common life of its members and the need of a function which will ensure the coordination of diverse purposes. Essentially the family community is a temporary one (although the institution itself may be permanent) since its common life is directly oriented to eventual dissolution, and the authority exercised within it simply by serving its purpose progressively does away with that very purpose. Human beings are such that only gradually can they grow into a state of responsibility for their own lives. The function of authority in the family, then, would seem to require no justification; its exercise, however, has certain characteristics which are peculiar to it.

Ideally such an authority would be based on superior knowledge, natural leadership (not without charismatic overtones), and legal function—but it is conceivable that only the last of these is significantly present. Since social structures and social thinking have already advanced far beyond the conviction that being male constitutes a title to both superiority and authority, there is no justification for asserting that the father simply as such is the one to exercise authority in the family (although he might effectively do so by virtue of the other enumerated characteristics or by an acceptable social convention). It is true, however, that only chaos could result if parents (as a sort of dual authority) were not to determine to a great extent the behavior of their young children. The parent–child relationship, however, is clearly a dialectical one, which means that in conditioning development it is in turn progressively conditioned by development. The whole rationale of parental determination is that it should promote the sort of self-determination which is ultimately the negation of the parental function. In practical terms the problem is one of time. It is certainly difficult, if not impossible, to say that any given age is in general the age when responsibility for self-determination has been attained, to say when—even in the particular case—the child has become a thoroughly autonomous, self-determining person. What remains is law, arbitrary as it may be, which determines both the duration and limits of parental responsibility for the actions of the child, on the assumption, of course, that responsibility and authority are correlative and co-terminous (although it is a mistake not infrequently made to think that the extent of merely financial responsibility defines the extent of authority). In any event neither the temporal duration nor the extent of parental authority is to be determined by considerations of what is "natural" or simply legal; the concrete situation demands a judgment—not easy to make—regarding the pace at which parental control diminishes and self-determination takes over. What is important to realize in this context is that parental authority is geared to cancel itself out, and the pace of this self-cancellation can be determined only by circumstances—and by a process of evolving social awareness.

THE SCHOOL

There is another form of community and, therefore, of authority which resembles the first not only in the unquestionableness of its prerogatives but also in the transitoriness of its effectiveness. The goal of this community is the disciplined formation of the young (intellectual, cultural, and even moral) in ways which cannot be accomplished by the family alone, by the day-to-day give-and-take of ordinary human relationships, or simply by the spontaneous activity of the to-be-educated. We can call this community the "school," and to the extent that it is carrying out the educational mandate of the parents—which, presumably, it is doing on the elementary level and which, for the sake of argument, we can concede that it is also doing on the secondary level—there is no great need to consider the authority exercised therein separately from that of the parents (remembering, of course, that the school is an instrument not only of the family but also of the larger community of which the family is a part). On the higher levels of education, however, it would seem there is question of a different kind of community and, thus, of a different exercise of authority. Without seeking to designate any precise point in the developmental process at which the student becomes a "full partner" in the educational venture, we can say that, on the higher levels, the educational community becomes one in which the primary relationship is between those who are being educated and those who are doing the educating. (Nor, again, need we forget that such a community involves multiple relationships to the larger community—or communities—of which the individuals engaged in the process are members.) The question here concerns simply the nature of the community, the authority which enables it to function purposefully, and the exercise of that authority, that is, in what areas, to what extent, and by whom. Practically speaking, this comes down to a question of the manner in which and the extent to which "educators" determine the educational process—what sort of authority is theirs, how do they exercise it? Although, unfortunately, there are obvious and perhaps even numerous aberrations in this area, it seems necessary to suppose that they have the authority of professional competence (although superior knowledge in a discipline need not be equated with competence in educating). It would be comforting, too, if we could suppose the authority of natural and even of charismatic leadership. The question to be considered, however, is that of functional leadership in an organized venture, in which spontaneous activity is not sufficient for the end in view, the authority of office whose exercise is necessary if something is to get done. Here, it would seem, multiple models are feasible, and the primary criterion for judging their validity is the efficiency with which they get the job done (on the assumption that we are clear in our minds as to just what job is to be done). All of this, unfortunately, does not advance us very far, since it makes the concept of authority in education a function of an educational philosophy which all too frequently consists in a conviction that the way it was done in the past is the way it should continue to be done or in a dissatisfaction with the way the job is being done coupled with rather arbitrary but frequently vociferous convictions both as to what job is to be done and as to the manner of doing it. We are left, then, somewhat up in the air, cherishing perhaps the hope that "educators" and the to-be-educated can come together to find the answer to two questions: (1) What job is to be done? and (2) How is authority to be exercised if the job is to be done? Suffice it to say that if an answer is to be found to either or both of these questions, it is to be looked for in the dialogic relationship of the partners in the process. As partners they must co-determine the job to be done; as partners they must agree on the degree of authority necessary for getting the job done—thus recognizing that the teacher has as much authority as he can persuade the student to grant him for the purpose in view (if the student grants too much or too little the educational process will suffer).

THE STATE

By this time it could well seem that the only purpose served by our inconclusive venture into the school has been that of diverting attention from the main question, which concerns authority in the larger community and its exercise by those who hold official positions in the community. In fact, however, it prepares us in a number of ways to investigate that larger community called civil society, which on its most thoroughly articulated level we call the state. Like the communities we have already observed, the state consists of a multiplicity of individuals united together for a common purpose and coordinated by an authority whose function is to ensure unified action. Whereas, however, it is essential to both family and school that both the community and the authority operative within it be temporary, it is indispensable to civil society that both community and authority be at least relatively permanent. Like the individual human being, whose history from birth to death is one of progressive disintegration, the family tends by the very dialectical nature of the relationship which constitutes it to disintegrate. Only if the family is constantly replaced by other families which spring from it can life go on. By the same token, although in a somewhat different way, the community we call the school is characterized by the temporariness of the relationship between its members. It is essential to the dialectical relationship of educator and to-be-educated (or, if you will, of authority and subjection to authority) that it be one of disintegration—the educator as educator manifests his usefulness by rendering himself useless. Thus, it is not merely that the overall membership in family and school is not constant (the facts of birth, death, and changing attitudes take care of that in any community), but that the dissolution of the authority–subjection relationship is a necessary condition for the survival of the community as a permanent institution. It is, on the other hand, indispensable to the civil community that the relationships which constitute it be fundamentally permanent; the dialectical relationship may disintegrate, but it is not essential to it that it do so—even in Marxism it is not seriously believed that the destiny of the state is to wither away. This is not the only difference between the larger community and its constituent communities, but only if this difference is understood will others be understood.

The purpose of the civil community, which is both the good of the community and the community of the good, may in the concrete evolve with changing requirements of human living; it does not cease to be a goal which is common to both the community as a whole and its members as individuals, nor is the achievement of the goal inextricably bound up with the cessation of the community relationship. Precisely because this is so, however, we are forced to say that the authority which serves such a community is resident in the community itself in such a way that those who exercise the authority are designated neither by nature, as in the family, nor by professional competence, as (ideally) in the school. There has to be some way in which the community as a whole designates those who are to exercise its authority function. At this point, of course, there arises a whole complex of problems, both theoretical and practical. What can it mean to say

that the whole community designates those who are to exercise authority? Is it all or only some of the members who do the designating?
What does it mean in a democracy, for example, to say that those who
exercise authority in the community have been designated by the
membership, when a substantial segment of the membership—the mi-
nority—has quite specifically indicated its opposition to those whom
the rest—the majority—have designated; is it legitimate in these circumstances to relinquish the responsibility of self-determination and
hand it over to the will of others?

Here it is that the concept of "the consent of the governed" must be
invoked—and interpreted. If the authority function resides fundamentally in the community as a whole—and no other formula would seem
to be meaningful (the authority of God is at this point not even part
of the question)—then it is for the community as a whole to agree on
the exercise of an authority which, practically speaking, cannot be
exercised by all. Still, historically speaking, such universal agreement
has been at best interpretative. Apart from periodic elections of officials within a framework which itself has not been chosen by those
who do the electing, the authority structure in a community is for
most, if not all, of its members a given into which they are inserted by
the mere fact of birth within the community (even those who enter
the community from outside are accepting an already given structure).
One could argue, of course, that by entering the community or by remaining within it the members are ratifying given structures, but for
the vast majority of members there is no live option to do otherwise.
Consent, then, to the structure itself is for the most part no more than
tacit, and this is true no matter what the original means whereby the
structure was instituted. It was true of the Greek city-state as well as
of the Roman Empire; it was true of the feudal principalities of
medieval Europe as well as of the emerging constitutional states of the
eighteenth and nineteenth centuries; it is true today of the established
nation-states, like the United States, France, and Great Britain, as well
as of the proliferating "people's republics" throughout the world. People live in and "consent to" structures which they have not chosen
and with regard to which they retain no effective live option.

History, of course, is witness that changes can and do take place,
and over the long run some of these have been complete changes in
structure. The point is, however, that the "consent" which is constitutive of both the structure and the authority function within the structure is determining only in a very broad sense of the term, and it is
secured in a way which for the most part favors stability rather than
change. More than that, even though it can be said not only the-
oretically but practically that the dialectical constitutive relationship

between the consent of the governed and the exercise of authority is a constant, the very exercise of authority permits a manipulation of consent which makes the effectiveness of the latter for change extremely dubious, except where that intangible but unmistakable thing called a "climate of opinion" gradually brings about reluctant transformations.

Authority is a moral, not a physical, power; it resides in the community in whose service it is exercised; its exercise is conditioned by the constitutive consent which designates those who are to exercise it; and in the concrete its competence is defined by the purposes of the community, which in a certain sense at least means that it is limited by what the governed in constituting it are consenting to. This last, of course, might well seem to be opening up a Pandora's box of individualistic—even anarchistic—interpretations, but it must be remembered that it can be understood only within a framework where authority continues to be a real function and where the unlimited exercise of individual autonomy is recognized as productive of chaos. The point is that authority has its limitations and that these are functions not only of the kind of community in which it resides but also of the inviolable autonomy of human individuals as such. It is true that human liberty is meaningful only when limited (or when operative within a community in which the needs of others and of the community as a whole channel freedom toward effective action); but it is not true that effective liberty is defined by the granting power of those who exercise authority. To enumerate even the general areas in which civil authority is not competent to limit or impede autonomy is a task rendered impossible by limitations of space. It is sufficient here to insist on a truth which Plato never tired of driving home: the physical power to get something done is not synonymous with the moral power to require that something be done (or not done). Civil government, for example, simply does not have the moral power to require that all segments of the population agree with its policies or that they do not express their opposition openly. It does not even have the moral power to impede efforts to organize opposition to its policies.

At this point a difficulty arises which is not readily resolved. In the ideal order the instrument of opposition to governmental policy would be rational argument, to which, obviously, government would also have the moral power to oppose rational argument. This, however, is not the way things happen in our imperfect world. The *de facto* instruments of opposition to government policy are not rational argument but propaganda, demonstrations, active resistance, and so on. Where such instruments are employed, it is almost inevitable that one or other of the opposing positions will secure an advantage which has nothing to do with reason. Where the instrument is propaganda, one party (presumably government) can effectively control the means of propaganda, and the advantage is obvious. Where this occurs, the instrument resorted to (at least in our contemporary society) becomes demonstration, which is, so to speak, the propaganda of the frustrated. In a society where the violent suppression of demonstration is not tolerated, this can result in the non-rational advantage of the few who can impose their will without submitting their arguments to impartial arbitration (if this latter is, indeed, possible). Where the instrument is active resistance, its opposite number is coercion, and we have experienced the difficulty of assigning justifiable limits to either. There is no theoretical solution to these difficulties, since in practice the solution is going to be different in each instance, and, no matter what the solution, each party is going to remain convinced that the other party is wrong.

In general it can be said that the competence of government in the exercise of authority extends to such matters as are necessary to the survival or well-being of the community. Whether or not the basic law of the state is contained in a "constitution," and whether such a constitution has been ratified by a vote of the citizenry or simply promulgated by government itself, it is generally assumed that the limitations of governmental competence are part of basic law, as are the "inalienable rights" of the citizenry. What is important to note, however, is that when we speak of either limitations of authority or of inalienable rights of individuals we are speaking in moral and not merely legal terms. The relationship, then, which we have called a dialectical one, constituting both the community and the authority operative in it, is a moral relationship. Obviously the functional details which determine the manner in which the relationship operates will be spelled out and made more precise in legal language; it may even be necessary to specify the use of physical force to ensure the functioning of the relationship or to impose sanctions for impeding that function; still, the relationship itself remains a moral one. This means that both the exercise of authority and the response of the community to that exercise are to be judged in the light of moral criteria. This is not to say that law is amoral or that the existence of law plays no role in moral decision, but it does say that both the decisions of authority and the laws in which such decisions are embodied always remain subject to moral review.

The real problem, however, does not arise on this theoretical level. Nor on the practical level is there always a problem of determining when the demands of morality outweigh the demands of law; but there is a serious practical problem of effectively retaining authority in the grasp of the whole community once its exercise has been put into the hands of officials, and of making the consent of the governed a concrete constitutive function in the social structure and not merely something which is manipulated by those who have the power to do so. Ideally speaking, of course, the periodic recurrence of elections keeps control in the hands of the electorate, but in the practical order this control is frequently little short of farcical. As states grow larger and the communications media more powerful, the opinion of the electorate can be so manipulated that informed control by the community is effectively eliminated. It is for this reason that criticism of officialdom—as was the case, for example, in many of the attempts to oppose United States policy in the Viet Nam war—is not to be construed as disloyalty to the community, even though it is convenient to government to interpret it as such.

What comes out of all this is the paradox (perhaps most obvious in the civil community but also, as we shall see, manifest in the Church) that although authority exists for the preservation of liberty—whether against those who would take it away or against the chaos which is the negation of significant liberty—still, almost inevitably, its existence also poses a constant threat to liberty, since only by limiting freedom can it ensure freedom. The paradox, it would seem, is with us to stay, but the refusal to take it for granted that a resolution has been achieved will at least ensure the kind of dialectical tension between the exercise of authority and the consent of the governed which will permit authority and freedom to live with one another effectively.

THE CHURCH

At this point we might seem to run the risk of prolonging the present discussion beyond all proportion if we take up the question of authority in that other great community, the Church. Still, the discussion will unquestionably be truncated if we do not institute some sort of comparison between the civil and ecclesiastical communities, each with its own authority structure. Traditionally they have been likened to each other in that both are called "perfect societies," that is, societies which in themselves dispose of all the means necessary for achieving the end for which they exist. By the same token they have been contrasted in terms of the different ends (temporal *vs.* eternal) for which they exist, differing manners of institution (natural need *vs.* divine will), and differing principles of coherence (legality *vs.* love). There is little point in discussing here the traditional distinctions, both because they say little to what is at issue (save, perhaps, the distinction between legality and love) and because they have contributed more toward obscuring than toward clarifying the problem of authority.

We can, I think, say with the Fathers of Vatican Council II that the exercise of authority in a community whose bond of union is love must be a function of love, but I prefer in the present context to take those characteristics of the authority–community relationship which we have already examined to see how they apply to the ecclesiastical community.

At the outset we can eliminate any discussion of the kinds of authority which go with superior knowledge or competence, natural leadership, or charismatic gift—not because these qualities are not present in the church community but because there is no demonstrable connection between the possession of these qualities and the holding of official position in the Church. Thus, we are forced to say that the authority with which we are concerned is that which has its roots in the community situation, not in the personal prerogatives of those who exercise it. Renaissance theologians, who still seem to guide official theorizing on the subject, were convinced that civil authority resides primarily in the community and only by designation in its officials, whereas ecclesiastical authority resides primarily in officials, at whose head stands the pope. Without going into the complexities of the argumentation upon which this claim is based, it would seem that there is little validity to it since it argues not so much from what Christ did or said in instituting this community as upon what he must have meant if he intended the kind of community which the theologians conceived the Church to be—modeled on the monarchical civil society with which they were familiar. What is more, the arguments they use to show that civil authority resides in the civil community would seem to apply equally well to any voluntary community (as opposed to a "natural" community, the only clear example of which is the family). Against this it was argued that by divine right Christ possessed all authority, that in instituting the Christian community he conferred authority over it upon the Apostles as a body and supremely upon Peter as its head, and that his will for the permanence of the community implied not only the decision that the successors of Peter have the same authority but also that those successors be the bishops of Rome!

There is obviously no need to dispute the authority of Christ; nor is there need here to dispute that he instituted a community which we call the Church, or, for that matter, that he personally designated its first head. Without clear evidence to the contrary, however, it seems imperative to dispute that he intended a community in which the community–authority relationship differs from the dialectical relationship which the very concepts of community and authority seem to demand. It would be far better to argue that he intended a community in which resides an authority corresponding to its nature, needs, and purposes—which would not preclude the development of structures. If, as I have argued earlier, the being and exercise of authority are meaningful only where there is community, then the existence of community is a pre-condition for the being and exercise of authority (that is, as a need of the community). As a consequence, it would seem, authority in any voluntary community—not merely in the civil—is mediated through the community, and its exercise is a function not only of the existence but also of the structuration of the community, which structuration is not static but dynamic. Historically the church community has structured itself; it has designated the officials who exercise the authority necessary for its functioning; it has retained the capacity to develop its own structures and is not bound to a structure which did evolve and which was solidified only at a relatively late stage in its evolution. There is no evidence to be found either in the nature of the community or, for that matter, in the expressed will of its founder that its structure at any given period was intended to be or should be unchanging. It is a mistake to conceive of any human authority as static, that is, explainable on the basis of a single model. Authority is a relational function in a framework of interrelation among free beings. As the overall manner of interrelationship evolves, so does the authority relationship.

There is no question that the Church is a unique community; that it belongs to the economy of salvation history and not merely to that of world history; that its nature, needs, and purposes go beyond the merely temporal; and that the relationships of its members to one another, to Christ, and to the community as a whole differ from those which are proper to other communities. At the same time, however, it is a community in which (as in every other community) the exercise of authority is a service to the community, the consent of the governed is dialectically constitutive of the authority function, and accountability to the community is inseparable from the exercise of authority in it. When one reads those theologians for whom the weight of papal pronouncement seems to equal that of divine revelation, one gets the impression that authority in the Church enjoys the unique prerogative of defining itself, rather than being defined in an existential relationship to the response it elicits. Whatever else this response may be, it cannot and must not be an abdication of personal responsibility; nor can it be a relinquishing of the right to demand that authority be not arbitrary in its exercise (or, perhaps worse still, a blindness to the possibility of such arbitrariness). Ecclesiastical authority is not divine, it is human; as such it must constantly be aware of the grant of authority contained in the consent of the governed, which

means, in addition, that it never has the right not to be questioned—
and where the questioning is wholesale, as it is in our contemporary
authority crisis, there is at least the suspicion that authority has exceeded its competence.

The problem of the authority relationship in the Church has been
complicated by two factors which we have seen to be operative in the
state but which are operative in a unique way in the Church. (1) If
there is to be order in a community, it would seem to be the responsibility of those who exercise authority in the community, and not of
anybody and everybody, to determine the means for obtaining that
order. Correlatively, this means an obligation on the part of the members of the community to take the means thus determined. Strictly
speaking, this concerns what they may or must do or not do. In the
Church, however, this obligation is extended to include what its members may or must say and not say, think and not think—which could
very well be, and sometimes is, interpreted as signifying the inadmissibility of the sort of questioning and criticism of which we have spoken.
It is not inconceivable, of course, that speaking and thinking can be
prejudicial to the legitimate ends of the community, but only great
vigilance and great honesty will prevent the claim that they are from
being arbitrary and an abuse. (2) The second factor is similar to the
first. We have seen that government, particularly in large bodies, can
so manipulate the consent of the governed that questioning or opposing government policy can be interpreted as disloyalty to the community itself, thus inhibiting a response which is, in fact, loyal. This
is further complicated in the Church by the fact that what can be interpreted as disloyalty to the community can also be interpreted as sin,
than which there is no greater deterrent to thought, word, or action!
If we add to this a tendency—observable also in civil society but more
fraught with consequences in the Church—to identify government or
administration with the community itself, we have a situation in
which both the nature and the exercise of authority are almost inevitably corrupted.

When, for example, it is asserted that the schools and churches of a
diocese are the "property" of the diocese and that, consequently, members of the community who enter these premises without the approval
of the administration are "trespassing," it might be conceded that such
an assertion can make sense. It is conceivable, certainly, that some
members of the community could violate the rights of the community
as a whole. It is difficult, however, to concede that administrators alone
can decide when such rights are, in fact, being violated. Buildings
which serve the religious and educational purposes of the diocesan
community are, it is true, the property of the diocese. This means,

however, that the whole community, not merely the administration which serves it, owns these buildings.

The example, of course, may raise more problems than the one it seeks to illustrate, but the point should be clear. Whenever the body of those who exercise a right (or better, administer its exercise) is confused with the body in which the right resides, there is bound to be a falsification of the relationship expressed by the right in question. The same applies to authority. There is little question that it cannot be exercised by all but only by those designated to do so. Nor need there be question that the members of a community have an obligation to respect both authority and the exercise of it. This respect, however, cannot take the form of an abdication by the community of an authority which continues to reside in itself or of a submission to its exercise which absolves that exercise from accountability to those in whose interest it functions. The dialectical relationship which we call authority does not cease to be dialectical with the appointment of administrators who supervise its exercise—which is but another way of stating that there can be no once-and-for-all establishment of structures which then function as though the relationship they express were not dynamic. It is scarcely conceivable that community could function effectively without the exercise of authority; but it is no less inconceivable that the authority function can become so fixed that it is no longer constituted by and thus changeable with evolving social relationships, with evolving social consciousness.